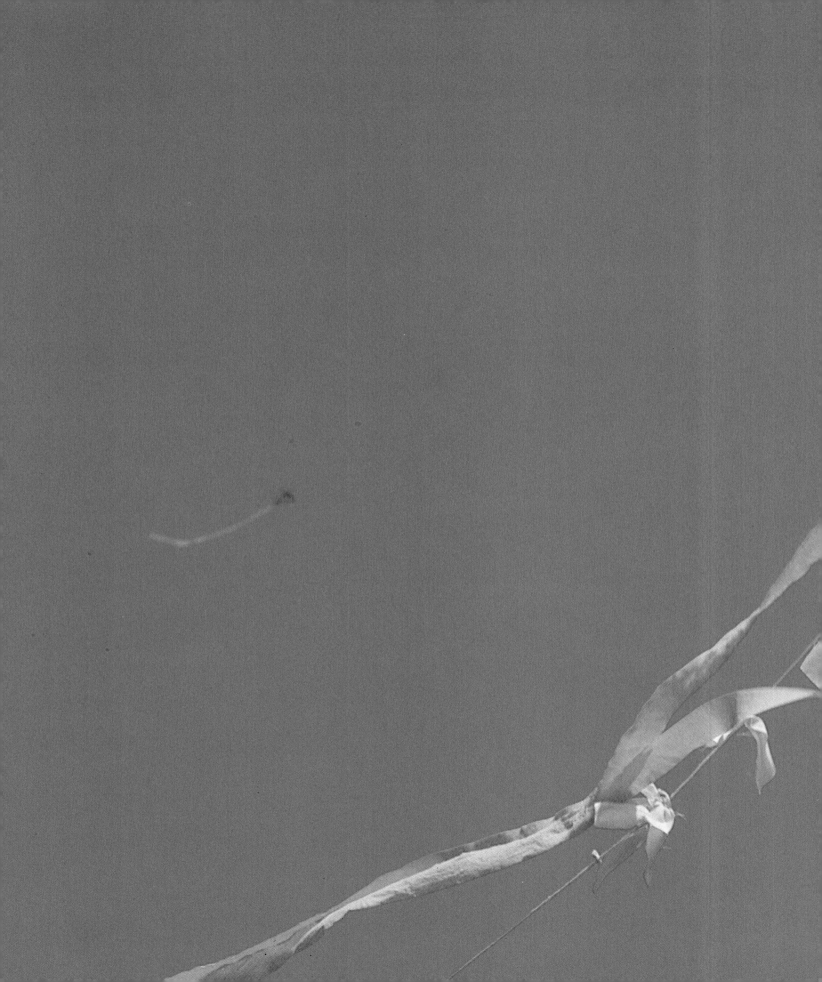

THE SMITHSONIAN EXPERIENCE

SCIENCE–HISTORY–THE ARTS . . .
THE TREASURES OF THE NATION

The Smithsonian Institution
Washington, D.C.
1977

Distributed to the trade by
W. W. Norton & Company
New York, N.Y.

TABLE OF CONTENTS

Introduction 13

Enter the Smithsonian's doors, or turn the first pages of this book, and you'll see: a white tiger cub at the National Zoo (page one); the incomparable *Spirit of St. Louis* at the National Air and Space Museum (pages two-three); the blazing eye of a carousel horse and the deck of a ship model at the National Museum of History and Technology (pages four-five & six-seven); an entry in the kite flying contest on the Mall (title page); or a feathery Indian at the Folklife Festival (opposite).

Fifth Printing May 1984
©1977 Smithsonian Institution
Library of Congress Catalog Card Number 77-9213
ISBN: 0-89599-000-8
ISBN: 0-89599-008-3 pbk.

The Smithsonian Institution
Secretary, S. Dillon Ripley

Staff, THE SMITHSONIAN
EXPERIENCE

James K. Page, Jr., Director
Russell Bourne, Senior Editor
Alexis Doster III, Chief of Research
Mimi Dince, Administrative
   Assistant

Editors: Joe Goodwin, Judy
   Harkison
Copy Editors: Dana Gibson, Ann
   Beasley
Research: Caren Keshishian

Index: Toni Warner

Picture Editor: Jane Ross
Picture Research: Pat Upchurch
Picture Consultant: Caroline
   Despard

Design: Wickham & Associates, Inc.:
   Jay Williams, assisted by
   Vicki Valentine, Sally Summerall
   and Flash Fleischer

Separations and Engravings:
   Lanman Lithoplate, Inc.
Typography: Carver
   Photocomposition, Inc.
Printing: Rand McNally and
   Company

Marketing Consultant: William H.
   Kelty

Photography by Susanne Anderson,
Lee Boltin, Ross Chapple, Chip
Clark, Betsy K. Frampton, Peter
Garfield, Kjell Sandved; and others,
including the photographic staff of
the Smithsonian Institution (see
Photographic Credits, page 256).

Cartoons by Paul Hogarth

The major essays in this volume
were written by members of the
Smithsonian staff (identified on the
first page of their essays). Other,
shorter sections were written by
Wayne Barrett, Editor of *American
Cyclist;* Cynthia Field, research
associate of the Smithsonian;
Edwards Park, member of the
Board of Editors of *Smithsonian*
magazine; Marvin Sadik, Director
of the National Portrait Gallery;
Stephen E. Weil, Deputy Director
of the Hirshhorn Museum and
Sculpture Garden; Melvin B.
Zisfein, Deputy Director of the
National Air and Space Museum;
and members of the staff of THE
SMITHSONIAN EXPERIENCE.

Outside the Castle:
a lone reader.

When one is dealing with a national legend—and that is where the Smithsonian stands at this writing—one should be careful but not necessarily serious. It's well to remember that at the base of the Smithsonian Castle, that improbable, romantic building swathed in ivy, are several botanical signs identifying species of flora; one of them quirkily but accurately proclaims, "Poison Ivy."

The Smithsonian Institution, and the myths and historical facts that surround it, has been growing like a kind of a magic plant ever since 1829. That year James Smithson—an Englishman—died, leaving the curious bequest described on pages 20-27 of this book. What in the world is an institution that embraces a number of museums but is not a museum itself? What kind of place can expound science, history, and the arts; house the nation's treasures; nurture what at first seems the most arcane research yet translate it for laymen; play host to queens and presidents; and, on Washington's formal Mall in sight of the dignified halls of Congress, erect a carousel for the delight of seven-year-olds?

Given the assignment to capture all this, the editors pondered the question: how to reflect the institution's almost limitless diversity as well as its special charm—and even its humor—in a single volume? As H. L. Mencken said of human problems, there is always a solution that is simple, neat, and wrong. To be right, this book would have to be, like the institution itself, complex and perhaps even a bit unpredictable. Some new paradigm was needed and in our search for that exemplary system, we found ourselves looking again at the Smithsonian museums themselves, all resplendent from their Bicentennial celebrations.

Good museums are full not only of objects well displayed, but of surprises—and even curious juxtapositions. Visitors to the National Air and Space Museum usually expect to see the *Spirit of St. Louis* but are taken by surprise to find Julia Child on a television screen explaining the recipe for "primordial soup." To leave the quiet amplitude of the Freer Gallery of Art and enter the exuberant clutter of the "1876" exhibit in the Arts and Industries Building, the great mechanical orchestrion thundering cheerfully in your ears, is to experience a pleasant form of culture shock. Could, then, a book be like a surprisingly good museum? Perhaps. Could it show all the facets of the Smithsonian? Not at all, anymore than the million or so objects on exhibit here are anything but a tiny fraction of the 70 million objects and specimens in the institution's care.

The foyer, or opening section, of this book-museum demonstrates (in case anyone should forget) that the Smithsonian is a public space, with most of its support coming from the federal purse but with a curious, vital inmixing of private funds. And the foyer also reveals this book's own exhibition techniques: informal introductions and conclusions to each section, excursions sometimes in the form of fantasies into the nooks and crannies of the institution's present and past; picture stories that reflect the panoramic beauty and the intricate detail of the Smithsonian's collections; and insightful essays by distinguished scholars and administrators, such as the first one on the founding of the Smithsonian written by Wilcomb E. Washburn, Director of the Office of American Studies.

Thus oriented, the reader moves from the foyer into the book's galleries.

The seven successive sections of the book focus on places and people where the Smithsonian is particularly active: up front with the exhibits, behind the scenes with the objects and the collections themselves, in the laboratories and out at the zoo with natural history scientists, looking at the human condition with anthropologists and folklorists, exploring the realms of art with curators and children alike, launching into space for a short course on the universe, and coming back to earth to ponder with Secretary Ripley the proper functions of an institution that seeks to offer a truly "open" learning experience.

None of these excursions would have been possible without the enthusiastic cooperation of innumerable and wise friends in all corners of the Smithsonian. To have attempted the construction of a book-museum was presumptuous enough; if we have succeeded to any degree it is because of their patience and, more importantly, their zeal to inform people about what they know best and what they feel is terribly important. We thank these Smithsonian colleagues warmly—and hold them blameless for whatever omissions they find in our exhibition.

The Editors

13

PART ONE

An Establishment of Learning

Look east from the Washington Monument and you are struck by the unimpeded view of the Capitol—an architectural scheme worked out by planners long ago. They knew the power of a vista. But on the periphery of your vision stand two hedges of monumental buildings—seven of the Smithsonian Institution's 14 museums, planted firmly but politely in the presence of the government buildings of the United States of America.

Americans—the most successful inventors of democracy, high technology, and the belly laugh—can be cheered that on the Mall exists a remarkably diverse collection of buildings, each planned in its time as an architectural statement. Thus, the Mall speaks with many voices— voices heard on the following pages.

Americans can be humbled that it was an Englishman who, for reasons obscure, ignited the fire that now burns so steadily parallel to the Mall's greensward. They can also feel comfortable in that our disputatious congressmen of the time did not fritter away the Englishman's gift, but, as historian Wilcomb Washburn chronicles, created a curious, multifaceted cultural complex devoted to research and education, independent but tied inextricably to the aspirations of the nation.

But, remember, the Smithsonian is no shrine though it harbors some of the most revered artifacts of American history. It is not only a source of precise scholarship but also a place of popular learning. It is a home for good humor, a ride on a merry-go-round: the stuff of dreams as well as hard facts.

15

I Wonder What Happens at Midnight

The Smithsonian Institution in Washington, D.C., has a staff of some 3,500 directors, curators, assistants, scientists, researchers, clerks, secretaries, stenographers, technical experts, maintenance people, security people, grounds people, and one person who wanders around from museum to museum with a mixture of awe and bemusement. I'm that last. It's a pleasant job as long as I don't take it too seriously. Nothing snaps the ground out from under my feet so quickly as seriousness. You'll see.

Certain exhibits at the Smithsonian Institution have made use of animated contraptions to get across some museum story, some theme of an exhibit or facts about a display. They're called by my Smithsonian colleagues "talking heads." I recall Uncle Sam, almost embarrassingly real, telling me how he was born in the minds of Americans. There was also a testy ship's captain in the old Maritime Hall who kept chewing out his first mate, and an air traffic coordinator at the National Air and Space Museum telling us about air traffic control systems.

I suppose I'm especially sensitive to these devices, being the sort of person who averts his eyes from unclad dress mannequins and says "I beg your pardon" when he stumbles into his wife's six-foot avocado plant on the darkened front porch. Anyway, they bother me. The illusion is simply too good. I find it hard to look them in the eye as they fix me with their filmed stare and tell me their stories. And even though I may be late for an appointment, I am compelled to hear

them out rather than leave them orating to an empty hall. I wait until the tape has obviously run its course, and then I murmur "Thank you," and slip away.

Being this sort of person, I have often wondered whether they don't possibly talk to each other in the dark reaches of the night when no

guards are around. Perhaps one would forsake his prepared text and call downstairs to the other: "Hey, Captain! How are things on the high se-e-e-a-a-s?" And the answer would echo back through the marble halls: "Finest kind, Uncle! Finest ki-i-n-d!"

And then, I would wonder, what next? Would 42 First Ladies, all elegantly gowned, all caught in gracious poses amid White House settings, be inspired to indulge in gossip? It must surely be seething in their plastic heads after all these years: Martha Washington, sweet and comfortable and endearingly naive, speaking of her monumental husband as "the old man;" Abigail Adams, brilliant, acerbic, devoted to whatever half-stated ideal her John espoused plus a few of her own; Dolley Madison, impressively self-assured, delightfully witty, sternly patriotic; red-haired Emily Donelson, Old Hickory's niece, serving as First Lady in the place of his late wife. She would be twitted perhaps by the other mannequins because of the talk of bigamy that smeared her uncle and also, perhaps, because her uncle chose to walk rather than ride along Pennsylvania Avenue after his inauguration.

What a hissing of whispers would arise from that display whenever the guard turned away from it! Mrs. Lincoln complaining of the capital, its climate, both political and natural; "Lemonade Lucy" Hayes defending

her teetotal White House dinners; young Frances Folsom Cleveland, recounting her wedding in the East Room and gently ignoring whispers about her husband's illegitimate child; the two Mrs. Roosevelts arguing social reform.

Soon the conversations would be interrupted by the political figures in the campaigning exhibit nearby. The candidate's oratory would ring from the observation platform of his campaign train, punctuated by the cheers and jeers of the gallus-snapping farmers in the audience. Soldiers and sailors clad in the uniforms of America's past would clump downstairs to restore order. The cacophony would stir life into the neoclassical statue of George Washington, who would lower his indefatigable right arm, pull his toga about his chilled marble shoulders and stride, towering, from his plinth to see what was up.

And with Washington's overwhelming presence departed, the rest of the Museum of History and Technol-

ogy would waken and move, its figurines calling out to each other from every display that contains them. The three carpenters working on the Hart House from Ipswich, Massachusetts, would leave their

tools and take a break. At last even the 18th century couple, endlessly about to kiss in order to demonstrate the spark of static electricity between their pouting lips, would grasp each other gloriously and consummate their embrace without that disconcerting snap of miniature lightning.

This, to my mind, should be enough to stir blood into every statue, every mannequin in the Smithsonian. Up the Mall at the Museum of Natural History, a host of native peoples would carry on the work that is stopped in mid-career for the benefit of students and sightseers. Indian weavers would pass the yarn across their looms; South Seas drums would thump and

17

Mrs Lincoln   Mrs Wilson   Mrs Polk

bare feet would raise dust as figures danced in their habitat groups. The splendid African statues by Herbert Ward that line the gallery of the rotunda would relax from their tight-muscled depictions of human moods, contemplate their toes (polished to bright brass by the surreptitious touches of thousands of visiting schoolchildren) and, I think, relax into smiles.

Across the Mall at the great National Air and Space Museum, the figure of Wilbur Wright in his rounded collar would turn his head and move his controls, searching frantically for a place to land before crashing through that wall of glass that bars

him from the Mall. The wing-walkers in the Exhibition Flight Gallery would complete their hair-raising transfer from one Curtiss Jenny to another. The pilot of the slow-rolling Spad fighter in the World War I Gallery would complete his victory roll and so allow, at long last, the blood to drain from his head. Other pilots in other cockpits would stir, wobble their controls, adjust throttles, raise gloved hands in salute. And among the space exhibits, astronauts in their $150,000 space suits would continue their action, stepping off for a space walk or a lunar landing, guiding their craft toward reentry and splashdown.

And so the statues and figures wake and move all around the Mall and beyond. At the Hirshhorn the Burghers of Calais come anxiously to life and continue their dire argumentation, each picking up his existence where art froze it. In the Arts and Industries Building, the scarlet robed figure of Gambrinus, mythical inven-

tor of beer, blinks and sighs and thankfully downs the foaming goblet he has been holding on high amid the "1876" displays. In front of the Castle, solemn Joseph Henry, first Secretary of the institution, turns about on his pedestal with a swirl of his scholastic gown in order to look again at the old building whose construction he supervised and in whose rooms he spent so many years.

Given this dream, surely there also would be a sympathetic rattling of the restless bones of James Smithson within his stone sarcophagus in the Castle. Since Alexander Graham Bell of the Board of Regents brought Smithson here at the turn of the century from his threatened grave in

Italy, the Castle has felt his presence. Elevators have been called up to empty floors at midnight, typewriters have twitched and jumped upon their tables, guards have suddenly fled from their posts of duty and never returned to the job, much less explained what happened.

Now I see the transparent shade rise from his vault (a short man, strongly built, according to anthropologists who have examined the dust of their institution's founder). I see him seize upon the great Smithsonian mace displayed beside him and, leaning upon it, climb to the topmost tower of the Castle. Another ghostly (but real and present) inhabitant, the tower owl, hovers over him; shooing it off with the mace and limping a bit from unaccustomed exertion—and from an old injury (it left a mark upon his left femur), Smithson hobbles across the roof to the flagpole which in the light of day displays the institution's sunburst banner. His

pipe is firmly clamped in his teeth (dental wear indicates he smoked a pipe habitually).

From this point James Smithson looks down upon the Mall—that splendid corridor of grass and trees that opens up the heart of this great American capital which in real life he never saw. Along the Mall, from 4th Street nearly to the Washington monument, he counts nine great buildings that house most, but by no means all of the collections and activities of the institution he founded. He also distantly glimpses the National Collection of Fine Arts and the National Portrait Gallery. He does not, I think, see the Renwick Gallery near the White House, nor can he possibly see the National Zoological Park far out on Connecticut Avenue. Neither can he see the Silver Hill Facility at Suitland, Maryland, where air- and spacecraft are prepared for display at the National Air and Space Museum, nor the zoological research center in the mountains at Front Royal, Virginia, nor the Chesapeake Bay Center. The Cooper-Hewitt Museum in New York City, the Astrophysical Observatory in Cam-

bridge, Massachusetts, and the Tropical Research Institute with its foci in Panama and Honduras can only be summoned to his mind from previous, ghostly inspection. James Smithson, I fancy, does not see these now from the Castle roof, nor the work that is going forward in archaeology, in the biological sciences, and in ecology all over the world. I think he probably knows about them, however. I'm not altogether sure of the facts when it comes to ghosts, but I'd lay odds on his knowing.

He might be bewildered by what has happened to his half-million dollar bequest. He did not foresee museums; he sought a research center, a sort of laboratory complex, one presumes, like those he was accustomed to in England. The research is here, of course, both broader and deeper than he could possibly have dreamed in detail. Yet the museum complex, which started after the original Smithsonian building, the Castle, was completed, is sure to win the old ghost's approval. How better to "diffuse knowledge among men" than with these creative displays that supplement the entire learning experience? Smithson would like them. And he would approve the caperings of statues because he would know that, just as his institution celebrates human life, so does it also show aspects of life by arresting the action at a selected moment. That's what a display is.

So he would suck at his pipe, rest on the mace, nod benignly at the midnight revelry, then stump back to his resting place. I'm quite sure of it. Why, only recently there was a light flickering and a framed portrait swinging on the wall above that long-haunted vault. Everyone should realize by now that James Smithson was simply settling down after a midnight excursion.

by Edwards Park

19

A National Museum

by Wilcomb E. Washburn

The American sculptor, Horatio Greenough, passing along the south side of the Mall in 1851 after a nine-year absence in Europe, paused as he saw the battlements of the Smithsonian Castle looming against the horizon. "Suddenly as I walked," he wrote, "the dark form of the Smithsonian palace rose between me and the white Capitol, and I stopped. Tower and battlement, and all that medieval confusion, stamped itself on the halls of Congress, as ink on paper! Dark on that whiteness—complication on that simplicity! . . . 'Bosom'd high in tufted trees,' the Smithsonian College must, in itself, be hereafter a most picturesque object—the models whence it has been imitated are both 'rich and rare'—the connoisseurs may well 'wonder how the devil it got *there*.' "

From its highest turret the Smithsonian still aggressively "flaunts" its "little banner for Académe" against the monolithic government buildings which, in the words of the present Secretary, S. Dillon Ripley, "all seem to be lying down . . . sleeping in the sun . . . like a pride of lions." The Smithsonian still exists in mysterious complication, if not medieval confusion. And it still provokes millions of Americans to wonder "how the devil it got there."

The answer, while not simple, is not impossible to fathom. On his death in 1829, James Smithson, the illegitimate son of one of England's most powerful men, the Duke of Northumberland, left a will which gave to the United States of America half a million dollars to found, in the city of Washington, "under the name of the 'Smithsonian Institution,' an establishment for the increase & diffusion of Knowledge among men." The United States was not the direct beneficiary; it was, in lawyer's talk, the contingent residuary legatee. But none of Smithson's heirs, legitimate or illegitimate (he attempted to provide for them in either case), survived. The money therefore came to the United States.

Why the United States, a country which Smithson had never visited and with which he had no known ties? Perhaps the situation of the United States touched a responsive chord in him; in the eyes of most Englishmen the

Wilcomb E. Washburn, Director of American Studies at the Smithsonian, is author of several studies of the institution, with which he has been associated since 1958. He has also written extensively on the American Indian; his latest book is entitled The Indian in America.

U.S. was the rebellious and illegitimate offspring of the mother country (despite Burke's urging in Parliament before the American Revolution that "the Americans are the sons, not the bastards, of England"). Smithson had remarked that though the best blood of England flowed in his veins, it availed him not at all. Although educated at Oxford and distinguished as a scientist, Smithson could not inherit his father's titles or position. He had to make it on his own. And that was not easy in England. But he was determined to leave his mark. As he put it, "the name of Smithson shall live long after the names of the Percys and

The bronze Smithson medal, created by Paul A. Vincze of London.

Northumberlands are extinct." His prophecy, though not yet fulfilled, has in another sense been justified. It was not as easy as it might seem to accept the gift and build the institution. Some Americans thought it was beneath the dignity of the United States to accept the private gift of a foreigner. But for most the problem was determining to what purpose the gift should be put. The number of plans for spending the money was legion. Former President John Quincy Adams, then a member of Congress, had in 1836 been instrumental in drafting the necessary legislation to accept the "high and solemn trust which the testator has committed to the United States." Soon after, Adams was appointed chairman of the Select Committee of the House of Representatives charged with recommending an appropriate disposition of the fund. Adams found himself assailed on all sides by those who wanted the money applied to support an existing university (the struggling Columbian College—now George Washington University), or to create a new university, or to support the National Institute for the Promotion of Science (then tottering along with an amateurish program of museum exhibits), or to some other benevolent purpose. Adams wrote wearily in his diary in January 1839 that he worked "with a heavy heart, from a presentiment that this noble and most munificent donation will be filtered to nothing, and wasted upon hungry and worthless political jackals."

Few members of Congress shared Adams' intense and almost religious commitment to preserve and utilize the gift in the spirit in which it had been given. While Congress debated, the funds were invested, over Adams' objection, in Arkansas and Michigan state bonds which promptly sank precipitously in value. Many members were content to write off the loss, and the institution, as the victim of fate. But Adams, with his New England conscience, insisted that in accepting the trust, the United States had assumed a sacred obligation to preserve intact the original fund. At his urging, Congress made good on the dissipated inheritance. The irresponsibility of his colleagues saddened Adams and he confided: "I despair of effecting anything for the honor of the country, or even to accomplish the purpose of the bequest—the increase and diffusion of knowledge among men."

In 1840 Adams' committee on the Smithson Bequest presented to the House of Representatives an amended bill, with a report and various supporting documents urging the creation of an institution and incorporating the purposes of the testator in various specific provisions. In the next six years this and substitute bills were debated in Congress. The bill sponsored by Adams' committee called for the creation of an observatory, which Adams had long urged (it was part of his 1825 State of the Union address). But important men opposed the plan, including Secretary of the Treasury John C. Spencer, after listening to Adams talk about the project in 1843. Adams noted that Spencer "pronounced the prejudice against my plan of an astronomical observatory insurmountable, because I had once called observatories light-houses *in* the skies. My words were light-houses *of* the skies. But Mr. Spencer sees no difference between the two phrases."

Late in 1844 Senator Benjamin Tappan of Ohio, with the support of Representative Robert Dale Owen of Indiana, took over the fight for a Smithsonian bill from a tiring Adams. The Tappan bill provided for an agricultural college, chemical laboratories, a museum, and popular lectures. Both Tappan and Owen were anxious to communicate practical knowledge to the common man, and the plan they supported for the Smithsonian emphasized these utilitarian elements. At Owen's insistence, the new bill was altered to include provisions for "judiciously conducted common schools" and a professorship of common school instruction to be located in a national normal school. Owen wrote a friend that "Adams' hobby, though not suffered to reign paramount, had not been neglected," since Owen had specified astronomy as one of

About his portrait painted by George Caleb Bingham c. 1844, John Quincy Adams (1767-1848) noted in his diary that the sitting took place in "a small hut or shanty at the foot of the capitol hill."

the subjects to be taught by the institution.

But neither Adams' nor Owen's pet schemes emerged dominant in the jockeying that went on. Instead, proponents of a big national library, most notably Senator Rufus Choate of Massachusetts and Representative George Perkins Marsh of Vermont, succeeded in establishing the notion that a large portion of the funds should go for this purpose. Choate set forth his vision of the Smithsonian as a great national library in a speech on January 8, 1845, asking: "Does not the whole history of civilization concur to declare that a various and ample library is one of the surest, most constant, most permanent, and most economical in-

21

strumentalities to increase and diffuse knowledge? There it would be —durable as liberty, durable as the Union: a vast storehouse, a vast treasury, of all the facts which make up the history of man and of nature, so far as that history has been written."

In supporting Choate's vision of a great library, Marsh ridiculed some of the alternative suggestions: "We are promised experiments and lectures, a laboratory and an audience hall. Sir, a laboratory is a charnel house, chemical decomposition begins with death, and experiments are but the dry bones of science. . . . Without a library, which alone can give such training and such discipline, both to teachers and to pupils, all these are but a masqued pageant, and the demonstrator is a harlequin."

Owen, however, who in 1845 had succeeded Adams as chairman of the House Select Committee on the Smithson Bequest, attacked the "bibliomaniacs." "Are there a hundred thousand volumes in the world worth reading?" Owen asked. "I doubt it much. . . . It grieves me not, that the fantastic taste of some epicure in learning may chance to find, on the bookshelves of Paris, some literary morsel of choice and ancient flavor, such as our own metropolis supplies not. I feel not envy, if we republicans are outdone by luxurious Europe in some high-seasoned delicacy of the pampered soul."

Yet Owen's alternative to the library, a national school for the training of teachers, was so offensive to Adams that he vowed he would rather have the whole sum of money thrown into the Potomac than appropriate one dollar to the scheme.

On August 10, 1846, after years of acrimonious debate and expedient compromise, the Smithsonian bill became law. The act was a grab bag reflecting the varying interests and influences that had been brought to bear on the subject. It provided for the construction of a building "with suitable rooms or halls for the reception and arrangement, upon a liberal scale, of objects of natural history, including a geological and mineralogical cabinet; also a chemical laboratory, a library, a gallery of art, and the necessary lecture rooms. . . ."

However, the fight over what the institution would become was not over; it was merely transferred to those designated to carry the plan into operation: the Board of Regents—the governing body—and their chosen representative, the Secretary. Of these men, the most influential was Joseph Henry, professor of physics from Princeton who was chosen first Secretary of the Smithsonian Institu-

Joseph Henry (1797-1878), the resolute first Secretary of the Smithsonian, appears in an oil portrait painted one year before his death by Thomas Le Clear.

tion on December 3, 1846. Henry came to Washington reluctantly. Alexander Dallas Bache, director of the Coast Survey and a regent of the newly established institution, had urged Henry to come: "Science triumphs in you my dear friend and come you must. Redeem Washington. Save the great National Institution from the hands of Charlatans! Come you *must* for your country's sake."

Some of Henry's friends, on the other hand, urged him to decline the invitation. R. A. Tilghman wrote Henry that he certainly did not undervalue the importance of an institution like the Smithsonian when in "proper hands" and in a "proper sphere of action; but I believe that *both* these are essential to extended utility and the desert of Washington seems to be the last place in which such a sphere could be obtained." In other words, Tilghman regretted that the institution had not been placed in a more cosmopolitan center like Philadelphia.

Henry, with unblushing confidence, proceeded to redefine the purpose of the institution, incurring even the suspicion of John Quincy Adams with whom he consulted on his proposed "programme" for organizing the Smithsonian. Adams remarked testily to Henry that he had thought the institution had already been organized by Congress. Henry, like Adams, agreed that the true purpose of the donor was the *increase* of knowledge, and secondarily its *diffusion* throughout the world, but disagreed with Adams on what to do about the act of Congress establishing the institution. Smithson's purpose, in Henry's view, invalidated the scheme to spend the bequest on a library or a "mere museum for the diffusion of popular information to a limited community," and certainly excluded the earlier proposals for a university whose function, at that time, was not designed to increase knowledge, but to diffuse that which already existed. "No other interpretation of the will," Henry insisted in behalf of his own definition, "is either in accordance with the terms employed or with the character and habits of the founder."

Senator Choate had shaped the law to read that up to $25,000 annually could be spent on the library, and as a member of the new Board of Regents, was able to preselect a librarian—Charles Coffin Jewett. But Henry, in effect, chose not to spend the amount authorized on the library. Eventually, in a test of wills, he fired Jewett and managed to sustain his point of view in the congressional investigation that followed.

The historic act of Congress, which made no reference to original research and publication as the appropriate means by which knowledge might be advanced, was in effect amended by the insistence of Joseph Henry that the carrying out of the will of Smithson was inconceivable without recognition of the purposes a man of his character must have had in mind. Henry argued his case so persuasively and so boldly that he converted even members of Congress who had disagreed entirely with his interpretation. In 1852 Senator Stephen A. Douglas, the "Little Giant," was lecturing in the Smithsonian building at a convention of agriculturalists when Henry happened to walk

Social reformer, advocate of birth control and women's rights, Robert Dale Owen (above) carried on the fight for the Smithsonian in his capacity as Congressman from Indiana. He was delighted with the building committee's choice of James Renwick's Norman-style plan for the Castle. In later years, Renwick was portrayed with sketch of New York's St. Patrick's Cathedral in hand (right).

in. The trend of the senator's remarks was to suggest that the Smithsonian should be converted into a society for the promotion of agriculture. Henry, as he later described the scene in a letter to Bache, rose and stated ". . . that the money was not given to the United States exclusively for its own benefit but for the good of man—given in trust for a special object. And that it would be an everlasting disgrace to our country if the trustees of this fund should divert it from its proper object and devote it to their own use etc. I was very much excited and I fear was rather severe in my remarks. The whole however passed off very well and Judge D. found he had made a mistake."

Henry's ability to keep the shadow of partisan politics from the door of the Smithsonian was an achievement of no small proportions since, as he put it, "There is no place in this country where *motives* and *acts* are more critically examined than in the City of Washington. There is none in which *capacity, honesty of purpose,* and a *prudent, straight forward course* are more necessary to continued success, and none in which *deviations* from *right,* whether intentional or otherwise, are more readily detected and exposed."

Yet Henry was able to sustain his interpretation of the meaning of Smithson's will against those who wished to promote the interests of the museum, the library, education, and other pursuits which Henry deemed inconsistent with the research mission of the institution. To the objections at first raised to his plan of organization, such as "that Congress has enacted laws in regard to the institution, which must be obeyed," Henry boldly responded: ". . .the resolutions of Congress may be changed, but the will of a dead man should be inviolable."

Henry had been fighting another battle with those who

sought to erect a grand edifice to house the Smithsonian's activities. This meant challenging Robert Dale Owen, regent and chairman of the Building Committee, whose architectural plan for the institution was, at Owen's insistence, published by the Smithsonian as its first publication. Henry, whose distaste for Owen grew as he came to know him better, successfully met the challenge of the "builders" by obtaining a delay in the construction of the Smithsonian Castle until the interest on the Smithson fund could produce sufficient revenue to support its early operations. "Though I am an admirer of good building," Henry wrote his wife about the plans of "young James Renwick," the architect, "yet I do not choose to be its victim." Henry kept Renwick on a tight leash, forcing him to choose simplicity over ornateness whenever he could effect the change. He was unsuccessful, however, in having the two wings of the building eliminated. By 1855 the Castle was largely complete with Henry and his family inhabiting an apartment in its east tower.

Joseph Henry maintained an even longer fight against the pressure to create a large museum with the proceeds of the Smithson fund. The objects collected by the Wilkes expedition to the South Seas (see page 164) had been turned over to the Smithsonian, and Congress saw an opportunity to free itself of the responsibility for maintaining other such collections· by a similar transfer. Henry was faced with the prospect that Smithsonian funds might be consumed in the upkeep of the national collections. His friend, Professor Benjamin Silliman of Yale, wrote him that "If it is within the views of the Government to bestow the National Museum upon the Smithsonian Institution, the very bequest would seem to draw after it an obligation to furnish the requisite accommodations without taxing the Smithsonian funds: otherwise the gift might be detrimental instead of beneficial." Senator Jefferson Davis of Mississippi, one of the regents of the Smithsonian, compared the proposal to give the national museum to the Smithsonian to the gift of an elephant that the King of Siam might give to a minister whom he wished to crush. "The minister cannot refuse the present, because it comes from the King, but the expense of keeping the present crushes the minister."

Henry's objections to becoming the nation's museum keeper were not merely financial. "The tendency of an Institution in which collections form a prominent object," he wrote, "is constantly towards a stationary condition. . . . There is indeed no plan by which the funds of an Institution may be more inefficiently expended, than that of filling a costly building with an indiscriminate collection of objects of curiosity, and giving these in charge to a set of inactive curators." Henry was induced in 1857 to accept the national collections on the understanding that Congress appropriate money for their upkeep. Nevertheless he estimated in 1876 that fully one half of the Smithson income

had gone to house and take care of the collections. With some bitterness, he noted that "every civilized government of the world has its museum which it supports with a liberality commensurate with its intelligence and financial ability, while there is but one *Smithsonian Institution*—that is, an establishment having expressly for its object 'the increase & diffusion of knowledge among men.' "

Powerful Senator Stephen A. Douglas wanted the Smithsonian to concentrate on agriculture. His portrait above was painted as decoration for 1860 election campaign—which he lost to Lincoln.

Henry worried most about the political consequences of a huge museum complex that might overshadow the research mission of the Smithsonian. "The Museum is destined to become a very large establishment, commanding considerable patronage and is at all times liable to be brought under direct political influence: the association while advantageous to the Museum is dangerous to the future of the Institution." He feared that the Smithsonian, as it became dependent upon skillful lobbying every year to convince Congress to appropriate money for support of the national museum, was liable to "fall under political dominium, and, finally, be presided over by some distinguished politician."

Henry was not opposed to original research which required, or produced as by-products, museum objects:

"Nothing in the whole system of nature," he wrote, "is isolated or unimportant. The fall of a leaf and the motion of a planet are governed by the same laws. . . . It is in the study of objects, considered trivial and unworthy of notice by the casual observer, that genius finds the most important and interesting phenomena. It was in the investigation of the varying colors of the soap-bubble that Newton detected the remarkable fact of the fits of easy reflection and easy refraction presented by a ray of light in its passage through space, and upon which he established the fundamental principle of the present generalization of the undulatory theory of light. Smithson himself, the founder of this Institution, considered the analysis of a tear as nowise unworthy of his peculiar chemical skill."

The Smithsonian Institution continues to mystify its friends and confound its enemies. "Dark on that whiteness, complication on that simplicity" still stands as a judgment on the Smithsonian, unique among organizations established by the government with more practical missions. Perhaps the confusion is inevitable because of the ineffable character of the mission: "to increase & diffuse Knowledge among men."

Certainly the infinite variety of opinions about how that sublime object is to be achieved underscores the confusion. When Samuel P. Langley, secretary from 1887-1906, sought a modest appropriation to support his researches in aeronautics, he had to face cynicism and disbelief in Congress and ignorance and jest from the press. Before the era of the airplane, the common wisdom was to assume that if man was meant to fly, God would have given him wings. The Smithsonian as an institution pushing back the frontiers of knowledge has frequently met with the jeers or suspicion of those situated comfortably within the limits of existing knowledge. As a result, the Smithsonian has tended to support with its private funds what might seem bizarre and useless to those who provide the institution with its public funds. When a program ceases to be bizarre and becomes obviously useful, then the Smithsonian is inclined to transfer its operation to some agency more concerned with the obvious.

Examples of this practice are numerous. Joseph Henry instituted the procedure of obtaining simultaneous telegraphed reports on the weather in different parts of the country in order to come to a more scientific understanding of meteorology in the country. As soon as the utility of such an operation became obvious, Henry encouraged the formal organization of the task outside the Smithsonian. The result was the U.S. Weather Bureau.

After the War Department withdrew its support from Secretary Langley's aeronautical experiments, which had achieved theoretical successes but practical failures, the Board of Regents, in 1913, reopened Langley's aerodynamical laboratory and created an advisory committee to organize further research in aerodynamics in cooperation with other government and private agencies. The committee was the forerunner of the National Advisory Committee for Aeronautics, which in 1958 became the basis of the National Aeronautics and Space Administration (NASA). Under Secretary Charles Doolittle Walcott, (1907-1927), the Smithsonian provided financial support to the pioneering experiments in rocketry of Robert H. Goddard as well as publishing, in 1919, his "A Method of Reaching Extreme Altitudes." As Dr. Wernher von Braun recalled, only a handful of persons in Europe and America then comprehended the significance of Goddard's experiments. Now that manned spaceflight is within the understanding of all, and its utility in peace and war obvious, it is appropriate that billions should be spent by the government itself on its development. The importance of the Smithsonian's role in advancing knowledge cannot be measured in the total amounts spent over the years but in the quickness with which fundamental intellectual problems were recognized and placed on their way to solution.

Had James Smithson been of a more cynical turn of mind, he might, like the donor in Mark Twain's story, "The Man Who Corrupted Hadleyburg," be suspected of having conducted an experiment to demonstrate how corruption and ignorance can normally be counted upon to obliterate man's puny attempts at benevolence and high purpose. But most observers would agree that rarely has a nation been more successful in administering a trust in accordance with the intention of its donor. Although the history of the Smithsonian has been, and continues to be, a history of intense controversy over the specific ways of carrying out the will of the founder, that will in its general purpose has remained inviolable.

Opening the curtain on his Philadelphia Museum, the first in the United States, Charles Willson Peale (self-portrait opposite, painted in 1822) displays the astonishing wealth of his collections. They include not only birds from expeditions to the West and portraits of Revolutionary heroes (rear wall), but also the fantastic "mastadon" skeleton which Peale had helped unearth and which filled the contemporary mind with delightful fears that such beasts still roamed North America. Beside Peale's left hand, which is held "in a gesture of exposition," is his painter's pallette; thus one sees the wide range of history, science, and the arts represented in his museum. It was precisely this "Cabinet of Curiosities" that Secretary Henry argued against as a pattern for the Smithsonian, saying it would not coincide with Smithson's intent and that it would require excessive space and funds. Yet it was indeed this kind of museum that second Secretary Baird perceived as beneficial, both for interested citizens and for scholars probing the collections, and therefore appropriate for the "increase & diffusion of Knowledge."

Shadows of Yesterday

Shapes of Tomorrow

A winter's setting sun projects the pavilion-like image of the Arts & Industries Building against the concrete curve of the Hirshhorn Museum.

They line the Mall—the diverse, distinctive buildings that house the Smithsonian collections. Each one speaks to its own time: there is the turreted Castle, the majestically domed Natural History building, the circular presence of the Hirshhorn, and the bold towers and sky-reflecting bays of the National Air and Space Museum. Together these structures present a panorama of changing architectural tastes in America.

The Castle of red sandstone, completed in 1855, was the

first home for the Smithsonian Institution. Robert Dale Owen, chairman of the building committee, was a firm advocate for a large and showy building. The future success of the institution, he believed, depended upon a structure which could make "conspicuous the work of the organization." Submission of 13 different plans heightened public interest in the proposed building. Two plans of Gothic and Norman style, submitted by architect James Renwick, were favored by the committee. Owen was delighted with the committee's choice of the Norman version which, he noted, "seems to me to have struck into the right road" and deserved to be designated as a national style of architecture for America.

The choice proved auspicious. The eight crenelated towers of this richly colored building stand etched against the changing sky. The unusually crisp execution of details and the rhythmic massing of the building have contributed to the creation of an image so strong that it has become a trademark for the institution.

The popular success of the 1876 Philadelphia Centennial Exposition prompted the construction of the second Smithsonian building, a repository for an enormous amount of Exposition materials. In 1881, the Smithsonian completed the home for the first United States National

"The Smithsonian College must, in itself, be hereafter a most picturesque subject," mused the American sculptor Horatio Greenough in 1851, four years before architect James Renwick's Norman design (opposite) gained acceptance. Picturesque in flames, too, the Castle suffered less extreme devastation from the 1865 fire than imagined by *Harper's* magazine artists (below). By the time your grandparents visited Washington, D.C., and sent home a tinted postcard from the site (left), the Castle was ivy-hung, tree-shadowed, and . . . picturesque.

Museum (now called the Arts and Industries Building). The flowing, centralized plan of this building on Independence Avenue east of the Castle recalls a traditional 18th-century French museum format; this architectural solution ex-

pressed the time-tested concept of the museum as a place for maximum display areas, a place to experience the multiplicity of things in the world.

In the exposition style, banners flying, the structure hugs the ground under a vast industrial iron roof—which has as many ups and downs as a merry-go-round. The building's material is common brick made of local clay in Washington brickyards, enlivened by gaudy splotches of glazed color. This first National Museum, proudly regarded as one of the most economical of federal buildings, was built for the modest cost of $250,000. Yet cheap construction proved costly later: plaster fell in patches from the ceiling; the Smithsonian annual report for 1881 records ominously that the situation "greatly endangered life and property in the Museum," requiring an entire summer for repairs.

No sooner was the new National Museum opened than there was an urgent need for more space. For 20 years Congress annually turned down appropriation requests. Secretary Baird in 1885 could only report in dismay that

Architects of the National Museum, whose oaken doors first opened in 1881, dramatized its national importance and cultural grandeur (right, top). Their early rendering of an inside hall (right) emphasized its engineering vigor and light-filled airiness. For the Bicentennial celebration, the Smithsonian returned this structure, now called the Arts and Industries Building, to its first function—display hall for machinery and other artifacts from the Centennial Exhibition in Philadelphia.

·NATIONAL·MUSEUM·
·WASHINGTON·D·C·

"the need is now much greater than ever before, as there is enough material in the way of valuable specimens of economic interest to fill a second building the size of the first one."

The initial idea to create, in the exposition style, a twin to the National Museum changed over the years to a totally classical concept. The ultimate design for the projected building on Constitution Avenue, now known as the National Museum of Natural History, featured a ceremonial entrance dressed by grandiose Corinthian columns. Controversy commenced after Congress had approved this approach. A major design battle raged over the dome. Praising this most sacred and imperial of Roman forms as a magnificent symbolic statement (whether it functioned for the purpose of exhibitions or not), the architects won out over the space-hungry curators.

The National Museum of History and Technology is totally different in concept and design; neither the old name nor the grand, classical image of a temple for the nation's goods seemed appropriate. What was wanted in that era was a non-image, a passive but dignified shell to house collections, not to glorify the institution or the nation. Yet the quality of this cautious, introverted structure captures the gray-flannel American mood of the late 1950s.

When the National Gallery of Art—with its formal, symmetrical design—was under construction in 1939, Congress appropriated funds for another museum that would be devoted to contemporary art. The father-son team Eliel and Eero Saarinen submitted a winning design for this proposed Smithsonian Gallery of Art in a forthright, modern architectural style, but lack of funds and the war years

A noble dome and arched entranceway were to proclaim the significance of the second National Museum, as shown in an architect's proposal, above. By its construction, 1911, it had lost some loftiness. But when glimpsed over Mall tulips, (below) much grace remains.

Largest of Smithsonian structures when built in 1964, the National Museum of History and Technology has room enough to hang a 71 foot pendulum to demonstrate earth's rotation. More utilitarian than grand, the building offers step seats for poolside lounging (opposite, below).

Like a crystalline hangar for man's star-bound chariots, the National Air and Space Museum is photographed above with Venus poised in the sky. The building, which opened on July 1, 1976, presents three vast halls gleaming between concrete masses that house 23 galleries.

Rising above the Mall's greenery—and even above the bold towers of the new East Building in the view below—the dome of the National Gallery of Art floats as a reminder of the beauties of another age. The two structures are linked by public spaces for gathering and dining.

aborted the innovative plan. Yet the Smithsonian never lost sight of its desired role as an active center for contemporary art, and 30 years later ground was broken for the Hirshhorn Museum and Sculpture Garden.

A highly individualistic, functional American design emerged: the Hirshhorn is a concrete cylinder 82 feet high and 231 feet in diameter. Lofty walls frame it. Its enduring

impact upon the popular imagination seems to be as a modern fortress, a protector for the valuable art inside the walls. Once inside the fortress, however, the exciting paintings and sculpture dominate; the architectural presence is deliberately muted.

If the Hirshhorn turns inward, the National Air and Space Museum which rose beside it in 1976 opens itself to the outside. About the same size and shape as the National Gallery and of the same pinkish Tennessee marble, the Air and Space building was designed by architects Hellmuth, Obata, and Kassabaum to be "contemporary," a soaring structure in tune with man's fascination with flight.

Scheduled to open in 1978, the latest Mall structure is the East Building of the National Gallery of Art. (The National Gallery, although formally established as a bureau of the Smithsonian, is an autonomous and separately administered organization governed by its own board of trustees.) The bold new addition stands free yet in a balanced relationship to its imposingly formal parent. Architect I. M. Pei worked on an architecturally demanding site to create a building which is comprised of an exhibition center of three towers connected by bridges clustered around a central court, and a study center with offices arranged around a six-story library well.

Each of the Smithsonian's buildings is an expression of the perceived role of the institution in the culture of its day. The Smithsonian's first role, to be a center for learning and inquiry, is still embodied in the scholastic medievalism of the Castle. The successive buildings housing the treasures of the nation create sharply different images as they march eastward from the Castle down the Mall, as seen on the chart on page 82—from the gaiety of Arts and Indus-

Tubular steel roof trusses of the Air and Space Building must support the enormous weight of exhibits hanging in Milestones of Flight (above); yet they remain open enough to bring in light and Mall glimpses.

tries to the efficiency of Air and Space. The Freer Gallery to the west of the Castle (built in 1923, page 188) retains the stern privacy of a Renaissance palace—an astonishing contrast to the East Building of the National Gallery of Art that stands so beguilingly on the opposite corner of the Mall.

This architectural panorama, with its variegated patterns and purposes, reflects the efforts of the Smithsonian Institution to serve the constantly changing needs of the American people.

by Cynthia Field

Regent's Choice

Once a Regent, I tell my friends here, always a Regent. Even now, more than a century after I was forced in most untimely fashion to leave the Board and my dear family to venture to these heavenly altitudes, I still retain a proprietary feeling about the institution. Our most important task then as now was the selection of the chief executive officer, the Secretary. And while pride and self-satisfaction are frowned upon in these parts, I must confess that my colleagues and I have been remarkably perceptive in the eight choices we have made over the years.

field of learning, but unlike college presidents, secretaries of the Smithsonian are unencumbered by the often messy exigencies of student bodies and alumni. The Secretary holds a lordly position in the worlds of science and the arts. He guides and often personifies one of the few organizations—if not the only one—associated with the United States government that has a world-wide reputation for doing *only* that which seems best.

Second Secretary Spencer Fullerton Baird, his wife Mary, and daughter Lucy.

Consider for a moment the Secretary's job itself: an administrative post of unparalleled appeal. It carries the rank of cabinet officer but is insulated from the variable breezes of party politics that drive—and eventually drive out—all cabinet officers and their chiefs. It bequeaths upon its holder the role of leader in the

With wife and daughters, Joseph Henry relaxes in a c. 1865 photograph.

Yet a remarkable—even exasperating—thing is that in most instances when the Secretary's job has been proffered, it has been accepted only with strings attached and sometimes with what smacks of reluctance. Of course, when Joseph Henry was urged in 1846 to become the founding Secretary, the institution existed only in name, the job had to be "created" by its holder, and Washington—with its unfortunate climate

and its frightful lack of social sophistication—was hardly an attractive place for any but those afflicted with an incurable lust for politics. Why would the nation's leading scientist, a pioneer in the study of electricity, the inventor of the induction coil (a device which made possible the telegraph), a man who refused to patent his inventions out of a deep-seated belief in the purity of science . . . why would such a man leave his work to do battle with an argumentative and egotistical array of Congressmen to build an institution of learning on the edge of a swamp?

Indeed, Henry wrote: "I could not hesitate about accepting (the position of Secretary), though from the first I had much misgivings as to the propriety of the course, but I considered that I was the only available candidate of a scientific character, and that it was my duty to endeavor to direct the funds of the liberal Bequest by Smithson to some useful end, and not to suffer it to be wasted on unworthy objects or chimerical projects. Views of this kind, rather than thoughts of personal aggrandizement, led me to accept the position. . . ."

I can say with complete assurance that Henry's successor, in 1878, was also the best man in the country at the time for the job: Spencer Fullerton Baird. He welcomed the assignment when it came. He had, even as a young man, wanted to be associated with the Smithsonian, applying in 1847 by letter to Henry for the job of curator. An unequalled collector of natural history specimens, he had, by the age of 19, amassed so many ornithological specimens that Audubon himself gave the young naturalist his own not inconsiderable collections. (I have reason to suspect that finances played a role in Baird's interest in the Smithsonian: as an associate professor at Dickinson College in Pennsylvania, he earned a salary of $650, less than half of the salary he would earn at the institution.) Eventually Joseph Henry took him on—not as a curator but as Assistant

Samuel Pierpont Langley, the third Secretary of the Smithsonian, sits for a formal photograph.

Secretary and head of the new National Museum, and Baird arrived in Washington in 1850 with two train-car loads of specimens weighing some 89,000 pounds. Thus was the Smithsonian launched solidly into the amassing of specimens in spite of Henry's sometimes voiced misgivings toward collections.

Secretary Langley studied vultures in flight at the National Zoological Park.

The insatiable natural history collector and the ascetic physicist got along very well despite their different emphases. Having created what has been called the "Bairdian Period of Ornithology" by publishing *North American Birds*, Baird switched to fish, became the country's leading icthyologist, and in 1871 was named by President Grant as the first Commissioner of Fish and Fisheries, a

post he held in addition to his duties at the Smithsonian. He was a superb administrator, eking money out of every nook and cranny for research and collecting expeditions. One of his curators wangled a huge amount of material from the Philadelphia Centennial Exposition which, once it was housed on the Mall, formed the basis for many of our collections today. (Forgive me; "our" slips in quite naturally.)

But, you see, it is the Fisheries connection that proves the point I'm making. In 1878, when Professor Henry died, my colleagues and I were delighted to offer Baird the position of Secretary. He accepted with characteristic enthusiasm but at the same time retained his position with the Fisheries Commission. Indeed, he established a laboratory at Woods Hole, Massachusetts, which itself has gained a certain repute in the intervening years. And, furthermore, while Secretary, he spent his summers and other times of the year there on Fisheries business. I used to twit Baird about this at those Regents' meetings I attended before coming here, but I later came to understand that his double role was beneficial to the institution. The Smithsonian flourished. As the nation settled the West and industrialized the East, the institution explored, collected, learned. It became the National Museum.

Not until a decade after it occurred did I hear the sad news of Spencer Baird's death in 1887. (Communication up here is very slow . . . and why not, after all? No one here is in much of a rush.) The new Secretary, Samuel Pierpont Langley, was a gentleman I had met once when he was a young professor of physics at the Naval Academy. Later, at the Allegheny Observatory in Pennsylvania, he established the system of standard time distribution to train stations and other interested parties, the time being set by the observatory. Such a man—of thought and practical action—would, I believed, be a good Secretary.

And so he was, as I later found out. Under his leadership the institution continued to flower. The collections grew, research was encouraged, the National Zoological Park was established, and Langley also founded the Smithsonian Astrophysical Observatory of which he named himself director, pursuing not only astronomy but his other first love—heavier-than-air flight.

Langley experimented with the engines and airfoils needed for flight, and between 1891 and 1903 he built a number of models including a steam-driven model with a 15-foot wingspan that flew 3,000 feet on two occasions. No less than President McKinley asked Langley to develop a larger, man-carrying machine—but unfortunately this plane, the Aerodrome, was a failure. Though Langley was personally humiliated by the failure and was haunted by it until his death in 1906, he had nonetheless launched the Smithsonian into what I, in earlier times, used to call the heavens.

Langley's successor, Charles Doolittle Walcott, kept his gaze firmly fixed in the opposite direction: on the ground. As Director of the U. S. Geological Survey, he had founded the Reclamation Service, the Forest Service, and the Bureau of Mines. When he became Secretary he advanced and expanded the institution's activities, while spending every summer in the Canadian Rockies, studying Cambrian and Precambrian formations and amassing vast collections of fossils for the Smithsonian.

Walcott's successor later wrote: "It is said of Walcott that seventy percent of all knowledge of Cambrian paleontology at the time of his death

was due to Walcott, and three-quarters of that seventy percent he had discovered while Secretary. . . ." The writer, Charles Greeley Abbot, had succeeded Langley as Director of the Astrophysical Observatory and then succeeded Walcott as Secretary in 1928. This, of course, was an era called the Depression, not a particularly good time for

Paleontologist Charles Doolittle Walcott, the Smithsonian's fourth Secretary, visits the Grand Canyon. His field work added greatly to knowledge of the Precambrian and Cambrian periods.

expanding the institution's range. Nevertheless Abbot succeeded in such delicate tasks as retrieving the Wright Flyer from Great Britain where it had resided ever since the Wright brothers had had a tiff with

the Smithsonian. A man of remarkable vision, he had earlier given financial and moral support to a "crank" named Robert Goddard (who, of course, flew the first successful liquid propellant rocket). Later as Secretary and afterwards until his death at the age of 101, Abbot patented devices designed to turn the sun's energy into useful power—a matter of even more concern on earth these days, I hear.

When Alexander Wetmore succeeded Dr. Abbot in 1945, the institution had at its helm one of the world's leading ornithologists, a man who had been director of the National Zoo and later of the National Museum. Dr. Wetmore was, and remained after his tenure as Secretary,

Charles Greeley Abbot, pioneer solar scientist, with a chart showing the relationship of precipitation and solar activity.

one of the nation's most prodigious researchers in the field of living and extinct birds. To him we owe a major portion of our knowledge of avian evolution as well as of the living birds of Central and South America.

The period from the 1920s to the 1950s was, it appears from here, a necessarily quiet time for the institution. What with the Depression and the War, the Smithsonian performed its functions of research and curating collections sturdily but generally out of the public eye. But in the 1950s, the nation was again a booming, bustling place, flexing its muscles.

The new Secretary, Leonard Carmichael, set about the business of flexing the Smithsonian's muscles. He had been a psychologist but had become primarily an administrator at Tufts University before coming to Washington. Carmichael applied the insights of his field to the institution itself. As an educator and a psychologist, he focused much of his energies on developing new exhibition techniques, building the National Museum of History and Technology, where his ideas could have a fresh garden in which to grow.

Then in 1964, the Regents selected the eighth secretary. My information is a bit behind the times, as usual, but from what I understand, this man S. Dillon Ripley, a Yale man, is off to a good start. He has acquired the splendid old Patent Office Building for some of the Smithsonian's art collections and is talking about a museum of modern art with a gentleman from New York. Through his prodding, a new field in biology—called ecology—is being practiced: heaven knows what *that* is. (In fact, heaven *doesn't* know yet.) And Mr. Ripley is an expert on, among other things, waterfowl and the birds of India and Pakistan, and apparently a considerable force in the conservation of wildlife.

I'm glad to know about these outside interests of Mr. Ripley's. It seems to me, after a century of thinking about the matter, that an institution so redolent of the nation's history requires continuity as well as a willingness to face new challenges. And an administrator who engages in scientific research keeps himself in touch with the best of the past. He shares the exacting rigors of his curators, and keeps his feet planted firmly on the shoulders of the giants whose patrimony he nurtures for the future.

A remarkable photograph portrays the most recent of the eight Secretaries. From left, current Secretary S. Dillon Ripley, Charles G. Abbot, Alexander Wetmore, and Leonard Carmichael.

Well, enough of that. I'm off to a Regents' meeting. We keep on holding them up here. It may seem a bit silly since we're behind the times but even so, we can't help believing that they have some kind of beneficial effect. Once a Regent, always a Regent. That's what I say.

by James K. Page, Jr.

39

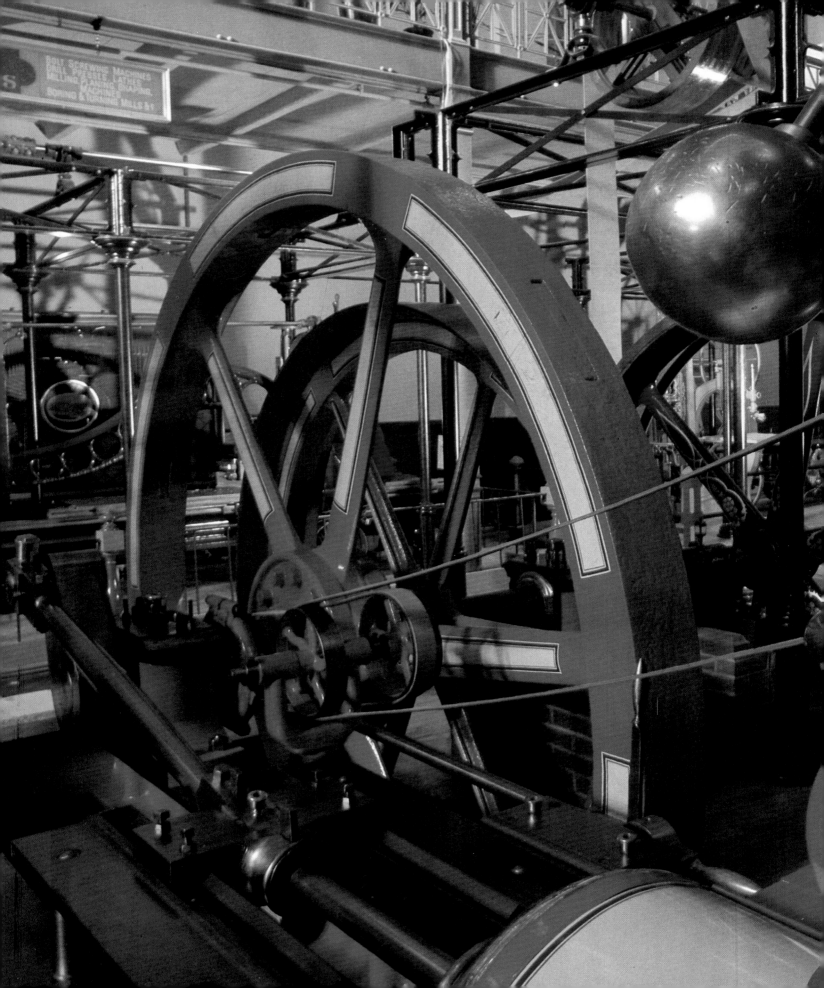

PART TWO

The Art of Exhibition

When wheels, belts, and governor weights turn all at once, this big steam engine makes a wonderful sound. It's like farmers honing scythes in unison. Sight and sound convey the knowledge that many old external-combustion engines whispered while they worked. At the Smithsonian most exhibits educate on several levels. Appealing to the mind through the senses, they impart understanding, perspective, and feeling, as well as cold hard fact (as the next story attests).

At the Museum of Natural History, furthermore, you can step back 700 centuries to experience life—and death—among Neanderthals. After meeting some of them and the craftsmen who prepared their exhibit in our picture essay, you'll feel as if you know these resourceful men and women of the Ice Age.

Marilyn Cohen and Benjamin Lawless then take you farther behind the scenes and into the past to introduce you to decades of Smithsonian exhibit styles.

As for the exhibit viewer, the general rule is HANDS OFF! But as Susanne Anderson's photographs show, there are hundreds of exceptions—including the entire navigation bridge of the aircraft carrier U.S.S. Hancock, a pickled rattlesnake, and a rock from the moon.

Finally, see the institution's exhibits through the eyes of the guards. Once somebody tried to break loose and steal the moonrock on display for people to touch. Pistols ready, guards had the culprit in custody and out of the building in seconds. To this day you can see the mark made on the moonrock by the would-be thief's wrench.

41

Exhibits You Can Hear

The great, green Southern Railway locomotive that stands on the lowest level of the Museum of History and Technology has inspired numerous stories in the press. It chugged onto the Washington scene before the building was completed—in 1961 to be exact—and stirred up all sorts of questions like: How does a 275-odd-ton monster on iron wheels negotiate Constitution Avenue without destroying that famed thoroughfare? How do you get it into the building? How would you get it out again? Does the floor have to be reinforced to take the weight?

The newspapers answered all the questions: very carefully on a monstrous flatbed truck; through a huge window in that wall; you wouldn't; you bet it does.

But my favorite story about that engine has to do with its sound effect. It's my story because I saw it happen.

The engine sits there on the reinforced floor, its wheels gripping a scrap of track. It's an overpowering sight—huge and gleaming with its green paint and silvered connecting rods. And then the sound comes on. You hear this deep, powerful *huff* along with a concert of hisses and ticks, and if you belong to the right generation your mind is snapped back to some childhood day when you saw a similar locomotive standing at a station platform, hissing and ticking and occasionally huffing, while steam wreathed up from around its funnel, making the buildings beyond shimmer in the heat waves. The engineer in his billed cap that seemed made of mattress cloth would stick the long spout of his oil can into various crannies in all that warm machinery, and the fireman, looking languidly out of his open window, would wink solemnly at you.

The sound effect includes those mysterious groans and sighs and squeaks that emanated from couplings and joints as the cars settled down to rest at the depot while the new passengers got aboard. And then you hear the distant cry of the conductor. It's a shout as stylized and as indecipherable as the calls of the fruit vendor or the rag-and-bottleman in those places fortunate enough to have them. It's a badge of the conductor's profession, proudly learned and here perfectly transmitted to the sightseers at this museum.

It is followed by the first great CHUFF of the engine, and you know before you hear more that the wheels will slip on that shiny track, and that first thunderous pulse of power will surely disintegrate into a ripple of senseless little puffs unless the engineer adds sand and the wheels begin to grip at the second CHUFF. And the second CHUFF reverberates, and the third, and the fourth, and you hear the wheels creaking forward and the hot breath of the cylinders as the great pistons plunge and drive.

And it was at just this point, when I was listening along with a group of tourists, that a man of my age reached out to his three-year-old grandson who was staring up at the front of the monster, and gently pulled him off the track.

The sounds at the Smithsonian work this sort of magic on you. You hear the Southern Railway locomotive pass you by, its voice receding, and you *know* that there must be a crossing ahead that will demand a whistle. And sure enough, there it comes, rising above the clack of the last cars on the rails—that indescribable multi-note wail that stirs up our nostalgia and fills us with undefined longings: whoooeee: the blues in the night. As it fades, you turn away, climb a few steps, round a corner into the display of old cars, carriages, and bikes in the Hall of Transportation, and suddenly hear another sound, filled with meaning. A bright red 1903 Winton two-seater is starting up. From under its shiny hood comes a long, cyclical grinding as some invisible force—surely not a hand crank?—is trying to get that inefficient two-cylinder engine running. At last the first gasping explosions erupt, then smooth out to a flowing pant of modest power as another—or perhaps the same—unseen hand adjusts choke and advances spark.

You are sure you can see the hood quiver with the engine's vibration and the blue exhaust rise triumphantly in the clear country air of 1903. You are certain you smell the fumes—that delirious odor recalled from childhood, when you thought that no harm could ever come from such a seductive scent. You can even visualize the driver and his companion in dusters and goggles, he with cap turned around, she with a scarf pinning down the broad brim of her hat. You may well wonder why the American automobile industry spent all the intervening years taking the fun out of automobiles.

No sooner has the Winton two-seater worked its magic than another sound across the room takes over. This comes from where the carriages are parked. It has a light, scratchy, grinding sound punctuated by rapid and uneven pulsations. Vastly more generations of humans lived with this particular music than ever knew the song of the Winton, and so, perhaps atavistically, you recognize it—carriage wheels crunching along a gravel

A first—the 1903 red Winton made the coast-to-coast trip in 44 days.

road with the hoofbeats of a pair of horses clopping away in front.

And again your imagination fills in the gaps: the white dust rising from the thudding hooves, the scent of hayfields and roadside lilacs, of warm leather and of horses. The sight of that beautifully preserved old carriage cannot, alone, transport you in this way. The sound of it does.

Airplane engine noises, of course, are especially effective. Over in the National Air and Space Museum there is ample opportunity to make the displays talk to you with their voices of power, but the technique is used with restraint and so has a special impact. In the Exhibition Flight Gallery there is a film taken by a camera that is obviously attached to a biplane. The scene is a country airstrip, and the action consists of the camera plane following another biplane through takeoff, slow roll,

loop, and finally landing. But it's the sound of that engine that plays the major role, for it permeates the gallery, speaking for all those exhibits of old barnstorming planes and of the stunts that were done with them. Hearing it from outside the gallery, you are drawn in to sniff the heady fragrance of high octane fumes, to feel the cool air beat at your face in an open cockpit, to sense the small kicks and buffets in the seat of your pants as the plane makes its way through the restless currents of the air.

In the Apollo to the Moon Gallery, you would expect the terrible thunder of a Saturn rocket's lift-off, that sound that beats upon your chest so that you almost gasp for air. But, cleverly, the story is largely told by video tapes—President Kennedy addressing Congress, the build-up toward the moon shot—and also, marvelously, by the voices of Apollo 17 astronauts Eugene Cernan and Harrison Schmidt as they guide their lunar module *Challenger* toward the ultimate American moon landing, December 11, 1972. Their terse statements, heard from within a mock-up of their lunar module, take on meaning that is new to most of us. They are not just dramatic words, but, spoken at the control console of that vehicle, logical and necessary.

President Woodrow Wilson used the 1905 cabriolet in WWI to save fuel.

Sounds play a part in other museums. Headsets at the art galleries offer insights to what you're seeing; at the Museum of Natural History they give you the sound of an elephant trumpeting, a whale singing, a dozen other beasts sounding off. But it's at the Insect Zoo, which is in that latter museum, where the sounds surround you with amplified volume. These roars and squeals and mighty chirps and chitterings are not at all familiar. They open an unexplored area to you and fill you with new knowledge and wonder.

My favorite of all the "talking" exhibits is back in the Museum of History and Technology, in the Nation of Nations exhibit. Here you find a prairie scene. You are in a farmyard looking off at gently rolling land, bare of trees. A windmill stands in the foreground, its rough timbers rising to the vanes spinning overhead. And you hear it. You hear the whir of the shaft and the rhythmic squeak of the pump rod. Especially you hear the endless sigh of the wind, gently stir-

ring across that open land, a vast, soft movement of continental air that picks up a little dust now and then, kicks along a tumbleweed occasionally, rustles the wheatfields, and, right here, turns a windmill.

The audio part of this scene continues with the sounds of chickens and hogs, the slap of a door being shut, the bump, rattle, and clink of chores. But the prairie wind permeates the whole scene so that you suddenly know what life is like there. It is as crystal clear to you as if you had been brought up beside that creaking windmill and known it for the better part of your life.

by Edwards Park

45

A New Image For Neanderthals

Photographs by Chip Clark

Some 70,000 years ago a young man was buried according to accepted ritual in a cave in southern France. The body, knees drawn up under the chin and probably bound in place with rawhide or plant fibers, was laid on a bear skin in a limestone-lined pit and covered with a massive stone slab. On this were placed votive offerings of stone tools, haunches of bear meat, and a deer antler, all covered by a cairn of pebbles. Bones of brown bears *(Ursus arctos)* arranged decoratively in older cairns nearby bore witness to a religious cult that must have flourished for many generations.

A dramatization of the burial—unearthed in 1957 in the Dordogne region of France about 90 miles east of Bordeaux—is part of the Hall of Ice Age Mammals and the Emergence of Man in the Smithsonian's Museum of Natural History. The scene presents our Neanderthal antecedents in a startling new light. Heretofore, they were thought to have been beetle-browed, lame-brained, hunchbacked creatures who shambled along like apes, wore dull expressions on gargoylish faces, and grunted "ugh" when moved to speak. Such first impressions were based on the widely accepted misconceptions of noted French paleontologist Marcellin Boule, who wrote early in this century

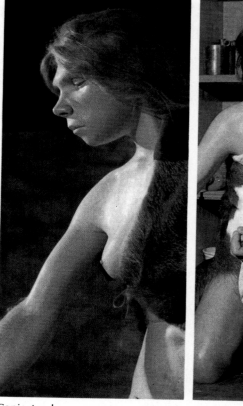

Conjectural mourners at an ancient funeral, these solemn but strikingly modern looking figures of a Neanderthal woman and boy were created after careful study of Neanderthal skeletons from sites in Europe and the Middle East.

of the "brutish appearance" of Neanderthals. They were "uncouth and repellent," echoed an English anthropologist, with a "peculiarly ungraceful form."

They were, in fact, upright individuals astonishingly like people of today, comparable in size and build, although having a somewhat larger, longer head with a pronounced brow. And, far from being the "bestial kind" that Boule perceived, Neanderthals possessed, as finds in burials have attested, traits characteristic of mankind. Yet, the loutish caveman cliché persisted in people's minds.

At least part of the Neanderthals' image problem can be traced to the scarcity of complete skeletons. Studying a

few fossils, often of greatly different ages and dating from the late Ice Age of 100,000 to 40,000 years ago, anthropologists have agreed only that Neanderthals were *Homo sapiens*. But were they precursors of modern man? Or an aberrant offshoot of the ancestral stem that died out, to be replaced by modern man? Or a combination of both? Or neither? The answer is hotly disputed.

In recent times enlightened people have sought to rehabilitate the Neanderthals' reputation. Within the Smithsonian, scientists of various disciplines have joined with artists and craftspeople to project a fresh image of Neanderthals, one that would be both credible and dramatic.

The Natural History Museum, planning the Hall of Ice Age Mammals and the Emergence of Man, envisioned a multi-faceted geological and paleontological panorama, encompassing the last three million years in a series of fossil displays, dioramas, murals, and tableaux. Visitors would walk by skeletons of giant ground sloths, saber-toothed tigers, mammoths, mastodons, and other Ice Age animal life in almost life-sized murals, while a theater's slides would present the grinding, scouring advances and retreats of the great Pleistocene glaciers.

In the midst of this sweeping montage of the ice ages, a speculative but vivid recreation of a Neanderthal burial scene would find a natural stage. Recreation of the scene suggested by the Dordogne finds won enthusiastic approval; a Stone-Age funeral was deemed more meaningful—and less trite—than, say, a hunting scene in which Neanderthals spear a bear.

Overseeing the creation of the Neanderthal figures was Dr. Lawrence Angel, the Smithsonian's Curator of Physical Anthropology. Dr. Angel examines ancient skulls and ponders personalities. He conjectures that the man of the Dordogne burial, because of his large parietal lobes, "was something of a dreamer and a poet." He was fair skinned,

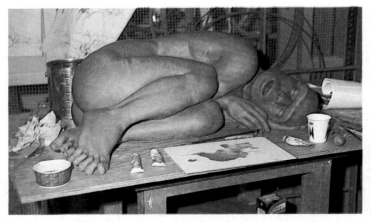

Representing the only known participant in the Dordogne burial, this recreation of the dead man nears completion on the sculptor's bench.

Dr. Angel believes, and like modern Europeans, quite possibly blond. "We decided to make the shaman in the exhibit red-headed," the curator revealed, "because shamans always have something unusual about them." A conjectural figure, as are all in the exhibit except the dead man, the shaman stands ramrod straight: "There is no evidence that he was less erect than we are."

When Alfred McAdams, chief designer for the hall, asked for a model for the shaman to guide sculptor Vernon Rickman, Dr. Angel glanced about the hall and spotted photographer Roy E. "Chip" Clark, bearded and built like a fullback. "There he is," the scientist said. Clay studies of a

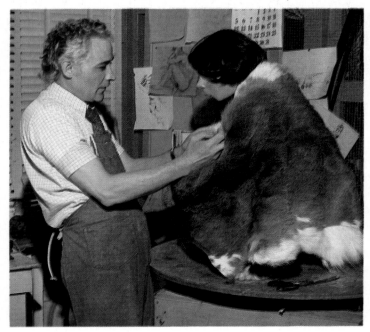

Clark-shaped shaman were soon ready for inspection.

It was McAdams's task to translate words into physical reality. He chalked off areas, sketched ideas, tested small scale models. He played mental games, assuming roles of visitors: "What should I see? What can I touch?" He tried dummy rails at varying distances from the Neanderthal exhibit to keep specimens just beyond arm's length. He elevated the observation ramp to give viewers the illusion of

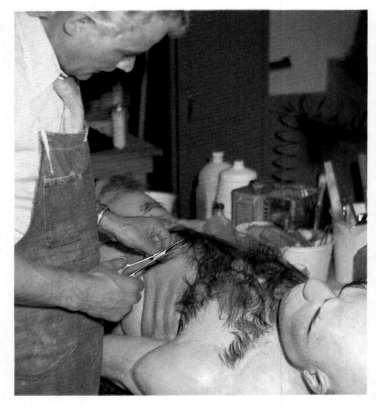

Barber and haberdasher to Neanderthals, sculptor Vernon Rickman knows them man and boy. After adjusting a fur cloak for the youth, he trims the shaman's hair to proper shagginess with surgical scissors.

looking into a cave. The intensity of light, the size and placement of printed legends, the colors and textures of fabricated items—"making them appear as real as possible"—typified the problems to be solved.

The evolution of the Neanderthal exhibit—from thumbnail sketch to a full-scale, three-dimensional tableau—challenged nimble minds and skilled hands. Heather Banks, technical information specialist, was pressed into service as a model for the Neanderthal woman cast as the widow of the dead man. Besides posing with an arm outstretched to simulate an offering of food, "I was even scrutinized for skin color."

The Neanderthal figures, modeled in clay around styrofoam cores used as armatures, were cast in fiberglass. In painting them, artist Rickman mixed wax with oil colors—"the Rubens method"—to give luminosity. He glued on inexpensive wigs bought at a downtown shop. An

walk superintendents, they were outspoken in their observations. Model maker Bruce Hough recalled that as the shaman was lifted into place, a little girl gasped: "He looks like my gym teacher."

That remark succinctly summed up the purpose of the exhibit. Neanderthal man was no monstrous brute. He was an acceptable member of the family.

by Wayne Barrett

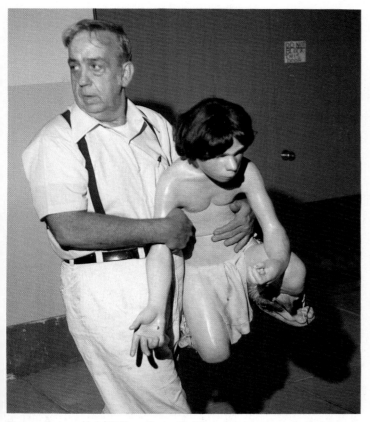

Brawny but careful, William Donnelly is one of the dozens of exhibit specialists who spent over 3,000 man hours creating the burial scene. (The boy, it should be noted, has shed his cloak, as most boys would.)

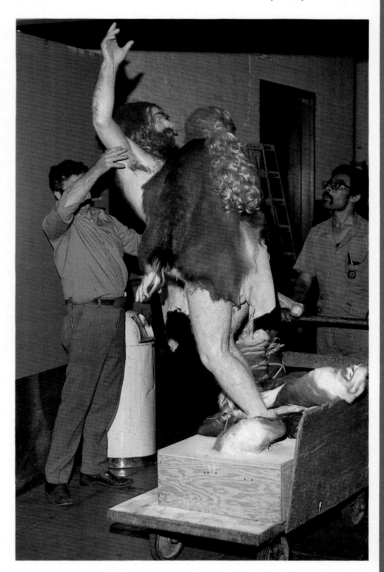

excessively mod style on the little boy in the exhibit forced the decision for a last-minute haircut. At Dr. Angel's suggestion, Rickman singed the shaman's beard with a soldering iron to impart a rough, natural look. The shaman's painted face derives from ochre crayons discovered at Neanderthal sites.

The stones in the exhibit were fashioned from polyurethane and cut into various shapes. The walls of the cave are papier-mâché and coated with water-base paint. After months of painstaking labor the Neanderthal exhibit was ready to be assembled. Crates were trundled into the hall to a circular area chalked on the floor. Although wooden barriers closed off the place, curious onlookers previewed the exhibit through cracks and peep holes. Like all side-

Wigged, booted, and clothed, members of the Neanderthal funeral begin a short but slow journey toward installation in the burial tableau.

Overleaf: the completed Neanderthal burial exhibit highlights the Ice Age Hall's story of human evolution.

The Smithsonian Style

by Benjamin Lawless and Marilyn S. Cohen

In the spring of 1954, Secretary Leonard Carmichael decided to paint the interior of the old Arts and Industries Building of the Smithsonian Institution. The colors he selected—a pink, a warm yellow, a sky blue, and a wondrous green—were as unexpected as were the painters who arrived with spray guns primed and covered in two weeks that which had not been painted in 76 years. Visitors to the exhibits, in the opinion of this experimental psychologist, were likely to be favorably impressed, but certain members of the Smithsonian staff felt the move rash and suggested that the standard grey-green recommended by Curator George Brown Goode in the 19th century was a more lasting color.

"Matches dirt exactly", said one cost-conscious historian, "you can hardly tell where one leaves off and the other begins!"

Carmichael was not persuaded and, as he looked about for other ways to brighten up "the Nation's Attic," as some newspapers were calling the old Smithsonian, he found exactly what he was looking for in the Exhibits Modernization Program begun a year earlier under his predecessor, Alexander Wetmore. Substantial amounts of museum money began to flow toward renovation of exhibits, and people who had grown accustomed to writing a memorandum to justify buying one tube of paint suddenly found themselves awash in a cornucopia of materials.

At the time two exhibits were being redone: the First Ladies' Gowns, which for generations had been displayed in the Arts and Industries Building in standard museum cases little differently than if they had been animals or birds, and an assembly of pre-Columbian artifacts displayed as a type collection on the upper floors of the Museum of Natural History.

The work was going slowly, and the people involved, curators for the most part, were becoming discouraged by what seemed to be an endless imposition on their professional time. Exhibits, the Smithsonian was discovering, were something more than "considerations of upholstery

Benjamin Lawless, an Assistant Director at the National Museum of History and Technology, is in charge of exhibitions.

Marilyn S. Cohen serves as supervisor of the Exhibits Evaluation Program at that museum.

beneath the dignity of an institution of learning" (as one 19th-century curator called them). They required people with special kinds of knowledge and experience.

Within a few months, new faces began to appear among the Smithsonian staff, young faces for the most part. These Exhibit Workers, as they were called in those days—designers, illustrators, typographers, and preparators—looked upon the great collections stacked from floor to ceiling with a mixture of horror and anticipation. Their entrance into the ranks of the Smithsonian professional staff would dramatically alter the status quo of 100 years.

And so the workload for the exhibit personnel increased. Two new Indian exhibits were completed in the Natural History Museum, while planning began on three other exhibits—Mammals, Birds, and Life As It Was Lived in the Colonial United States. A Hall of Health appeared in the Arts and Industries Building. Its vivid demonstrations of bodily processes culminated in a life-sized transparent woman who spoke in strange accents of the mysteries of womanhood as lights glowed and winked over various portions of her glass-like anatomy.

An exhibit worker was dispatched to the Cretaceous chalk beds of Kansas to search for a fossilized fish desperately needed for an exhibition. He eventually found the fish, but the search took five weeks and nearly ruined the timetables which had suddenly appeared on everyone's wall. Fossil fish, warned these charts—even rare ones from the chalk beds of Kansas—must appear on schedule if exhibit deadlines were to be met. Efficiency was becoming a word often heard in the dusty offices of the Smithsonian Institution.

Exhibitions at the Smithsonian were taking on a professional look. Joseph Henry had nothing like this in mind when he became the Smithsonian's first Secretary. The primary goal, he felt, ought to be original research. Collections for display were relegated to odd corners of the red sandstone Norman Castle, unattended and, more often than not, identified in Latin. After a time, as the holdings of the Smithsonian increased, Henry relented somewhat and requested congressional appropriations to defray the cost of displaying specimens. In 1850 he hired Spencer Fullerton Baird as an assistant, never realizing that Baird's interest in public education would, within eight years, foster a "museum" within the great hall of the Smithsonian building. For a beginning, this museum was an extraordinary effort. The graceful wooden exhibition cases were designed by the Architect of the Capitol, Thomas U. Walter. The arrangement of specimens, labeling, and taxidermy were as good as could be found in any other scientific museum in the world. Guidebooks were printed to assist the

"A rapid stroll through the halls" should acquaint one with the exhibits at the Smithsonian, wrote curator George Brown Goode in the 1890s. By the 1930s, the First Ladies' Gowns could only be scrutinized as rare, isolated specimens.

visitor as he toured the displays and these were expanded to include the Biological Sciences, Ethnology, and Fossils.

A "style" of exhibition began to evolve. At first the exhibition halls of the Smithsonian resembled nothing more than an enlarged version of the Cabinet of Curiosities used by wealthy European collectors to exhibit everything from unicorn tusks to mastodon bones. In 1849, with the transfer of 18,000 devices from the Patent Office collections, the Smithsonian and the U.S. suddenly had a "cabinet" that was unsurpassed in size and variety by anything in the Western World.

The Smithsonian artifacts were presented, according to Henry, "for the satisfaction of the mature man of science," and shelved, as in a library, by category. Only gradually through an increasing involvement with national and international expositions did the Smithsonian begin to concern itself with attracting the public into its exhibit area.

"The greatest fair of them all," the Philadelphia Centennial of 1876, was to increase the institution's concern for the public dramatically. First, Congress appropriated $67,000 for Smithsonian participation at the Centennial. For that time this was an astronomical sum—exceeding by 16 times the institution's budget less than 10 years before. And then, after the Centennial, literally as the exhibits were being dismantled, a young Smithsonian curator, George Brown Goode, who had set up the government and Smithsonian displays at Philadelphia, secured for the institution 34 displays that had been sent from foreign nations and almost all of those from the states and territories.

The magnitude of acquisitions was greater than anyone had anticipated. It proved an understatement when Joseph Henry, in his last year as Secretary, guessed that his institution's involvement in the Philadelphia Centennial "would have a greater effect on the future of the establishment than would at first be apparent."

He had no idea that within another year Congress would

approve funds for a building to house the Centennial collections. Situated next to the Smithsonian Castle, and called the United States National Museum, this building was the most advanced structure for exhibitions in the country when it opened in 1881 (see page 32). Yet it was this museum, unchanged by the middle of the 20th century that helped earn the Smithsonian its late sobriquet, "the Nation's Attic."

In the beginning, Goode, under the benevolent eye of Spencer Baird, Henry's successor as Secretary of the Smithsonian, established a set of guidelines for exhibitions that in sophistication and philosophy are eminently suitable even today. Goode organized the collections into coherent rational categories. He was concerned for the physical wellbeing of both visitors and objects. He had exhibit cases arranged in neat rows spaced far enough apart to offer unobstructed vistas. He attempted to develop exhibits on two levels, one for the serious student and one for the casual visitor. To this end he devised the multi-layered exhibition hall which allowed a rapid appraisal of the collections on a walk through the primary aisles. A more thorough investigation of subject detail could be obtained by exploring side avenues off the main path.

Goode published voluminously on the subject of exhibitions and museum principles. When he died in 1896 at the age of 46, some said it was from exhaustion due to his strenuous efforts to make the Smithsonian collections understandable to all people.

Four years later, Samuel Pierpont Langley, third Smithsonian Secretary, had in mind a museum just for children within the original Smithsonian Building and planned to include all things that would appeal to young eyes. There would be bright-plumaged birds and tiny nests and eggs. Low shelves would hold aquaria filled with colorful fish and baby turtles. The children's museum would be a sunny

Lithograph of Children's Room devised by Secretary Langley for Castle shows stained glass, bird cages, and aquariums.

spot, comfortable, attractively designed, and conducive to wonder. It was most discouraging to Langley therefore, when he read the label his scientists had prepared for the European robin: "*Erithacus Rubecula* (Linn)." He rewrote it on the spot: "Robin Redbreast, one of the best beloved birds of England." The administration of this new museum, Langley realized, must rest with someone who understood the interests of children. So, as Secretary of the Smithsonian, he appointed himself Honorary Curator. In a letter to himself accepting the appointment on behalf of the children of America, he said he hoped that now they would have the same opportunity to enjoy a museum as adults had always had.

In 1903 a new Museum of Natural History was under construction across the Mall. For many years the scientific staff of the Smithsonian Institution had felt increasingly confined in the National Museum as their collections in anthropology, geology, and biology increased at a rate of a quarter of a million objects a year. Two departments, Industrial Arts and History and a National Gallery of Art, were wedged in among all of the natural history collections; Assistant Secretary Richard Rathbun, who was in charge, despaired of ever making sense out of the place. In an uncharacteristically passionate statement in the 1906 Annual Report, Rathbun complained that both the Smithsonian Building and the National Museum had been turned into warehouses, and that year by year as the exhibition cases were nudged closer together public enjoyment of the museum was being diminished. He felt that the experience of seeing steam engines, farming tools, Indian clothing, and marble statues all gathered under one roof, while perhaps impressive, was not exactly inspiring.

The 10 acres of new exhibition space in the Natural History Building solved a part of the problem. But there was a new condition which had to be dealt with. The public was becoming accustomed to seeing specimens in other museums exhibited in a fresh condition and in orderly display cases. Because of this, preparation of the Smithsonian displays took longer than was expected, and the exhibition spaces were still not completed two years after the building was occupied. The Natural History Museum, pressed for a deadline, invented the phased opening of exhibits, an accommodation which did not displease 281,000 people who toured the unfinished facility in 1910.

Meanwhile the Arts and Industries Building, as the old National Museum was now called, was declining into creaky old age. Exhibits of startling novelty in 1881 were by 1918 merely antique. As floor space disappeared under an avalanche of objects representing the best of American arts and industry, a new means of displaying things had been discovered. Specimens began to be suspended from the ceiling joists. At first this seemed merely eccentric, but with the inclusion of aircraft, overhead exhibits took on a new meaning. Some didn't like the idea at all. One assistant to a curator, called to task for his long absences from his desk, explained that his visits to the washroom were now taking him nearly 20 minutes. Since the washroom was only a short distance away, the incredulous curator asked how a trip which normally took less than a minute could possibly take that long. The hapless assistant replied that he was afraid the airplanes overhead would fall and so had plotted a circuitous route that took him completely around the inside of the building but "never underneath one of those danged flying machines."

After World War II the Smithsonian, reluctant and kicking, finally found itself pushed into the 20th century—just in time, for the century was almost half over, and the exhibition halls in three separate buildings looked very much as they had in 1910 and before. Some of the younger staff members returning from military service decided to do something about the situation and began pushing for yet another building to relieve the congestion of exhibits. Congress had heard all of this many times before, however, and was not in a mood to accommodate the Smithsonian at that time.

Subtle measures of persuasion were developed as curators and artistically inclined junior staff members began a surreptitious renovation program, redoing one case at a time in various parts of both the Natural History and the Arts and Industries Buildings. This was a delicate business, as work on even small-scale exhibits was costly and in those postwar years there was very little money to go around. The Smithsonian secretariat took a benign view of these projects, however, and extra money was usually available for a tube of paint or a box of cardboard letters. Things went very slowly until an appropriation was sought, not for a new building, but for upgrading 11 existing museum halls. This time Congress felt more generous, and slowly the doors of the great American treasury opened.

People were hired who knew how to draw, who knew about color and design and lighting. Model builders appeared who could faithfully reproduce any object at any scale. Arrangements were made with government architects to review the museums for the rebuilding of exhibition spaces. New curators were employed who had an interest in displaying their collections and they began to write scripts, a curious literary form that other museums seemed to find useful when doing exhibits. Thus the Museum Exhibits Program was born.

Exhibition designers were recruited to work alongside the curators and immediately there developed what has since been euphemistically dubbed "creative tension." The Smithsonian discovered, as other museums had before, that exhibition designers and museum curators look upon the collections from two entirely different points of view. The curatorial departments were amazed to find that the designers assigned to their exhibit halls often felt that explanatory labels, if not entirely superfluous, were frequently too long. The curators, although deeply committed to the written word, made heroic efforts to reduce their texts to a minimum—only to be told by a label editor that their minimum was his maximum. For a time the relationship between a drastically edited label and the curatorial temper was direct and measurable. But the innovation of silkscreen labels with their graphic flexibility made long labels easier to design and locate, and this particular irritant was minimized.

In 1956 the Smithsonian was given funds to build a Museum of History and Technology, the first new structure on the Mall since the National Gallery of Art in 1941. And this time, everyone said, the exhibits were going to be different and exciting, informative, compelling, and irresistible. They were also going to be democratic in that they would appeal to everyone who walked through the front door including Professor Henry's "mature man of science." Additionally and especially, this new museum was going to explain to a curious public all about stellarators and other hitherto mysterious objects of science.

An exhibits preparation laboratory was set up in a rented garage a short distance from Georgetown and nearly a hundred designers, artists, and preparators were soon at work prefabricating exhibits for the new museum. One hundred of anything is a difficult number to work with, but 100 creative, expressive, and imaginative people were almost more than the Smithsonian could absorb. There was an immediate confrontation between the personnel office and management about what "those people" were going to be called. The exhibits people thought "Exhibits Workers" hum-drum, and the hive hummed with dissatisfaction. Management hemmed: wasn't "Information Specialists" a trifle top-heavy? It was a question of professional tone—too little, or too much? A compromise was discovered—"Exhibits Specialists" pleased all.

In celebration, the model builders, who had been working on a series of miniature Civil War cannon, fired them off and tore a hole in the side of the garage. This was more of a celebration than anyone had in mind, and only quick work by carpenters and painters prevented the incident from being noticed by the garage owner, who would certainly have raised the rent or found less rowdy tenants.

A new line of exhibition cases was designed, the first since 1920, but this time the basic structural material was hardened aluminum and steel instead of mahogany. Panel systems took form as did a new kind of museum lighting that could pick out a postage stamp at a distance of 50 feet.

The building, a monumental structure five stories high and filling an entire city block, grew slowly from the great sink where Tiber Creek had flowed before it was rechanneled under Constitution Avenue.

A quarry in Georgia, last used 20 years before during the construction of the National Gallery of Art, was reopened for its blocks of fine pink marble, to be used on the new museum's exterior.

The exhibition halls took shape as gangs of workmen toiled in a wet darkness plastering and painting to the designs of McKim, Mead, and White, the great architectural firm of the 19th century, whose last building this would be.

The Director of the new museum, Frank Taylor, modified George Brown Goode's multileveled exhibition hall plan of 1881, and called it the parallel gallery, suggesting that this was a way of presenting museum objects both to historians and casual visitors.

Across the Mall in a World War I tin shed a Fokker D-VII and a French Spad (with the wonderful name of Smith the IVth), a giant seaplane hull, and many other examples of pioneering aircraft and engines were undergoing their first cleaning since becoming museum specimens 40 years earlier. The National Air Museum, created by Congress in 1946 and long an orphan among the more established keepers of scientific and technological apparatus, was finding that the public had an interest in things that flew, and it began to shop for more ample space on the Mall.

The old Patent Office Building north of the Mall became a part of the Smithsonian holdings and the National Collection of Fine Arts found a permanent home. A new National Portrait Gallery was settled alongside in an arrangement that is still uncertain in respect to the sometime overlapping of good historic portraiture with paintings as fine art.

One wing and then another were added to the Museum of Natural History, and after half a century the building was finally completed.

On January 23, 1964, the Museum of History and Technology opened to an enthusiastic public who in their great numbers and eagerness promptly began to wear out everything that was not made of casehardened steel. New techniques had to be learned about crowd control, dust, and security as 10 million visitors strolled through the exhibition halls touching all that was within hand's reach. Barriers were invented that were unobstrusive yet protective; alarm systems were devised that buzzed quietly and then loudly; exhibits were created that pulled visitors past areas of congestion toward less populated zones. (But this was forgotten and only rediscovered when the new Air Museum, now called the National Air and Space Museum, opened its doors 12 years later.)

Curators, designers, and fabricators were horrified at the damage caused to specimens by the sheer number of people passing by them. A facility for conservation opened within the Museum of History and Technology, and the microscope and air monitor became both tools and burdens to curator and designer alike.

In 1965 a new Secretary, S. Dillon Ripley, celebrating the 200th anniversary of the birth of James Smithson, turned the statue of Joseph Henry away from the Smithsonian Building toward the Mall, symbolizing his interest in all of the Washington museums now under his leadership.

He asked for a new style of exhibition from the curators and designers, one that would involve people in the common fabric of their lives. It would no longer be enough to collect and display the rarest and the best; what Ripley suggested was to get at the meaning of things.

Curator and designer hesitated, but only long enough to agree that audio-visual aids were probably exactly what the Secretary had in mind. So was born the Audio-Visual Program, a program that would baffle and frustrate the best of minds within the institution. Odors were thought to be a way of introducing the meaning of things to people, and mouth-watering aromas of chocolate and caramel were introduced into a period room of a 19th-century confectionary shop, triggering instant and painful hunger symptoms in anyone near the place at lunch hour. A special smell of perspiration and the barnyard was developed for a display of a Maryland sharecropper's house. A visiting scholar was inadvertently sprayed with the odorous mixture as he was being shown the exhibit and he later wrote that his trip home on the Metroliner was a great success, as he had most of the seats in the car all to himself.

Sound effects were added to the exhibits at the request of Secretary Ripley and these were not only economical to install and maintain, but they seemed to spark interest in observers at minimal cost. Sounds of the great Southern

Railway locomotive instantly increased visitation to that hall whenever they were turned on, and in the Natural History Building an elegant program of African music was placed alongside several beautifully crafted instruments as a way to let visitors experience the sounds of Central and East Africa.

The Bicentennial celebration began to dominate the thinking of the Smithsonian Institution by the end of the

Gone from Smithsonian exhibits are immutable brass plaques. Instead: silk-screened labels, which allow quick switches. Above workers raise a screen used for July 4 banner.

1960s. Ideas for exhibits were received that ranged in scope from spectacles costing millions of dollars to smaller projects within the budgets of the individual museums. A huge exhibition of immigration and emigration caught the fancy of the Museum of History and Technology, while at Natural History an exhibit on plant and animal life in caves, which had been in progress for years, became to everyone's relief a study of the changing land.

The exhibition staff, seasoned by 18 years of exhibition work, looked happily toward the Bicentennial years as a chance to display their many skills and talents. What they failed to realize was that their organization had grown in size and capability far beyond what the institution's directors had had in mind 18 years earlier when the exhibits program began. Now there were more than 200 exhibit specialists—artists, carpenters, designers, illustrators, molders, silkscreeners, electricians, filmmakers, sculptors, editors, writers, bracket makers—ready to move on an instant's notice to wherever the work was to be produced.

Such productivity, however, could be achieved only with tightly organized schedules. Group meetings were set up every Monday morning to define the scope of the week's production, who was to be assigned each project, and how much work was expected to be done by the first, middle, and end of the week. The meetings were long and often charged with tension as exhibit after exhibit was analyzed for progress or delay. But by 1973 the museums had had enough of tension and set about reorganizing the exhibits staff into smaller, theoretically less efficient but more compatible groups assigned to each museum. Under the awesomely mechanical title of "re-articulation," the act of dividing 200 people into four major groupings, each fully balanced through design and production, went forward. Certain old loyalties to individual museums created a kind of human poker game in which people wanting to go to one place were often assigned to another, only to trade themselves back by getting replacements who desired what they did not. When the dust had settled, the three major museums on the Mall each had an exhibit staff which would produce exhibits entirely for that building. A central exhibits core was the last remaining unit and was not assigned to a museum, but kept as a central supplier of design and production to all of the institution's museums as well as to the very popular Traveling Exhibition Service. Through the years this last had burgeoned into a major nation-wide distributor of outstanding exhibitions.

All was in readiness for the Bicentennial. The National Air and Space Museum staff, flexing its newly appropriated financial muscle, decided to create three exhibitions to prove that it knew what it was doing. The exhibits, it said, would be transfered almost intact to the new Air and Space Museum, the building on the next to last area on the Mall available for a museum.

The more experienced members of the Smithsonian community looked warily upon this kind of enthusiasm and candor, but to everyone's amazement the very same planning techniques that put Apollo 11 on the moon worked just as well in placing museum cases on an exhibit floor. There is no technology in the world that appears to the average person as difficult to understand as that of flying, but the staff of the Air and Space Museum chose to approach the subject with a mixture of science, history, and humor, and the combination proved irresistible. The museum visitor, as he walked through an exhibit of Life in the Universe, found Julia Child on television stirring a bowl of "primordial soup," or discovered an animated man sitting at a kitchen table talking about the development of air traffic control over the years while he grew older minute by minute. Impertinent puppets in a theater introduced children and many adults to the vagaries of crossing the English Channel by balloon, while an earlier exhibit of World War I flying featured one of the airplanes displayed upside down as though performing a combat maneuver. What in 1918 had seemed an alarming eccentricity—hanging airplanes from ceiling rafters—now convincingly made them appear as if in action. To cap all, the Air and Space curators had learned to write a museum label that for information and brevity approached the quality of labels written 100 years earlier by George Brown Goode.

The exhibits staff of the Museum of History and Technology created seven variations of an exhibit on immigration and emigration before finally turning the project over to a contract design firm who guaranteed that it would be finished during the Bicentennial year.

Without thinking too much about it, this same museum staff agreed to reproduce 60,000 square feet of the Philadelphia Centennial in the Arts and Industries Building, complete with objects, cases, and style of the period of 1876. Presently they began to comprehend the complexities involved in an exhibit on so great a scale, but by then the idea had taken root and to back down would have been unthinkable. They lured a designer from another museum and in the course of several months this young man so steeped himself in the attitude and feelings of a Victorian museum director that he knew what was required in design without excessive review of source material. With something less than enthusiasm initially, old specimens were brought to like-new condition, others were borrowed, and all were thoroughly checked for correctness of period. Teams of designers, production people, restorers, installers, and curators worked together on what proved the most satisfying exhibition ever mounted by the History and Technology Museum. To conform with the original of 1876, labels were omitted. Identification of the objects was left to costumed docents and an occasional sales brochure of the time.

On the stroke of midday, May 10, 1976, a flock of pigeons was released, a choir sang the Hallelujah Chorus from Handel's *Messiah*, speeches were made, and the exhibition opened 100 years later to the day, hour, and minute of the original Philadelphia Centennial.

With the same kind of teamwork, personnel of the Air and Space Museum battled deadlines and a bewildering variety of government contract regulations to open the entire new museum, complete with all objects and exhibits, on July 1, 1976. Of all the institution's major buildings, this was a Smithsonian first—both as to meeting a deadline and adhering to a budget.

A plaster "America" holding a generator-powered torch seemed most appropriate center piece for Smithsonian' National Museum Building, opened in 1881.

Other museums and facilities of the institution, both within the capital and beyond, rose to the occasion with similar imaginative flair and effective teamwork.

The National Portrait Gallery discovered a way to bring excitement to dusty portraits by associating them with items from the lives of the people portrayed. This idea of an imaginative museum director, so simple yet so elegant and effective in practice, drew crowds to the old Patent Office for the first time in a century.

Curators and designers of the Museum of Natural History dressed up the entrance to their museum and created Bicentennial models of Rock Creek Park over 10,000 years as an introduction to their massive collections.

A new laboratory for exhibition training and production was built for the Anacostia Neighborhood Museum, a museum whose primary focus is directed toward the history and local concerns of the community.

During 1976, Bicentennial exhibitions at various facilities of the Smithsonian Institution opened almost monthly: a marvelous painting exhibition, "America as Art", at the National Collection of Fine Arts; a display and discussion of Washington, D.C., city planning at the Castle; the collections of the Cooper-Hewitt Museum on display in Manhat-

tan for the first time in many years; an exhibit of city signs at the Renwick Gallery; and finally the exhumation, analysis, and classification of the bones of Mr. James Smithson and their reinterment in a newly furnished crypt in the original Smithsonian building. The work was done, all of it.

The Smithsonian staff looked at what they had accomplished and the realization dawned on them that they

When restored to original condition in 1976, the building appeared a recreation of the Centennial: some 15 percent of the objects actually appeared in the Exposition; the rest evoked the era.

knew how to do exhibitions. It had taken more than 100 years, but the lessons were truly mastered.

The original intent to do "Smithsonian" exhibits in the past had been interpreted to mean a style that would be recognizable in every museum, but what was apparent in that summer of 1976 was that the Smithsonian had developed many styles of exhibition, almost one for each museum, and instead of being a drawback and a sign of creative failure, this was dramatic proof of the vitality of the institution. Each museum approached its collections in its own way—in the museums of art with a taste for beauty and simplicity, in the history museums with a passion for the excesses and variety that is the story of the American genius, in the science exhibits with explicit demonstrations of the structural facets of our technological civilization.

The people behind the exhibitions, the curators, technicians, aides, designers, and producers, were proud of their work; so much so that, when a lady from South Carolina wrote that she had visited the old Arts and Industries Building for the first time in 40 years and was pleased to find it so little changed, they knew they had done their job exactly right.

Go Ahead, Touch It!

Photographs by Susanne Anderson

Inch-worm, inch-worm,

measuring the marigolds,

You and your arithmetic

You'll probably go far.

From the musical production,
Hans Christian Anderson

Children are like that, too, compelled to touch their surroundings. They compare with their hands and measure with their bodies. Youngsters learn from inch-worm arithmetic as they shinny up, scramble over, and dangle down from Uncle Beazley, the dinosaur on the Mall. Inside Smithsonian halls, children discover hundreds of touchables.

Uncle Beazley, a 22-foot-long fiberglass *Triceratops*, suffers of course from being a reconstruction. Also, he is a pip-squeak compared to *Brachiosaurus altithorax*, the bulkiest land animal that ever lived. To bridge the gap of 150 million years between him and us, Smithsonian scholars have set aside at the Natural History Museum a five-foot-long fossil *Brachiosaurus* arm bone for touching. A gentle rub brings no jinni, but the bone is real, and the simple fact of touching it brings home the reality of the

dinosaurs and their era to many children. And what enchanted lamp could produce anything more magical than the vivid mental movies children conjure, in this instance with themselves and the dinosaurs in starring roles?

Another kind of gap can be bridged by touching, this gap being 240,000 miles wide. For no matter how true recent history is, the stupendous fact that men have walked on the moon is almost beyond imagining. Visitors to the National Air and Space Museum can now reach out and touch a piece of the moon, picked up in December 1972 by the Apollo 17 astronauts.

The favorite "touchable" for many visitors to this museum is a recreated World War I military airfield near Verdun.

Uncle Beazley—the dinosaur on the Mall—beguiles children. And when they quit climbing on him they often go inside the nearby Museum of Natural History to touch the arm bone of a real dinosaur (below). Knock! Knock! At the Insect Zoo, kids tap on a hermit crab's house, an old seashell. Claws poke out.

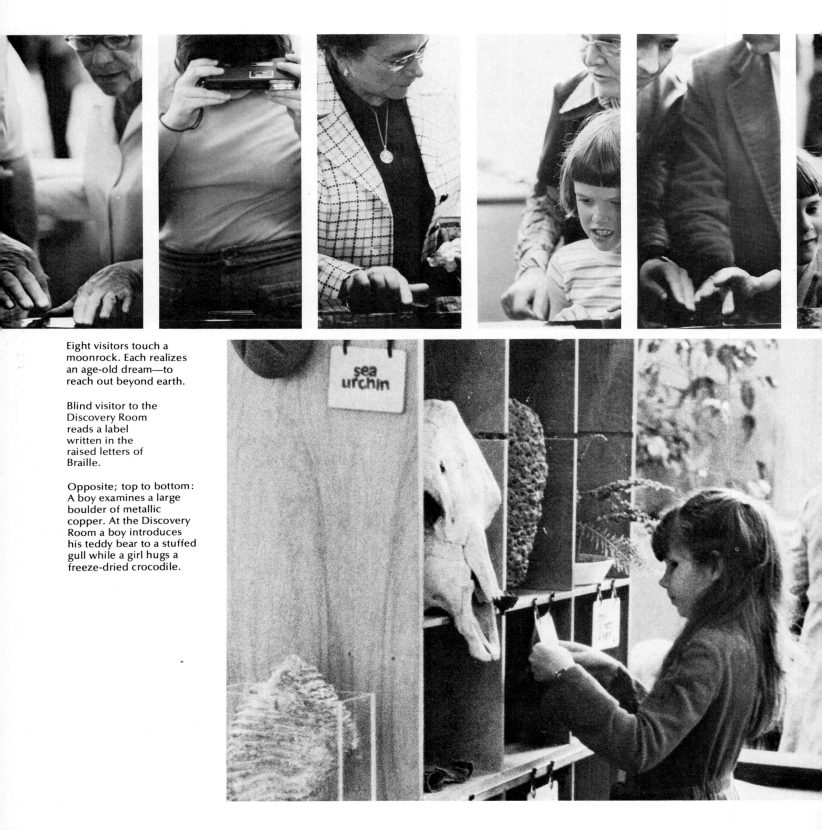

Eight visitors touch a moonrock. Each realizes an age-old dream—to reach out beyond earth.

Blind visitor to the Discovery Room reads a label written in the raised letters of Braille.

Opposite; top to bottom: A boy examines a large boulder of metallic copper. At the Discovery Room a boy introduces his teddy bear to a stuffed gull while a girl hugs a freeze-dried crocodile.

sea urchin

The time is November 9, 1918, just two days before the Armistice. The feel and smell of tent canvas, dusty sandbags, and shell-splintered wood add to the overwhelming sense of reality that hangs over the desolate scene. Further finger contacts with military hardware may be made on an aircraft carrier's bridge. The wheel and the levers work but, except in the pretend world of childhood, the museum won't sail away at flank speed on an alternate course.

For adults as well as children there is simply no substitute for hands-on experience. "I think with my hands," explains Paul Edward Garber, an early flier and now Curator Emeritus of the National Air and Space Museum. "The feel of an aircraft model coming into being as I work provides information of the real plane's characteristics and flight performance that sight alone can seldom reveal."

Blind people also think with their hands. At the Hirshhorn Museum, blind scholars can put on thin plastic gloves and touch sculpture. Since sculptors both think and feel with their hands, some blind people may have an advantage over sighted visitors in the "seeing" of sculpture. Seeing with the hands is something like standing before a great cathedral in pitch black night and shining the bright but narrow beam of a flashlight on one feature of the edifice after another. Each glimpse, however limited, adds depth, insight, and delight to the mind.

Much of the Smithsonian's touchable adventure occurs in the National Museum of Natural History. A number of mineral specimens from planet Earth, and some from the sky—meteorites—are meant to be touched. And in the Discovery Room, a mini-museum-within-a-museum espe-

Free-roaming bees travel a plastic tunnel to reach their hive inside the Museum of History and Technology. The girl who listens raises bees back home in Massachusetts.

Right: A boy at the National Air and Space Museum peers into a rocket motor built to boost a satellite into orbit. Now his pretend space travels will feature the real thing.

A most peculiar pottery beast resides at the Explore Gallery of the National Collection of Fine Arts.

cially for children, all the exhibits can be touched and even played with. A black boulder turns out to be a giant natural magnet, a lodestone; in its invisible magnetic field steel disks stand on edge and waggle. Elsewhere, young fingers encounter stuffed birds and reptiles, animal fur, fossils, seashells, and big whale bones. The star of the show is a pickled rattlesnake.

Experiences at the Discovery Room extend beyond the sense of touch to include smellables and tasteables. Young discoverers learn that the immature seeds of one spice, coriander, smell like bugs (the spice's name comes from the Greek word for bedbug).

Real live bugs can be touched at the nearby Insect Zoo. Scary but safe are big green hornworms, roaches, and a

non-poisonous centipede. The insects themselves have been bugged to provide recordings of their creepy sounding symphonies.

At Discovery Corner in the National Museum of History and Technology, student groups have shocking experiences with electricity. They feel tiny bolts of lightning from a generator of static electricity. Then they see how a model lightning rod draws away the spark. The current is low for safety, but interest runs high. In another corner young people can try on Revolutionary War uniforms and swing muskets to shoulders.

Elsewhere in the museum, curators sometimes take old-fashioned musical instruments out of the cases and make them sing. By special arrangement, visitors who are deaf or blind can touch the instruments being played and thus "hear" complex patterns of musical vibration.

An old carousel, still working well, combines motion and music. A Plexiglas tunnel penetrating the back-up Skylab Orbital Workshop invites you to walk through and imagine how teams of astronauts lived and worked for more than five months during 1973 and 1974.

To provide other historical and social experiences, a red double-decker bus from London rambles through Washington, D.C., on its free shuttle run between the Museum of History and Technology and the National Portrait Gallery. A country general store and post office from Headsville, West Virginia, was transported lock, stock, and calico to the Museum of History and Technology; it was reopened as an active post office, with its new postmark, Smithsonian Station.

Generally, nobody at the Smithsonian touches the Hope Diamond except the Curator, National Collection of Gems and Minerals, Paul Desautels. Recently, however, gemologist Robert Limon came in to remove the Hope from its setting, to examine it for hidden flaws, and to weigh it. Old records claimed that it was flawless—which it proved to be—and indicated a weight of 44.5 carats. But reweighed, the Hope tipped the scales at 45.5 carats. (No, it didn't grow; the difference is accounted for by changing standards for the carat over the years.)

All this goes to show the real value of touching and testing our surroundings. And though the sense of touch may appear slow and primitive, for many kinds of knowledge the hand remains quicker and surer than the eye.

by Joe Goodwin

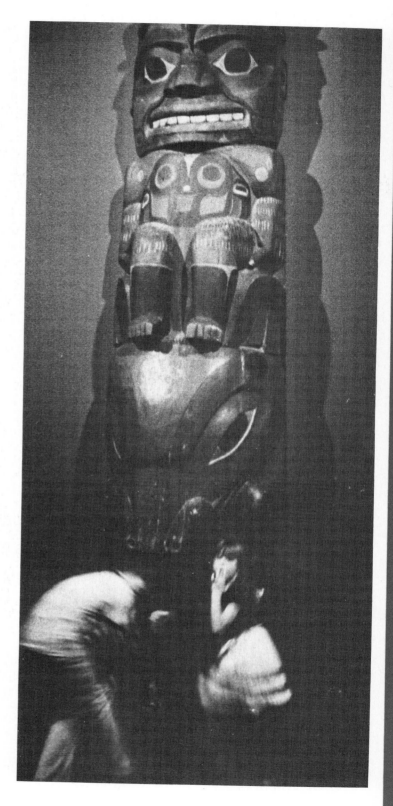

A brother and sister from the Midwest enter the door in a totem pole from the Pacific Northwest. Originally, the door led to a tribal building. And now, in the museum, it's quite all right to touch the totem and squeeze into the door.

What Happened When I Walked Off With the Hope Diamond

The event called for an institution-wide best foot forward. Henry Kissinger and a friend were about to pay a sudden visit to a couple of Smithsonian museums, squeezing a careful allotment of time between frantic scurryings to the Middle East. Very High Officials of the Smithsonian rallied to show off the Museum of Natural History and the Museum of History and Technology. Police appeared from nowhere to supervise traffic. Limousines hissed up to main entrances. Greetings were exchanged, guides introduced. The tour proceeded.

At the Museum of History and Technology one VHO of the Smithsonian and his wife followed along behind the Kissinger party, relaxed and pleased that things had gone so well at short notice. The tour route led past a newly opened exhibit which VHO's wife had not seen.

"Look at that gorgeous pewter," she said. "I wonder what kind it is." "Let's see," VHO said, and stepped gallantly over the restraining cordon to pick up a sample. And, as you by now have guessed, within a fraction of a second the entire party was surrounded by Smithsonian guards, guns drawn. The security system had been triggered, its full-fire blast fortunately squelched by timely explanations.

It isn't often that the Smithsonian guards have that much excitement or opportunity for unlimbering their sidearms. They are the young men and women who normally tell you how to find such-and-such an exhibit; who won't let you pass through "staff only" doors unless you're on business; who explain that, even though you've come to Washington from Butte, Montana, you're insane if you think you can park in one of the employees' lots; who keep children from falling into fountains, swinging on statues, and putting their fingers into spinning machinery. The guards are the first people you see when you visit the institution. Theirs is rather an awesome responsibility, as they are told in their training program. An officious guard can ruin your whole day.

The Smithsonian's security force—about 500 people—is composed of guards, policemen, detectives and four investigators. Guards, the basic category, by law are veterans. Policemen and detectives and investigators may be, too, but not necessarily. It doesn't matter to you much, anyway, since the uniformed figure you meet at the door is not there to demonstrate his proficiency with a mortar, but to stop vandalism or purse snatching, apply first aid if it's needed, and do other helpful things that are taught right here at the institution.

A new recruit gets four weeks of on-the-job training which he or she must pass. Then there's two weeks of police-academy-type schooling. Trainees learn about giving mouth-to-mouth resuscitation, how to handle crowds, how to "apprehend" (that marvelous word) criminals, all the other things that you recall from your TV shows. They make use of all the training facilities that the Washington Metropolitan Police, the Park Police, whatever other of the capital's many police forces have to offer. Rapport between the Smithsonian's little army and these powerful neighboring allies is very good.

Training ends with a graduation ceremony when the new people get their Smithsonian shoulder patches. Then it's out on the floors with them. Each museum has its own guard company, varying in size according to what is required of it. It doesn't take much supervision to keep things running smoothly at the Arts and Industries Building—only an occasional hard look at some youngster who wants to dive into the fountain pool

and retrieve some of the change that has been tossed in for luck. But at the National Air and Space Museum, with its vast area and enormous crowds, a lot of guards are needed to keep children (and some enthusiastic dads) from climbing into historic cockpits or reaching over the balcony to try and touch the wingtip of a suspended plane.

Flip-flops in the escalators are another category of problems at NASM. The escalators devoured these floppy little sandals when the building first opened in July, 1976. Guards stationed beside the devices ended the trouble.

At the Hirshhorn, the nature of the exhibits produces other problems. A modern sculpture that rotates slowly has proved irresistible to a few children and even to one or two adults. Guards have been shocked to find it occasionally carrying a couple of passengers round and round. And about the only paintings that are desecrated are those very modern canvases that seem to the uninitiated to be solid quadrangles of a single color. Sometimes—especially if the single color is light—the artwork seems to a child merely an empty area awaiting the scribbles of a more youthful talent.Out comes the pencil and *breep!* goes the guard's whistle.

In any museum, children get separated from their parents or school groups. A tiny youngster who has been told by a teacher to hold tightly to a classmate's hand will sometimes let go for a moment, perhaps in the squeeze around the Insect Zoo at the Museum of Natural History, and then quickly grab the first small hand he or she finds. And if it turns out to belong to a kindergartner from Newark, New Jersey instead of Pottsville, Pennsylvania, the guards have a small but vocal problem. They solve it by letting events take their sensible course. Teachers find they have either gained or lost a pupil; the pupil complains bitterly at being surrounded by strangers; guards are appealed to; the case is taken to the museum guard office; proper readjustments are rapidly made; no more problem. Lost children at the Smithsonian don't stay lost long enough to get a newspaper picture of them sitting on the sergeant's desk, wearing his cap and eating ice cream.

At night, the guard force drastically changes its ''posture'' (another evocative police word). From a paternalistically protective presence it becomes a tough and sophisticated defense force. Patrols include dogs. Sensory devices on display cases are beefed up. No one's going to mess with the smallest trinket from ''We the People'', much less the Hope Diamond.

The dogs can be quite terrifying. Pass one who is lolling about in a K-9 car, waiting for his handler, and he'll spring at the window with thundering barks that send you right out of your shoes. The guards say he's only being friendly. He's kept in his handler's home and he likes people except when he's told not to. Maybe. The effect of his presence—hair bristling around those bulging shoulders, gleaming eyes dourly surveying every rear end to determine which looks suspicious enough to be a possible target—has proved enough to rid the Institution of unwanted visitors. Even the winos who used to sleep it off on patches of grass or warm grills beside the buildings have moved on.

The Smithsonian guards can take credit for a sizable reduction of misdoings in the museums. Seldom is a lock tampered with. Very seldom is an act of vandalism found. As security authorities say, the nature of the Institution is the most effective damper on fooling around with exhibits. The Smithsonian belongs to everyone, and you don't deliberately smash things up in your own parlor.

In the "1876" exhibit at the Arts and Industries building stands a lovely old Steinway piano. It is sometimes played by costumed docents. And sometimes a tall young man comes in quietly, removes his uniform cap, and whips through some nice old songs while a crowd of sightseers gathers round watching a Smithsonian guard at another kind of duty. Obviously, at the Smithsonian, a policeman's lot is not necessarily an unhappy one.

by Edwards Park

69

PART THREE

A Collection of Things

During her lifetime Faith Bradford created this enchanting doll house. Now at the Museum of History and Technology, it reveals in affectionate detail the storybook life of Rose and Peter Doll and their family circa 1905.

In many ways, Faith Bradford's labor of love parallels the labors of certain Smithsonian workers. These curators acquire things of merit, study them, then assemble artifacts or specimens into collections that both delight and instruct.

Join Edwards Park of Smithsonian magazine on a odyssey in search of what curators call "museum quality." The trip reveals why a curator may pick up a tattered sign from the floor of a national political convention yet reject your grandfather's false teeth.

Paul Perrot introduces you to scientific conservators who protect acquisitions from the ravages of time. Other scientists work backward from tangible objects to reconstruct lost arts and neglected technologies employed by craftsmen of old.

At the Museum of History and Technology, Silvio Bedini helps detect counterfeit antiques and works to authenticate true heirlooms.

Finally, sit in that epitome of nostalgic furniture, a real ice-cream chair. Remember? You may recall poignant moments from the not-so-bygone era when ragtime was the rage.

Why We May Not Want Your Grandfather's Teeth

Any Smithsonian curator will tell you that hardly a day goes by without his receiving a letter, a telephone call, or a visit offering him some object that has lain long in someone's attic—and therefore must somehow be extraordinarily valuable to the institution. It may be a portrait, suspected of early Italian or Flemish connections. It may be a farm tool or a kitchen utensil or a brass telescope or an inkwell. It is either offered outright or only for appraisal. The Smithsonian doesn't appraise things it might accept for its collections. Of course if the Smithsonian reveals that your old umbrella stand is really a Ming vase worth a jillion dollars, and if you might decide to donate it to the institution anyway, we will doubtless accept it with considerable graciousness.

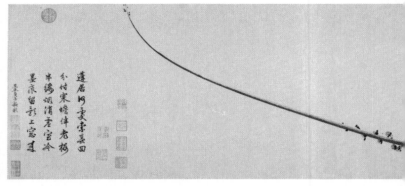

Detail from "Breath of Spring" by Tsou Fu-lei, Yuan Dynasty

A lot of people seem to think that anything faintly Oriental is a sesame to easy riches. The people at the Freer Gallery are besieged by requests for appraisals—so many, in fact, that the Freer sets aside every Tuesday from September through May to comply with requests and still finds that appointments fill those Tuesdays for months ahead.

Every week people bring in Oriental objects, and sometimes one of them has real value. Yet again, if it were offered to the Freer it might not be displayed because it did not fit the criteria. Not many works of art can claim the uniqueness of the ink scroll on these pages entitled "Breath of Spring." It's beautiful and it's also the only known work by Tsou Fu-lei of the Yuan Dynasty. The Bhutan devil screen (shown opposite) was designed to baffle evil spirits. It's intricate and interesting and tells a story. Also, it's not too big. All those things are criteria.

People who suggest sending their own mediocre family portraits to the

Life masks of Abraham Lincoln

The gallows hood, handcuffs, leg shackles, and cell key of the executed Mary Surratt

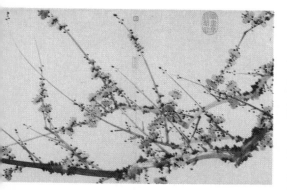

National Portrait Gallery might be forgiven if they have looked at the collection and noted, among other things, a rather bad portrait of Ulysses S. Grant. Surely, if the museum displays that, it might logically hang the dusty likeness of great-uncle Harker which you unearthed from under the eaves while trying to spot a roof leak.

But take a look at Grant's frame. That massive square of darkened hardwood is an intricate bas-relief containing acorns, oak leaves, and other kinds of vegetation plus the names of eight of the General's successful battles. That's a frame that's hard to beat. Also, it just happened that Grant was the 18th President and fits right into the museum's line-up between Andrew Johnson and Rutherford B. Hayes.

Bhutan devil catcher

There are other more straightforward portrait examples: a rather nondescript male figure of Major Whistler painted in 1858 after a lithograph. That's Whistler's father, son.

At the Museum of History and Technology long distance phone calls come ringing every day telling someone—any curator, it sometimes seems—that Grandmother's trunk has just been brought downstairs because the family is moving, and it's been dusted off and opened and here are the things inside. . . . The curators listen carefully and ask for a letter and a photograph of the ob-

Pictorial wool sampler in cross-stitch

jects that are offered. No one gives a cash value for this kind of object. Usually it is suggested that a local museum might be best for it.

Of course a life mask of Abraham Lincoln has no trouble making it into the museum. The one presented opposite in both bronze and plaster was done by Leonard Volk after the future President had been involved

in a Chicago law case. It was bought in the 1880s by 23 subscribers, each of whom got a copy of it as a sort of dividend. But they gave the original to the Smithsonian.

Five years after the life mask was made, Lincoln was assassinated, and the horrified nation quickly brought to trial the fellow conspirators of John Wilkes Booth. Four were hanged, including Mrs. Mary Surratt, the first woman to be executed in United States history. The institution was given the gallows hoods, handcuffs, leg shackles, cell keys of the prisoners, and also a piece of the scaffold. Unique and historic, these grim mementos have never been on

exhibit. Those relics pertaining to Mrs. Surratt appear on page 72.

I have seen Jimmy Carter peanut bags stowed away in a collection drawer in the Division of Political History after having been gleaned from the floor of the Democratic Convention hall by the curator. There seems little remarkable about them, but they are certainly cheap and compact (both criteria), and some day they will add value to the collection of political memorabilia. A number of campaign buttons and novelties like Teddy-Roosevelt-teeth

The Museum of Natural History gets its share of would-be contributions, too. I recall a "mermaid" that was shipped to one of its officials—a terrible looking little body with a monkey-like head and a fish tail. The top part was mostly papier-mâché and the lower part was actually a fish tail—old and stuffed—and an X-ray revealed a wooden frame that held the whole thing together. No, it

was photographed, of course, and then chalk lines were drawn diagonally across the wall and floor boards before they were pried apart and stacked on a truck. Back in Washington, all you had to do was reassemble the boards—if you got one out of place, you broke your diagonal line.

But why this kitchen anyway? Because, I learned, it fitted some precise requirements of the entire exhibition. The curators wanted people to see how earlier Americans lived from the distant to the recent past, moving roughly from east to west. There was a gap in mid-19th century west. This room filled it. Also, the room had an interesting history, well documented. That's important, because curators want their labels to be accurate. Also, that kitchen was available. It was serenely *there*, without a huge price tag attached to it (an important consideration for the Smithsonian, which watches costs like Scrooge).

Not far away is part of a balloon frame house, which was found in Illinois, torn down, and partly reassembled in its exhibit hall. Why? Because it tells of the technique of home building which developed after so many forests had been chopped down in our country that you couldn't count on finding lumber enough in your acreage to build your home. The balloon frame was lighter and easier to put together than the old hewn cabins and solid old homesteads of the early—and lumber-rich—colonial days. Two-by-fours and other elements of a balloon house could be carted to the site.

An Eskimo carving celebrates the killing of a seal.

flesh out the display dealing with American political campaigns. All of these once seemed as junky and trivial as the peanut bags.

didn't go on exhibit or into a collection. I don't know what the people there did with it.

Some time ago I listened to a history curator explain how a ranch kitchen, which is on display in the Everyday Life In Early America exhibit, came to be shipped here from California. It

We had a fine colonial house, showing construction with massive hewn beams. We needed this balloon house, so much to the astonishment of its owner, who was about to tear down the old shack since it lacked even plumbing and was no use to him, the Smithsonian leapt upon it with joyous cries.

On a smaller scale, one might ask what is so great about a model airplane? Why does the National Air and Space Museum have about 1,600 of them? Doesn't every schoolboy make models? Aren't they interesting too? Well, set forth at right is our model of a Navy torpedo bomber used in the early days of World War II—the Douglas TBD-1 Devastator. It has a number of features that most schoolboy models don't: It's mostly made of bronze; its engine cowl is removable and reveals a finely detailed miniature engine; its wheels

Model of the
Douglas TBD-1 Devastator

Headdress of toucan feathers with pendants of seeds, beetle wings, and bird skins.

retract; its wings fold; its cockpit has about as many details as the full-size cockpit. All of these attributes make this donated model plane part of the collection.

The institution, clearly, does a great deal more than entertain its 20-odd-million annual visitors by showing them all those thousands of displayed objects. Each museum has a role to play in an overall drama of . . . one hates to say "education," but it's close to the right word.

For few people come away from the Smithsonian without feeling that they're a little bigger than when they went in. They don't gain stature by having a hodge-podge of objects shoved under their noses. They do by becoming absorbed in a theme—a story that tells them something they didn't know. And that theme is presented with articles meticulously chosen for display, whether they be a cow weather vane with bullet holes in it, a Johnny Horizon hat, a necklace of Indian wampum, a scratchy record of an old campaign song, or a bad portrait of an early President.

by Edwards Park

75

Taking Care of Things

by Paul N. Perrot

Collections are the essential raison d'être of museums. They are the source from which the museum's unique role in the cultural fabric of society emanates. They are the basis of its contribution to scholarship, the instruments for its educational role, and the cause of public enlightenment and enjoyment. They are also one of the touchstones by which society can measure the importance of its own contribution in relation to humanity's past accomplishments and expressed hopes.

This vision of the museum's role places an unusual responsibility on those who have engaged in the various disciplines and crafts which make up the museum profession and on those elements of society who have pledged to give these institutions support whether it be financial, legislative, or moral.

Museums are essential vehicles of public education but even more important, they are the guardians of the tangible evidence of the past, whether manmade or the product of nature, and they are vehicles through which this evidence is safeguarded and transmitted to the future.

Such custody is an awesome responsibility. Although a museum may be described as an essentially "tomorrow" organization, its "tomorrowness," if one may use such a term, can only be assured if it serves the needs of the present, or, better still, if it anticipates those needs. For in collections we have not merely the testimony of man's previous accomplishments and aspirations, but perhaps more importantly in this age of multiplying needs and shrinking resources, we have the testimony of man's failings—of his occasional inability to recognize the unity between his being and a bountiful nature which he has often violated. In an age when serious minds forecast the possibility that some of the resources which we consider indispensable, if not for our survival at least for our wellbeing, may be exhausted in a few decades, it is good to know how past societies faced challenges. The solutions to our problems cannot all be found in museums, but a careful study of museum resources may provide some clues.

These considerations suggest that the cornerstone of the museum idea is preservation: the preservation of matter through which the history of ideas and ideals has attained tangible form.

No complex of museums, in the aggregate, has larger resources to preserve, interpret, and transmit than the museums of the Smithsonian Institution. Their collections range virtually across the gamut of human accomplishment, and, in association with the collections of the National Gallery of Art, they constitute a portion of the human patrimony which is unmatched in its diversity in the United

Dr. Rolland O. Hower records data in the specimen chamber, Freeze-Dry Lab.

States and hardly rivaled by any organization, under one administration, in any other part of the world.

For the last decade the institution has focused increasingly on the need to conserve this heritage. All of its museums have conservation workshops and trained technicians to monitor the condition of objects and practice remedial action when required. All matter is subject to change, and no sooner has an object been created than the process of decay starts. It may be infinitely slow or alarmingly rapid, but once started it proceeds relentlessly.

Conservation of objects, like medicine, can also be preventative. Measures taken to prevent or slow the deteri-

Assistant Secretary for Museum Programs at the Smithsonian, Paul N. Perrot is Secretary of the American Association of Museums. Until 1972 he was Director of the Corning Museum of Glass. His many publications focus on antiques and archeology.

oration of specimens include arresting decay or corrosion and subsequent monitoring of the environments in which the specimens are kept. High humidity, for example, can cause the deterioration of a wide range of objects, from wood or leather anthropological specimens to locomotives. Other environmental problems abound—indoors and out. The acres of windows at the new National Air and Space Museum required specification of glass to screen out the sun's ultraviolet radiation, particularly harmful to textiles, including a variety of goods from fabric aircraft coverings to spacesuits.

Conservation is often mistakenly called restoration. The confusion is natural, for, the visual effect of conservation often results in improved appearance. Or it may result in a marked reduction of the more obvious results of time, wear, or accident. Sometimes, of course, conservation results in the removal of the object for its greater safety. Yet there is a fundamental difference between restoration and conservation. While restoration is principally a cosmetic effort, true conservation seeks to attain the same aims by understanding causes of decay and deterioration and providing scientific solutions.

A museum's conservation laboratory may be confronted with repairing a scratch on a painting, arresting the corrosion caused by the juxtaposition of two metals which are not compatible, treating a warped wooden box, or determining by analysis of the constituents whether the stem of a goblet originally belonged to the bowl.

The conservator must combine the analytical approach of the scientist with the manual skills and understanding of materials characteristic of the sensitive craftsman. In his work he must be mindful that the measure of his success will be the effectiveness with which he has negated the passing of time and the blemish of accidents, while refraining from introducing into his work his own personality. In short, he must repress the all-too-human, subconscious desire to improve upon somebody else's work.

Since an active conservation laboratory is confronted with an enormous variety of problems, many of which are similar but no two absolutely alike, there are in conservation many specialities. Between the individual conservation laboratories and workshops of the institution's museums and the Conservation Analytical Laboratory (located in the Museum of History and Technology) there are relatively few problems which cannot be tackled authoritatively. Yet in conservation, as in other scientific disciplines, self-sufficiency is an illusion: complex problems are often solved only after extensive consultation and experimentation which may engage the talents of a number of laboratories in this country and abroad (see page 102).

Brought from Japan to the Natural History Museum, Terutoyo Fujimoto, a priest and ritualistic "polisher," reconditions steel samurai swords, never surpassed in strength and flexibility.

Sometimes, especially in the case of recently manufactured artifacts, industrial sources may be consulted on preservation problems. Some of the Apollo spacesuits in the National Air and Space Museum collection had been soiled and required cleaning. In addition, information was lacking on the suits' tolerance to ultraviolet radiation over long periods. The Apollo spacesuit manufacturer, ILC Industries, then of Dover, Delaware, devised dry-cleaning techniques and advised on display modes that would enhance the long-term preservation of these complex, but fragile garments.

When the conservators at the laboratory shared by the National Portrait Gallery and the National Collection of Fine Arts speak of repairing or retouching the paintings that come their way, they emphasize the difference between overpainting and "in-painting." The latter is a demanding process of applying paint (never oil paint, which might be difficult for later restorers to remove) to those areas of the canvas that have suffered paint loss; sometimes they prefer to use dry pigments along with the varnish with which the canvas is finally surfaced. All this meticulous laboratory work is done not under the high-

Aristotle, Ptolemy, and Copernicus highlight the frontispiece of a book by Galileo Galilei published in 1632, and now in the Dibner Library of the History of Science and Technology.

powered lights employed in many museums but under the strong, direct daylight that these Smithsonian technicians regard as the least tricky illumination for color-verification purposes. Their overall concern, furthermore, is preserving the museums' collections and permitting exhibition in the best possible condition.

The curious case of Thomas Hart Benton's self-portrait is but one chapter in the continuing story of how the conservators meet their peculiar challenges. The painting had been rolled up and roughly handled during a mysterious disappearance from the famous American artist's studio; the Portrait Gallery's microscopic examination of it revealed severe cracks beneath the grime. Notified of the painting's recovery, Benton—then in the declining years of his life—contemplated what should be done with it. After his death, the Portrait gallery attacked both the dirt and the cracks with a special regard for his original purposes. Detailed photographs of the laboratory operation show the gesso painted in the cracks as stark white against the vivid color on either side; subsequently, the appropriate color was applied over the dried gesso. The result, as lively and lusty as the artist intended, can be seen in the Gallery's second floor lounge, directly behind George Washington.

In the Smithsonian's Conservation Analytical Laboratory, chemists, mineralogists, physicists, radiographers, and highly trained conservators minimize the effects of accident and wear, and the impact of time on the objects in their care. They also study the basic structure of materials, the manner in which they have been combined with one another, and the technologies by which they have been formed. These studies give curators and historians different perspectives on their objects of research. For example, by analyzing the lead in an antique bronze sculpture or tool we may determine in what region of the world the lead was mined, and from this draw conclusions on trade routes, the possible influences of immigrations, the source of styles, the spread of beliefs, the flow of ideas, and a variety of other factors.

It is unfortunately true, however, that the environment of many museums, even the Smithsonian's, is inadequate to protect the objects in their care. This is particularly true of storage areas which are too often ignored for more glamorous parts of a museum. The institution has grown tremendously in the last few decades, and has now reached a point where storage facilities are no longer adequate to satisfy the needs for prompt retrieval, easy access, and far more important, atmospheric and other conditions which will optimize chances of preservation.

For this reason the Smithsonian plans to develop, some six miles from the Mall, a major Museum Support Center.

When received by the National Portrait Gallery, Thomas Hart Benton's self-portrait was dark and damaged (left). Restored (right), one could see bright details of the seashore scene.

This will include the most up-to-date environmental controls in storage areas and study and laboratory facilities equipped with the scientific apparatus necessary for the varied studies concerned with the preservation and interpretation of the Smithsonian's large collections.

A major aspect of the Museum Support Center will be an enlarged Conservation Laboratory which will carry out basic research, carefully monitor the condition of objects, provide for their care, and at the same time develop a program for training Smithsonian personnel and friends from abroad in the varied crafts of conservation—a field in which at the present time there is a world-wide shortage of trained personnel.

Though the museum collections of objects are essential for our understanding of the past, alone they are insufficient. To assess the importance of an object, curators must know where it came from, who made it, why it was made, when it was made, and of what materials. The conservator combines old records with his contemporary studies of an object to make decisions on preservation techniques. The Smithsonian's libraries, archives, and curatorial files, as well as those of other institutions, are the repositories of the specimens' pedigrees and vital statistics, and the preservation and organization of the documents themselves play an important role in conservation.

For example, files in the National Air and Space Museum's branch library, and at that museum's Preservation and Restoration Division, contain technical handbooks and notes on the manufacturing specifications and maintenance procedures for aircraft, rockets, and their engines, details that prove invaluable in the preservation process. Care of the large collection of Bering Strait Eskimo artifacts obtained by Edward W. Nelson (see page 157) in the late 19th century has been aided by the meticulous records Nelson kept, now lodged in the Smithsonian's Anthropological Archives. Whenever available, similar records are maintained—as much for the conservators' study as for the curators.

Today the Smithsonian's libraries have almost a million volumes. They are housed partly in the Central Library in the Museum of Natural History and partly in the libraries of the various museums, as well as in the dozens of departmental and specialized curatorial branch libraries.

To achieve maximum efficiency in the institution's libraries, new methods have been developed to accelerate acquisition and processing. Computers not only expedite internal work, but are connected to a national network which provides data in a few seconds that, in the past, might have required hours, if not days, to assemble.

The library collections grow through exchanges and gifts, but the major part is purchased. Yet funds are limited; it is not yet possible to acquire everything that is

A Smithsonian Exhibits Laboratory worker painstakingly hand paints the accent lines on a piece of heavy farm machinery scheduled for exhibit.

needed for scholarship. At present, no more than 70 per cent of that goal can be attained (yet, not so long ago, it was barely 50 per cent).

Nonetheless, the institution has achieved a worldwide reputation for its research capabilities. That reputation had the beneficial result of attracting the recent gift by Dr. Bern Dibner of his unique collection of manuscripts, incunabula, rare books, and documents on the history of science and technology. By this gift, the library of the Museum of History and Technology has become one of the most important in the world and the museum will have the opportunity to display next to its scientific objects those important theoretical works which illuminate their creation.

Collections of objects, books, or archives may be just space-consuming things that require more or less constant care but are substantially dead if one does not have the means to assess and care for them. With about 75 million specimens, distributed in dozens of museum galleries, laboratories, study, and storage areas, the role of the Smithsonian's Central Registrar is particularly critical. The Registrar must codify each item in such a way that it will have the greatest possible usefulness to individual scholars—as well as provide for the easiest interaction among the institution's museums and others in the city and the region and, eventually, the nation and the world.

In the past, registration was considered essentially to be a bookkeeping function: an object came in, was received, given a number, and a file was developed around it containing the name of the donor, lender, or vendor, and if known, its origin and date. These data were kept in an infinite number of files where they remained for the most part fairly static. Only rarely did the results of research, curatorial or otherwise, ever find their way back to this basic record. With the development of computers, and the growing realization that registration unrelated to scholarly functions is imperfect, a new perspective has opened. This new technological approach to registration—knowing the place and condition of things through entries in a computer—is still in its infancy, but with care and patience it will no doubt thrive and acquire the stature that older disciplines have already achieved on the Mall.

The functions discussed until now all assist the institution to act effectively as the keeper of the National Collections and fulfill its mandate which is to serve the nation in the fullest sense by "the increase & diffusion of knowledge among men." But how do these activities relate back to the general public and to the millions of visitors who throng through its various buildings? First and foremost through permanent collections which are well cared for, clearly interpreted, and exhibited with a sense of style.

Many of the exhibit activities gain special support from the Office of Exhibits Central which provides services to those parts of the institution that are not large enough to have an exhibit laboratory, and special services whose costs could not be justified if they were to be duplicated in a number of museums.

For example, Exhibits Central provides services in taxidermy—especially freeze-dry taxidermy, a new method essentially developed at the institution. Perhaps the most successful displays in museums of natural history are the realistic habitats which combine stuffed animals with botanical and geological specimens, often presented in front of elaborately painted backdrops which suggest the vast landscapes of far off lands. These habitats are especially effective teaching tools, suggesting the complex relationship between animate and inanimate things, and the impact of geography and climate on patterns of life.

In the past, many of the animals that were placed in these displays were produced by traditional taxidermy which consisted of stuffing the skin of the dead animal to suggest the most realistic form possible. In freeze-dry taxidermy, however, the entire animal, including all of his vital organs, is preserved. The technique, using extremely low temperatures in a vacuum chamber five feet in diameter by eight feet long, permits the elimination of all liquid matter and the arrest of bacterial action. By the manipulation of the specimen prior to its being subjected to the intense cold of the freezing chamber, an extremely realistic appearance can be achieved.

Freeze drying lends itself particularly well to the preservation of small specimens, such as small mammals, birds, and lizards, although creatures as large as a six-foot alligator and the 60-pound head of a Pacific crocodile have been freeze-dried. The technique has the added advantage that at a later date these can be sectioned and examined with all of their internal parts in proper relationship.

While a substantial portion of the exhibit staff concentrates on providing support for the institution's museums in Washington, at the National Zoological Park, and at the Cooper-Hewitt Museum in New York City, all parts of the nation are served by the Smithsonian Institution Traveling Exhibition Service, known as SITES.

Established over 20 years ago, SITES is now the largest purveyor of large and small traveling exhibitions in the world. Its catalogue lists over 200 exhibitions ranging in size from small panel shows which can be shown by libraries, schools and similar organizations, to major, international efforts bringing from afar priceless objects which enrich the offerings of museums throughout the land and indeed enhance the ability of some of the nation's major

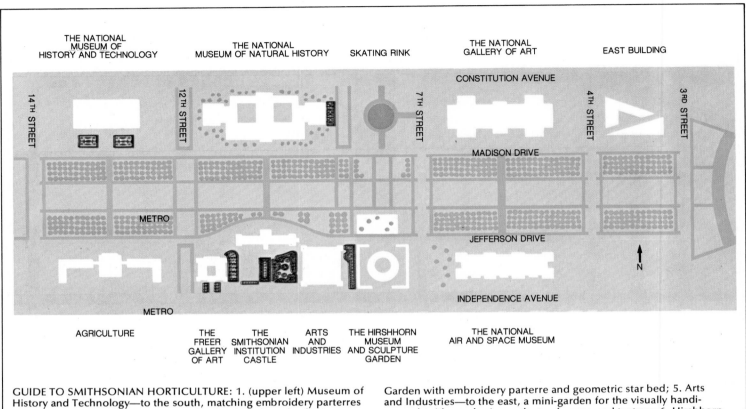

THE NATIONAL
MUSEUM OF
HISTORY AND TECHNOLOGY

THE NATIONAL
MUSEUM OF NATURAL HISTORY

SKATING RINK

THE NATIONAL
GALLERY OF ART

EAST BUILDING

CONSTITUTION AVENUE

14TH STREET

12TH STREET

7TH STREET

4TH STREET

3RD STREET

MADISON DRIVE

METRO

JEFFERSON DRIVE

N

METRO

INDEPENDENCE AVENUE

AGRICULTURE

THE
FREER
GALLERY
OF ART

THE
SMITHSONIAN
INSTITUTION
CASTLE

ARTS
AND
INDUSTRIES

THE HIRSHHORN
MUSEUM
AND SCULPTURE
GARDEN

THE NATIONAL
AIR AND SPACE MUSEUM

GUIDE TO SMITHSONIAN HORTICULTURE: 1. (upper left) Museum of History and Technology—to the south, matching embroidery parterres of 19th-century design; 2. Museum of Natural History—landscape plants serve as food and nectar source for the Insect Zoo; to the east, a border of perennials; 3. Freer Gallery—seasonal displays at south, west, and east sides; 4. Castle—to the south, a Victorian Pleasure Garden with embroidery parterre and geometric star bed; 5. Arts and Industries—to the east, a mini-garden for the visually handicapped, with emphasis on plants of aroma and texture; 6. Hirshhorn Museum—the Sculpture Garden contains evergreens and weeping beech trees; 7. National Air and Space Museum—to the west are seven *Sophora japonica* trees planted by seven Soviet cosmonauts in 1976.

institutions to provide varied offerings to their audience.

Among the objects in the Smithsonian's care are its own buildings, and the institution has always been conscious that its buildings were enhanced by their park-like setting. In the last few years, the Smithsonian decided to contribute to the richness of this setting by the care of its own grounds, thus implementing the visual harmony which was envisaged by the founding architect of the Nation's Capital, Pierre L'Enfant, and which has been the goal of succeeding generations.

Horticulture is not merely the craft of growing things; it is a historical discipline. The recent creation of the Victorian Garden, and the scholarly attempt to bring together the trees, bushes, and flowering plants with the attendant garden furniture of the 1870-1880s, is a new attempt at public interpretation. Horticulture inside and outside the museums plays an important adjunct role by introducing those plants and flowers which not only enhance visual appeal but provide a uniquely valid element to the exhibition's teaching function.

The small staff of the Office of Horticulture carries on research, and, with the help of volunteers, grows in greenhouses the hundreds of thousands of plants which are placed in and around our buildings to provide one more element of understanding and delight. It is planned, in the years ahead that, as millions of visitors come from the 50 states of the Union, they will find in various locations around the Mall, their state's flowers, trees, or bushes—the living symbols of the nation's unity and diversity.

Museums have been called "universities of the tactile," their professors are called curators. While the task of the museum is to expand and deepen and disseminate knowledge and enlightened pleasure, underlying all that is the fundamental curatorial role—simply stated, the job of taking care of things.

The elaborate plantings of the embroidery parterre enhance the 19th-century atmosphere of the Victorian Pleasure Garden.

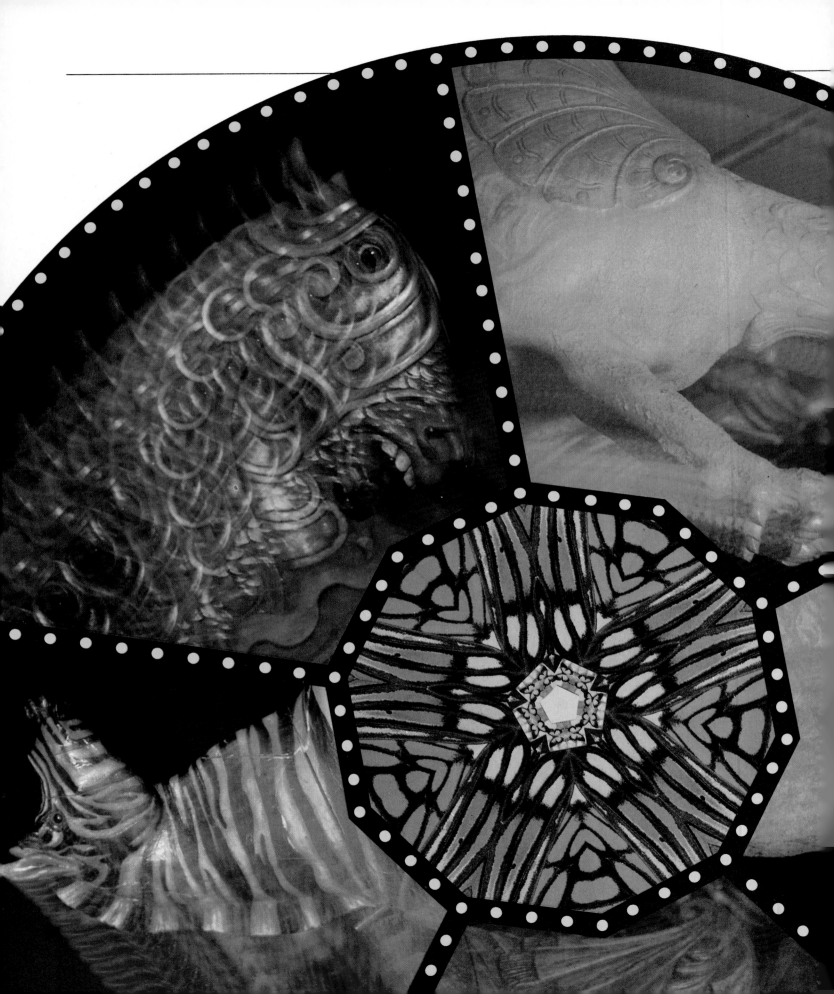

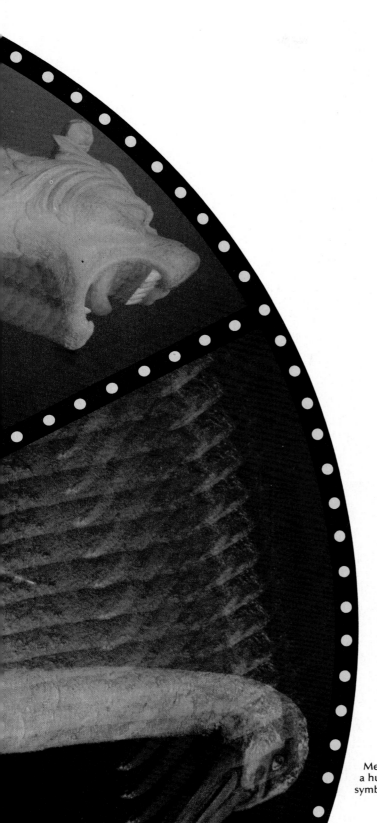

Smithsonian Through the Kaleidoscope

Seizing a kaleidoscope, a child presses the viewer to his eye and tilts the cylinder this way and that against the light. Ever-changing shapes of variegated color appear in an endless variety. A similar magic awaits the Smithsonian visitor. Of the 70 million objects and specimens in the catalogued inventory, only about three percent may be seen in the visitor's kaleidoscope—a mere fragment. Yet what is visible provides a dazzling array of treasures from this world and beyond: from dinosaurs and diamonds, peacocks and phonographs, to satellites and sculptures.

In the vast collections there is something for every one of the more than 21 million people of all ages and addresses who annually visit the Smithsonian.

At each step they find a surprise. A short distance from the fabled Hope Diamond in the carpeted Hall of Gems at the Museum of Natural History, the 330-carat Star of Asia sapphire blazes in its case. Nearby is a rival to that beauty—the deeply red Rosser Reeves Ruby. At the National Zoological Park, two endangered species, the golden marmoset and the Cuban crocodile, live but steps away from each other in adjacent buildings.

The collections run the gamut of superlatives. There are the "firsts": the earliest Secret Service mug book, American postal issue, machine-made pocket watch, U.S. manned spacecraft, and touchable moonrock. Then the curious: the remains of a certain Willelm von Ellenbogen which turned into soap after burial in the 18th century, the longest (17.5-foot) beard in the world, and Martha, the last passenger pigeon. Also the rare and unusual: a 3.1 billion-year-old fossil, the 1810 clock of early black craftsman Peter Hill, a 17th-century musical instrument in the shape of a sinuous snake. Fascinating people can be seen as well: carved in wood, cast in bronze, and portrayed in oils on canvas. Frozen forever in their moment of life, these figures are painted on a Meissen bowl, imposed upon a Wedgwood frieze, or carved on a weather vane.

After all this, what lingers for visitors is the infinite variety of the Smithsonian, a kaleidoscopic adventure that carries a built-in invitation to return.

Gems or gowns, animals or airplanes—what are the "beeliners" for the throngs of first-time visitors to the

Merry-go-round menagerie orbits
a hub of butterfly wings—a kaleidoscope image
symbolic of the Smithsonian experience.

Smithsonian? According to the 400 volunteers working at the Visitor Information Center at the Castle, people either know what they want to see—the Hope Diamond, the First Ladies' Gowns, the Air and Space Museum—or they ask, "What's in this building for me?" Trained volunteers, servicing the 11 desks seven days a week, are charged never to say, "I don't know."

Volunteers savor the occasional, unusual requests. For example, the Southern matron seeking information about a spice exhibit: a helpful volunteer checks out the Division of Industries at the Museum of History and Technology with the possibility that there is a new section devoted to herbs and spices; the bewildered woman turns aside the suggestion. "Spice," she says slowly and easily, "I mean Air and Spice."

by Jane Ross

Eight-ton African bush elephant greets visitors to the Museum of Natural History, while the view at the Museum of History and Technology begins with Francis Scott Key's "Star-Spangled Banner."

Popular exhibits surround the 45.5-carat Hope Diamond. Clockwise, visitors to the National Air and Space Museum can look up at the *Spirit of St. Louis*—can gaze at *Diplodocus* (one of the longest animals ever) at the Museum of Natural History—and can marvel over the gowns in the First Ladies' Hall at the Museum of History and Technology.

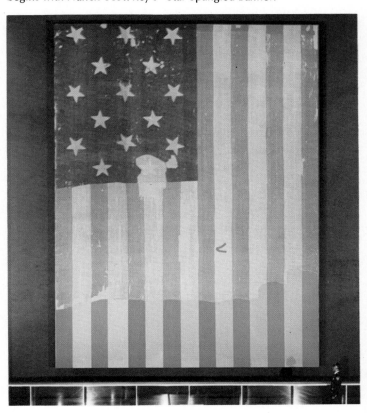

The rare and the curious, singular objects at the Smithsonian from the Museum of History and Technology include the most celebrated rarity among U.S. postage issues, the 24-cent invert of 1918; a set of George Washington's false teeth, made of gold and hippo teeth (upper), elephant and hippo (lower); and in the Division of Mechanical and Civil Engineering a Seth Thomas pillar-and-scroll shelf clock c.

1820, the second of five pre-production models built by Thomas before he settled on a standard group of working parts for the case. Symbolic of the American Indian, a Sioux Indian bonnet of more than 70 eagle feathers.

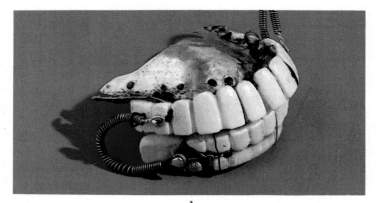

Clockwise, the lunar rover, called "the world's most expensive car," is an electric buggy like those used on Apollo missions. An 1804 silver dollar (at left) is the only surviving one with a plain edge: At right, a milled-edge 1804 coin. Radiocarbon-dated at 24,800 years old, a carved mammoth tusk symbolizes man's mastery of his environment—engraved lines on this replica may be an early map. The 1901 Pelton Wheel ran a Riedler pumping engine that furnished oil under pressure for the governing system in the first hydroelectric station at Niagara Falls. Oldest American man-of-war in existence, the Continental gunboat *Philadelphia*—sunk by the British on Lake Champlain in 1776.

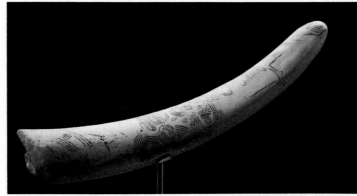

People are evident throughout the collections. Clockwise is a 10th-century Hindu goddess, Parvati, at the Freer. Sculptor Una Hanbury was so impressed by Rachel Carson's "tremendous vitality" that she created this bust (at the National Portrait Gallery) after one meeting.

"He stood there like an African prince, conscious of his dignity and power," reminisced Elizabeth Cady Stanton at the funeral of Frederick Douglass (1817-1895); this early portrait is attributed to Elisha Hammond. Below, a late 18th-century Wedgwood plaque portrays Heracles in the garden of Hesperides. Also at History and Technology is a Meissen porcelain bowl, c. 1770, painted with a drinking scene after William Hogarth's *Midnight Conversation*.

William H. Johnson (1901-70) painted (above), *Going to Church, c.* 1940-41 an evocation of his rural Southern boyhood. Better known as a mural painter, H. Siddons Mowbray (1858-1928), an American born in Egypt, occasionally did richly painted scenes like the two young women of *Idle Hours* (before 1900). Both of the above paintings are at the National Collection of Fine Arts. An 1872 caricature of Horace Greeley by Thomas Nast (1840-1902) portrays The New York Tribune editor in his unsuccessful bid for the presidency against Ulysses S. Grant. A pastoral group of Frankenthal porcelain c. 1772 from Germany enriches the Museum of History and Technology collection.

While living at his sister's home in London, James McNeill Whistler (1834-1903) painted some of his family in *The Music Room,* at the Freer Gallery. In a 19th-century lunette below, a playful Neptune emerges from a seashell as ornamentation on a paddle wheel housing, in the collections of the Museum of History and Technology. At left, a carved-wood Indian woman, late 19th century, advertises the wares of a tobacconist. Above, children climb a fruit tree in a detail from a Japanese screen of the Kanei era (1624-1643), at the Freer Gallery.

The first fully nude marble sculpted by Hiram Powers (1805-1873) is *Eve Tempted* at left, 1840-42; it predates the famous *Greek Slave* that became an international hit at the 1851 London Exposition. George Gershwin (1898-1937) completed his self-portrait in the summer of 1934 while he was creating the score of *Porgy and Bess*. Less than four inches high, the 16th-century pendant of a Triton was wrought in Italy of baroque pearls, gold, enamel, diamonds, and rubies.

Overleaf: An enlarged moth wing (center) from China, surrounded by other examples of the beauty of the natural world—all photographed by Kjell B. Sandved. How many can you name? See page 256.

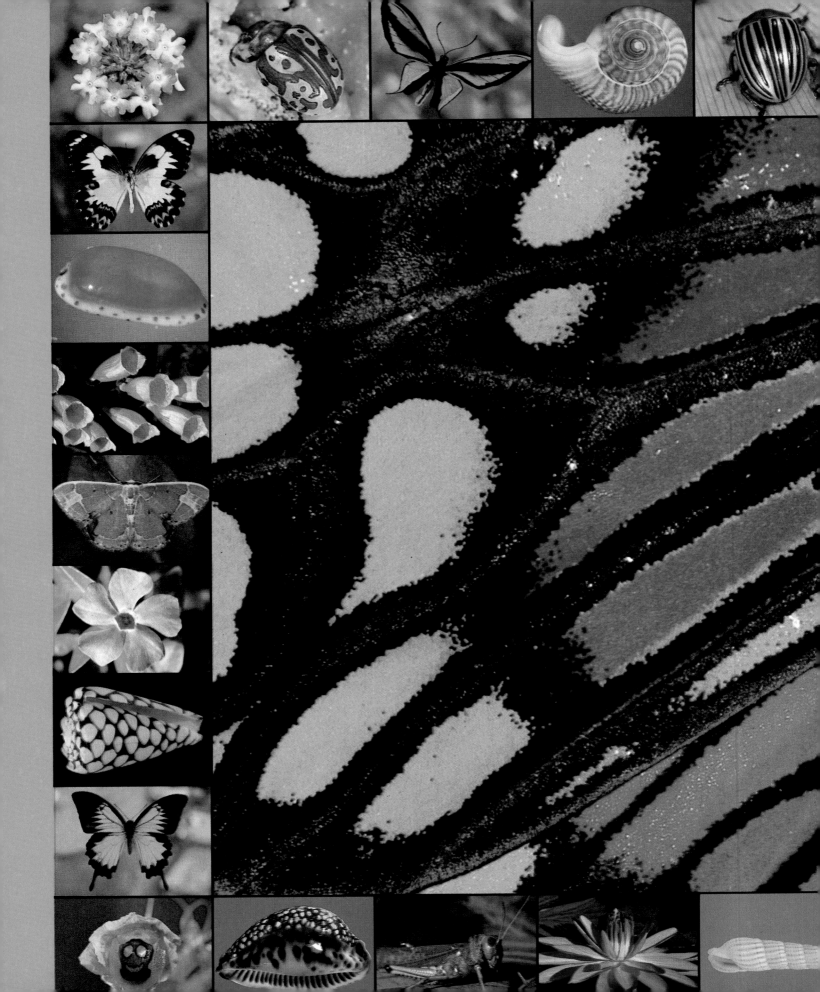

The Hardware of History

by Silvio A. Bedini

Recently a selection of two dozen Smithsonian UFOs (Unidentified Found-in-the-collection Objects) went on display as a "Whatsit?" exhibit in the National Museum of History and Technology. Each item was prominently numbered, and a nearby suggestion box encouraged visitors to make written guesses. Day after day, for over two years, the public enthusiastically deposited hundreds of suggestions. About half of the objects that stumped the experts were correctly identified by the public. Most were specialized tools once commonly used in the trades.

An outsize question mark dominated a "Whatsit?" display at History and Technology, challenging the viewer to identify these puzzlers.

That puzzling exhibit case became one of the most visited displays in the museum. Why? First, because the American public maintains an innate curiosity, even a preoccupation, with gimmicks and gadgets with roots in the tradition of native ingenuity. Second, and even more important, because the acknowledged experts in a great museum admitted they did not know everything. With almost 50 curators and as many museum specialists and technicians, the National Museum of History and Technology would, you might think, be able to identify any artifact from American material culture, national history,

Deputy Director of the National Museum of History and Technology, Silvio A. Bedini has observed the curatorial and research functions of the Smithsonian since 1961. A prolific writer, particularly in the field of horology, his most recent works are Thinkers and Tinkers (Early American Mathematical Practitioners) *and* The Life of Benjamin Banneker.

and the history of science and technology. Not always.

It was natural for the Museum of History and Technology to seek the public's help with its task, since the museum seeks to be a kind of translator between the American people and the hardware of their history. Much of the museum's work relates to the recovery and preservation of artifacts (see page 76); a great deal of its research lies in the interpretation of their historic use and meaning. Identification, therefore, is central to its efforts, and identification often depends on what might be called "tribal memory" and public interest.

As an example, a myth persists that American flags with 13 stars must be old and probably date from the period of the American Revolution. The fact is that extremely few were made earlier than the 19th century, and that 13-star flags continued to be produced for official use by the United States Navy, and occasionally by the United States Army, until 1916 and perhaps even later.

The flag with 13 stars was the official national banner of the United States from the enactment of the first Flag Act of 1777 until the second Flag Act of 1795, when the number of its stars was changed to 15. Thereafter the 13-star flag continued to be used for many years as the ensign on small boats of the United States Navy, and was frequently used also for commemorative events. Until an Executive Order of 1912, neither the proportions nor the arrangement of the stars were prescribed, and over the years many unofficial arrangements were devised by flagmakers. Only by technical examination of the fabric, sewing thread, and stitching can the date of a flag be determined with reasonable certainty. Whether it was hand-stitched or machine-sewn, whether the bunting is single or double-ply, whether the stars are made of linen or cotton, and the thread count are all factors in dating flags.

Flags made prior to the 19th century are stitched with linen or silk thread, although wool thread was infrequently used also. Cotton thread does not appear to have been used prior to the 1820s, and then only for attaching cotton stars. It was not until later that cotton thread was used for stitching the entire flag. The nature of the thread is extremely important for dating. For example, the 3/2 cabled cotton thread first came into use in the 1860s, and a 3-ply Z-twist silk thread or "machine twist" was first developed for use with the newly invented sewing machines in 1852. Although machine-stitching was initiated in 1850, hand stitching continued to be used throughout the 19th century. Mercerized cotton thread was introduced in the early 20th century.

As a consequence, positive identification of early flags is rarely possible but is achieved primarily by a process of

The earliest flag with 13 stars in the Smithsonian collections dates from the Mexican War, 1846-1848.

elimination, or what is best described as "negative" identification. The 13-star flag continues to be a subject of popular preoccupation, and requests for identification have been so numerous and constant that the museum's handbook on identification of 13-star flags has gone into several reprintings.

The same principles of identification and authentication apply to many other types of materials, such as metal objects produced in great variety and quantity in England and the United States over a period of many years in the same style and form. Often it is extremely difficult to determine whether an object of metal was produced in the 17th century or the 20th when it is made in the same form and detail without change. The presence of a patina presumably caused by corrosion and chemical change may be considered to be adequate corroboration of its claimed date of production, but it may not in fact be the case, for careful examination frequently proves otherwise. Objects made of brass were generally cast or made from hammered plate. By mid-19th century, later examples of the same type

would have been produced in rolled brass plate having a consistent thickness, quite in contrast to the earlier examples that varied minutely in thickness from one part to another because of the manner of production. Further examination might reveal that the patina had been artificially created with chemicals or by means of artfully applied paint to reproduce the appearance of corrosion and age.

With the ever-increasing mania for collecting in the past several decades, the supply of collectible items has fallen far short of the demand, with three results. Authentic antique items have sky-rocketed in price so that only museums and the very wealthy can acquire them. The less accessible they become, the greater the desire to own them, with the result that an immense variety of objects are being reproduced to satisfy the mania. The most ingenious techniques are applied in the manufacture of "authentic" antique items to delude the collector, with the consequence that the museum world as well as the collector and dealer must be ever suspicious and subject each piece to the most intensive examination. For the less discerning and more modestly priced market, many categories of collectible items are being mass reproduced, often rather carelessly, as out-and-out copies to meet the demand. Nonetheless, the incautious buyer is often led to believe, or he convinces himself, that he has acquired an object of value and joins the long lines of visitors trooping into museums for "show and tell" sessions with the curators. This situation has led to an increased alertness in identifying and authenticating such items and has produced new avenues of research and examination techniques to make the process more scientific and fail-proof.

Undoubtedly the most difficult items to authenticate are those claimed to have been associated with notable figures. If a piece is owned by a direct descendant of the original owner, and if documentary evidence of its original association and subsequent ownership in the family survives, the assumption may be made that the association is authentic. If no other negative factors are to be found, its association can be accepted with a fair degree of certainty. An examination of the object should ascertain whether it was made in or prior to the period of claimed association. The materials are studied to determine whether they are consistent with the period in question, and whether the maker, if identified, worked during or prior to the period.

As an example, this process of identification and authentication was applied to a gold watch claimed to have been presented by General Washington to the Marquis de Lafayette on the occasion of the surrender of the British forces at Yorktown on October 17, 1781. According to Lafayette family tradition, the timepiece was preserved by the Marquis among his most precious possessions through the events of the French Revolution. When he returned to the United States in 1824, he brought the watch with him and is said to have displayed it before the crowds that greeted him in every city. According to the story, the watch was stolen from him during the tour, and he returned to France extremely saddened by his loss.

In 1870 the watch was discovered and purchased in a sale of a pawnbroker's goods, and was brought to the attention of several members of the Congress. Through their efforts, a joint resolution of both Houses of Congress was passed

"One should always look a gift clock in the face," says author Bedini of many timepieces. But this handsome calendar alarm clock, is as authentic as it is brilliant in its gilt, brass case; made by Abraham Shegs in Nurenberg, about 1680.

and steps were taken to purchase the watch for the nation and to restore it to Lafayette's heirs. In December 1874 the American minister to France formally presented the timepiece in Paris to Oscar de Lafayette, the eldest of Lafayette's surviving grandsons. The watch descended in the family, and a century later it was placed on exhibition in the National Museum of History and Technology.

Because of its checkered history, Lafayette's watch seemed a perfect example to test by scientific methods. Had it in fact been presented by Washington to Lafayette? An exhaustive search of the Washington and Lafayette papers failed to reveal any mention of it, and consultation with Washington and Lafayette scholars brought no further enlightenment. On the other hand, it was a well established fact that Washington did not mention in his records or accounts the gifts that he made. Many of Lafayette's papers had been destroyed during the French Revolution, so other means had to be found to establish its provenance. A comparison of the style of watch with those known to have been purchased by Washington revealed that it was not of the type that Washington acquired for his own use. His watches were extremely simple and large in design, and he preferred timepieces by the foremost English and French makers of the 18th century. The Lafayette watch was small with a triple case, including an ornate repoussé case for dress wear and an outer case for street wear. The movement was signed "J. Halifax London." Specialists at the British Museum confirmed that the watch movement was actually of Dutch manufacture with the name and place added to enable it to be sold in England and its colonies, where English products were more highly prized and priced than foreign goods. Research in horological records confirmed that the watch had indeed been produced in the 1780s and the hallmarks on the case refined the date to a specific year within that period.

Laboratory analysis by specific gravity and X-ray fluorescence revealed that the two inner cases were of good quality, of approximately 22-karat gold, while the outer case lined with shagreen was made of mercury-gilt brass. There was no evidence of re-inscription or of other tampering to support history, and the watch proved to be indeed a high quality product of the late 18th century. It had received considerable wear, a condition consistent with the watch's adventurous career.

Despite the absence of documentation of the watch's association with Washington or Lafayette, it is nonetheless clearly identified as the timepiece purchased by the Congress and restored to the Lafayette family in 1874, and as such it remains a unique example of Congressional intercession for the preservation of a historical artifact.

The world of the collector and of the museum abounds with countless items of jewelry and furniture sincerely believed by their owners to have been associated with a notable figure at one time or another. The item can be proven to have been carefully preserved and handed down from one generation in the family to the next by word of mouth authentication, and there has never been any reason to doubt the claim by the family, because it has been well established that somewhere back in the family history there was indeed a contact with the notable figure in question. Documentation of such an association may even survive, recording the fact that on such and such an occasion the notable figure presented to a contemporary forbear an item the description of which seems to coincide unquestionably with that of the one that has been preserved.

Yet, upon careful, careful scrutiny, it may be discovered that the item in question could not have been produced in that time. It may be that its nails or screws were machine made half a century later, or that the metal stock was commercially manufactured. How could this have happened? The story in the family is eminently clear and documented. But in the course of time the family may have owned several similar pieces; inadvertently the story may have been switched from the original item to one similar. Meanwhile, the original may have been discarded or lost. Inasmuch as only one item survived, it was assumed to be the one having historical association. No one is to blame. The owner,

This watch may have been given by Washington to his French ally Lafayette. On the inner case (right) it says "Lord Cornwallis Capitulation Yorktown Octr 17th 1781."

however, becomes irate and unbelieving, and the competence of the museum curator may be questioned.

One of the most publicized instances of unpopular research technology resulted in a book-length publication in 1970 by Howard I. Chapelle and Leon D. Polland entitled *The Constellation Question.*

The *Constellation* was one of six frigates authorized by Congress in 1794 and built at Baltimore between 1794 and 1797. She saw action against France in 1798-99 and during the entire War of 1812 was blockaded at Norfolk. She later underwent numerous repairs and was employed until 1853 when she was "administratively rebuilt" as a spar deck corvette. During her subsequent career at foreign stations and as a training vessel, she was extensively repaired again and finally stationed permanently at Newport. After she became unserviceable, she was moved to Boston and there was considerable discussion as to whether she should be totally restored by the Navy. After World War II, at the request of a group of Baltimore residents who wished to restore the ship, the *Constellation* was delivered to them at Baltimore in 1953 by the United States Navy.

When this plan was first publicized in 1946, Chapelle raised the question of the authenticity of the vessel. The Baltimore Committee had proposed to restore the *Constellation* as the oldest American naval vessel afloat. They based their proposal on a memorandum prepared in late 1918 by Franklin D. Roosevelt, then Assistant Secretary of the Navy, claiming that the existing corvette *Constellation* was in fact the frigate built in Baltimore. Chapelle claimed instead that the ship had been so extensively rebuilt in 1853 that the surviving vessel was almost entirely a new ship, possibly with a few of the parts of the original frigate, and that as such it did not merit the investment and historical claim to fame that the Baltimore Committee ascribed to it. Chapelle, a maritime historian of towering repute, rampaged relentlessly through his evidence like a trial lawyer, laying low statements based on what he found

Weathering a gale, the U.S.S. *Constellation* rides the seas. This painting by an unknown artist depicts the ship as she appeared in 1833. *Constellation* was built in Baltimore and launched in 1797.

At History and Technology, the cotton gin model made by Eli Whitney before 1800 displays ginned cotton and seeds.

to be either non-existent or fabricated evidence.

Chapelle's contention led to an extensive correspondence published in *The Baltimore Sun* during the next several years. A committee of Baltimore citizens, formed to manage the reconstruction and perform the required research, opposed the evidence presented by Chapelle, and the debate continued until 1968 when he prepared a scholarly manuscript. The announcement of the forthcoming book brought a storm of protest from Baltimoreans who had already invested considerable time and funds in the restoration. Demands to prevent the publication came from various quarters. It was finally agreed that Chapelle's presentation would be issued together with a rebuttal from Leon D. Polland, technical advisor and Chief of Construction and Repair of the *Constellation* Project. The arguments were combined in a volume published by the Smithsonian Institution Press.

For some the *Constellation* question may never be resolved, but the debate between historians will remain one of the great examples of investigative research.

Similar problems arise in another form of research with which staff of the museum is frequently engaged, namely, the re-evaluation of the significance and achievements of notable historical figures involved either with national history or with the scientific and technological development of the nation—or, to put it simply, various claims to fame by noted Americans. Such re-evaluation is not easily or readily achieved in the face of persistent "facts," so often erroneous, that have been perpetuated in schoolbooks and popular histories for generations. Years of continued searching may be required to collect the bits and pieces of new evidence, to assemble it, and to confront the tra-

ditional renderings of past writers. An example is the case of Eli Whitney.

Whitney's name is familiar to every schoolchild; he is known to be the inventor of the cotton gin, a device which revolutionized the cotton industry late in the 18th century. He is also credited with having developed the so-called American system of manufacture by producing equipment with interchangeable parts.

The true pioneer in this field appears to have been a Frenchman named Honore Blanc, as reported by Thomas Jefferson in 1788. Whitney, however, was an entrepreneur par excellence. He claimed to have invented and produced molds and machines for making all the parts of muskets so that the parts produced were identical, and could be assembled without modification, and convinced even Jefferson of this achievement. Whitney's "invention" of interchangeable part manufacture was accepted by subsequent historians and biographers without question, yet was based in large part upon his own word. But research in progress at the museum has established that he never in fact achieved interchangeability of manufacture; this was demonstrated by a physical comparison of several of his muskets produced under government contract. It has also been proven that the invention of the cotton gin, while a valuable idea, was not a practical success and did not become useful until it was combined with a later invention made by another. At the same time, an intensive survey of Whitney's work has revealed that some of his less spectacular achievements and techniques have not received adequate appraisal or sufficient acknowledgement at the hands of past historians.

Research projects in the museum are often long-range,

and the product or derivative may not become available to scholars or the general public for years to come. Generally these inquiries are concerned with the preservation of specific collections, or ongoing compilations of data that require years of collecting. An example of the former is the detailed record for each of the gowns of the First Ladies. One of the most popular exhibits in Washington, the gowns were worn by hostesses in the White House from the first administration to the present. Although the dresses are maintained in a stable environment with carefully controlled temperature, humidity, and lighting, textiles have a limited life span. Accordingly, a skilled dressmaking instructor and designer has been at work making a careful study of each of the gowns—recording details of construction, decoration, and colors. From this study a drawing is produced, as well as a paper pattern and a muslin mockup, all requiring several months of work for each of the dresses. This ''package'' is filed for future reference by historians and students of costume design.

The museums' shops and laboratories process objects ranging from paper items including manuscripts, newspapers, broadsides, and many forms of illustration, to fabrics, models, instruments, and large machines. Take large machines, for example. Although automobiles and other vehicles have been the subject matter of museums for generations with standardized techniques developed for their preservation and restoration, such has not been the case for machines of immense size. In the planning for a new museum building that would encompass exhibits of

A ghostly squadron of aged airplanes had to be restored to like-new condition before National Air and Space Museum could open in 1976. At Silver Hill facility, craftsmen worked on such exhibited aircraft as the Douglas World Cruiser *Chicago*, one of two to complete the first around-the-world flight in 1924. Below, John Cusack, Walter Roderick lift wheel into place; above, Roderick punches holes for stitching new fabric to old wings.

power machinery and machine tools, it was necessary also to provide a facility for their restoration and preparation for exhibition.

Techniques and materials for stripping and cleaning had to be investigated and tested, and methods developed for creating missing parts. It was necessary to examine each machine to determine the original colors in which it had been painted, to recreate the proper method of belting, and many other features. The missing information was sought in trade catalogs, trade journals, and often in the records of the manufacturer. Lathes, grinders, milling machines, turbines, gas engines, and similar equipment had rarely been the subject of museum study and preservation, and as a result an entirely new resource of information was developed in the museum, to which other museums have had recourse. Similarly, a textile laboratory researches and develops techniques and materials for the cleaning and preservation of textile materials ranging from the most fragile item of 18th-century feminine wear to the most sturdy fabric, such as an army field tent.

Frequently special projects require the cooperation of other facilities such as the Brookhaven National Laboratory. One of these was an attempt to identify pottery shards found in Drake's Bay, California, to determine whether they had been left by Francis Drake's crew on his claimed landing there in 1579. After testing by means of neutron activation and comparing results with those obtained from similar examination of English pottery of the same period, the results proved to be inconclusive, indicating only that the bits of pottery were of the right period and origin and could have been left behind by Drake's crew.

Beyond restoring and preserving its own vast collection, the museum consistently attempts to track down objects of all types for care and keeping. Besides visits to other museums and repositories in search of specific items, curators request information from other museums, historical houses, and private collectors. Thus data is collected on materials such as medical instruments, music boxes, pewterware, and many others. This data is added to ongoing "national inventories" that are available to scholars and students. Data is also sought on the craftsmen who produced the objects. Curators search city directories, contemporary newspaper advertisements and accounts, records of vital statistics in government archives, business records, tax records, and numerous other potential sources for mention of craftsmen and manufacturers. The

George Washington's uniform, one of few to survive the Revolutionary War, was worn by the General, according to tradition, when he resigned as commander-in-chief in December 1783 at Annapolis, Maryland.

results are checklists, monographic studies, and often full-length books which become resources for other scholars and students. In addition, the curatorial staff has published a number of significant books on such widely diversified subjects as steam locomotives, American agriculture, American graphic art, chemistry prior to the 17th century, social reform in the U.S. Navy, and French privateers operating from United States ports during the wars of the French Revolution.

Investigative research as performed in the National Museum of History and Technology and other museums of history is distinctly different from the traditional research

With an elaborately painted lid and sounding-board case, this harpsichord, built by Benoist Stehlin in 1760 in Paris, has been restored to playing condition and is used in concerts at History and Technology.

of scientific disciplines as conducted in science-related museums and laboratories, and has rarely been fully described or studied. It is research related to artifacts, and consequently necessitates the development of numerous individual approaches and techniques. Research in a history museum takes many forms, and so do its fruits.

When the new museum building was being contemplated, it was decided to give voices to the collection of musical instruments. They were restored to playing condition and original musical compositions for them secured, so that once more they could be played with their own music for live audiences and for commercial recordings. An outstanding example is "Music from the Age of Jefferson," which was presented first as a public performance and then reproduced in a recording.

Another effort of this division, undertaken over a period of a decade by one of its curators and a conservator, has been to locate and assist in the restoration of 17th-century and later organs in Mexican churches. Some 75 instruments have been inspected and it is believed that others remain to be found. The team has been collecting information from the specimens themselves and has succeeded in arousing interest leading to their restoration. A derivative of the survey has been the invaluable information collected about the makers of these organs in Spain and in Spanish America, a comparative study of their distinctive architectural styles and structure, and recovery of the music composed for them. This undertaking has thus far resulted in the restoration of several of the instruments with the cooperation of Mexican authorities and technical and financial assistance from interested American specialists and organizations.

Other members of the division are engaged in an ongoing search and recording of the iconography of music, and research on colonial and later American instruments and their music.

Among the museum's numerous efforts to be relevant to the contemporary scene have been exhibits and an oral history project on the evolution of the computer, an exhibit analyzing American productivity, and another entitled "A Nation of Nations" occupying almost half of one floor of the museum and concerned with the peopling of America. More recent have been an exhibit on the history of the telephone and its commanding role in American life and one on nuclear particle accelerators. The public response confirms the view that Americans seek in museums not only a record of their past, but an understanding of the present.

During the past several decades the museum has sought and collected artifacts representing scientific and technological advancements with an awareness that the most modern achievement will soon become a relic of the past. The problem in any museum is the need to keep current with the fast-moving world of technological change. So rapid has been the advance that keen alertness is required to select and preserve those artifacts, or components thereof, that will become the milestones in this evolution. More than a century ago Joseph Henry, the first Secretary of the Smithsonian Institution, commented that "all knowledge is useful. . . ."

A Chair for Ragtime

The Smithsonian Museum
Washington, D.C.

Dear Curator:
You will note from my name and letterhead that I am residenced in Hooperstown, Illinois, south of Chicago. My family has lived here since the beginning of time, as anyone of prominence in the area will testify.

Because I am desirous of maintaining our home in the proper style, despite the deterioration of this older part of the town, I am anxious to have everything I possess—from the cellar to the garret—restored to mint condition. Certain objects of great value must be handled with special care and sensitivity. I am, therefore, writing you despite some fears that your attention is primarily devoted to engines and airplanes and sun spots.

The object I desire you to restore is an unusual chair, unusual both for its age (1912) and for what it represents. I do not wish you to display it to the public because I know a lot about the insecurities of your city. Nor do I wish you to "fix" it, because its very eccentricity is a part of its value. I am well aware that there is something the matter with the chair's seat; that occurred when it was occupied by a very big chief (whose name you would recognize as possessing enormous historical importance but whose personage I would rather not reveal, for reasons of both discretion *and* security).

I am enclosing a photo of the chair which I trust will answer any other questions you may have about this matter. You do repair historical items, don't you? Isn't this one of the benefits we get for our tax dollars? Taxes! The very word reminds me of this chair. If it hadn't been for Taft's defeat the previous year, would the Income Tax Amendment have been passed in 1913?

For all that, your statement that you will clean and otherwise restore the chair is awaited with anticipation.
Much obliged,

Horace Hooper
Horace Hooper

The Renwick Gallery
Washington, D.C.

Dear Curator:
How in the world my letter came into *your* hands I cannot conceive. Of all the possibilities in the world, the very last I desire is to have my chair displayed in your projected "Public Amenities of the Early Twentieth Century" exhibition. The smoothness with which you made that request went a-wasting; you should have paid more attention to my letter—all I want is to have the chair *cleaned*. Your further questions about the object simply served to confuse the issue. When I said that the person who had sat on the chair was a chief, I certainly did not mean an Indian chief—thereby qualifying the chair, you said, to be scrutinized by your Museum of Natural History's Department of Anthropology, of all things. I meant he was a great chief of The Party, the Republican Party.

Now obviously that would not have been a European. And to go on about how artifacts associated with European personages would properly belong in the Cooper-Hewitt Museum of Decorative Arts and Design (which I gather is in New York, so how can that be tied in with you in the first place???) is merely to leap from the bureaucratic to the absurd. Not to speak of your rather bizarre suggestion that the chief might have been Asian or African—which would have consigned my poor chair to yet another division of "Anthropology."

In order to lay this matter to rest, I must obviously state the facts in the case. Otherwise, dreams of your anthropologists dancing around in my attic will haunt me even after the grave. So, in spite of my real disinclination to entrust a private keepsake to your governmental hands, I will tell you enough more about my chair to ensure that you regard it appropriately.

On a spring day in 1912—a warm spring day, when all good minds turned to thoughts of sodas—Pres-

Teetering on bent steel rod legs, this ice cream chair, 35 inches high, helps document the ragtime era in the National Museum of History and Technology.

ident William Howard Taft came into my father's drugstore in Hooperstown. It was a day we had really been looking forward to: the band (those who hadn't sweated themselves into exhaustion or drunk themselves into oblivion by the time the President arrived) performed admirably; the bunting, though dirtied by all the mud that the automobiles' tires tossed up, survived the wind storm. It was hot and humid, but he was a big man, capable of carrying off the embarrassments of such occasions. It was only after he'd left that we noticed how the new chair, which had just arrived with the shipment of modern furniture from Chicago the week before, would never look quite the same way again. And of course Taft lost the election.

This having all been put forward, I trust that your museum . . . museums? . . . will now accede to my rather straightforward request. It seems to me little enough for a taxpayer to ask.

Much obliged,

Horace Hooper

Horace Hooper

Gentlemen lounged, soda jerk stood ready as 20th century dawned in Collins Pharmacy, Islip, Long Island.

The National Museum of History
  and Technology,
Washington, D.C.

Dear Curator:
You may very well have discovered that the chairs are called "Steel Rod Furniture," but in my day anyone who did not call them "ice cream chairs" would have been sent off to the state farm. As for the place of manufacture, I believe I told you that it and its companion pieces were sold to us by a totally persuasive young man from Chicago. His argument was that we should be ready for the new age that was then dawning; he also played ragtime very well and succeeded in getting a date with my sister, who had always considered herself, theretofore, a missionary type.

signature can be met with but one response: signatures exist on the chair exclusively in the seat's bottom as gum wads; they were added in years subsequent to its occupation by President Taft. Those were the years when

Campaign banners (opposite), tin plates, and cartoons rallied voters in Taft's colorful 1908 campaign.

I was privileged to serve at the fountain in my father's emporium. Though my friends thought it unfair that I could be "the Professor" and could work the gilded arms of that extraordinary machine, dispensing syrup and soda from the spigots and pumps, while they manned the mops and arranged the stock in the back room, those were my nepotic privileges.

More to the point, however, I recognized the truth of what my brother-in-law (as he later became) was selling: this was a marvelous new age; scorned and abandoned were the gloomy stores and Victorian spaces of yesteryear; into our parlor light flooded through colored glass, people gathered with a new sense of gaiety and civilization, the restrictions of the devil-fearing farmland around us forgotten. The music on the phonograph flowed and bubbled like the seltzer water I spilled on the counter.

Well, yes, that was too long ago to be pertinent to your concerns. But let me point out that we believed in progress then. When I went off to France (for which I do not blame Woodrow Wilson, guilty as he was of other fiascoes) we marched with our heads high. In fact, if I could give your generation anything today, I would give them *progress*—the very life-sap of American society. And therefore, despite my reiterated desire not to have my chair placed on display before the gawkers who wander through your dinosaur halls, I have informed my lawyers that I am shipping the chair to you as a contribution.

Take care of it; it will speak for itself. Please do not fix the seat.

Much obliged,

Horace Hooper

Horace Hooper

by Russell Bourne

It does, however, come as a considerable shock that you are, ultimately, more interested in the chair as a bit of technology than as art. There is a possibility that I would accept your argument if I knew what a Museum of History and Technology was. The proposition from your colleague at the Hirshhorn Museum that it would rank as art only if it bore an artist's

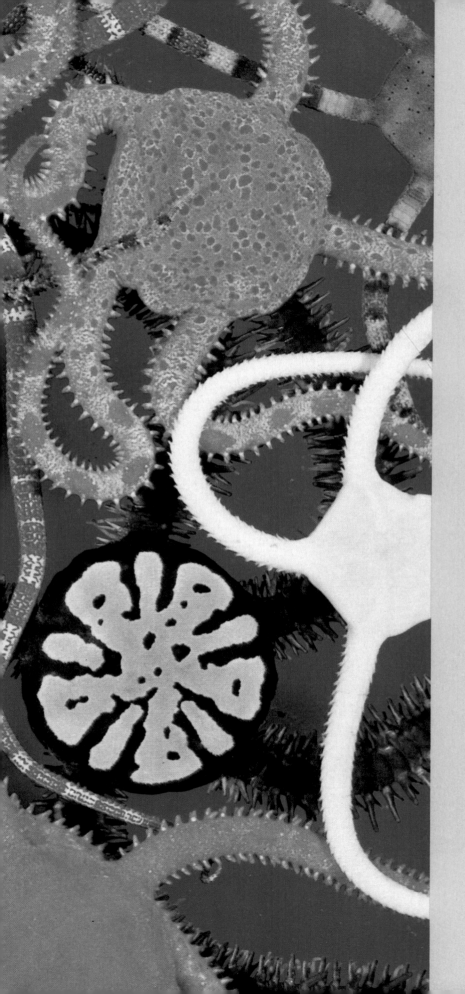

PART FOUR

The Natural World

Exuberant, colorful life crowds the seas and claims the land. And in few places on earth do so many scientists, with such vast study collections, know so much about life as at the Smithsonian.

Enter the mysterious realm behind the Museum of Natural History's closed doors where acres and acres of shelves line miles and miles of aisles, containing specimens for research.

Biological research is a long tradition at the Smithsonian and Edward Ayensu of the Department of Botany wraps it up, emphasizing the new directions that ecology-minded scientists are taking.

Our collections of creatures have also long included live specimens. In the mid-1800s, the nation's zoo had its beginnings on the Mall right next to the red Castle. And it has progressed a long way since then. Though the zoo always comes in at the tail end of alphabetical listings, in terms of human interest it comes in well ahead of the pack. A remarkable menagerie of zoo photographs shows the National Zoo moving into the field of research in animal reproduction. Like the Ark, the zoo is bent on saving as many endangered species as possible.

Silvio Bedini reminds us that live animals keep returning to the Mall, introducing several unexpected Mall-dwellers including Washington's first family of barn owls. They look down from a tower of the old Castle on the Mall.

109

Drawers and Drawers and Drawers

Every Smithsonian museum is blessed with a certain amount of built-in confusion. You enter the front door, and it all seems straight-forward enough. But the exhibits lead inexorably into a wilderness of corridors, lined with displays, of side rooms that entice, of stairways that lure, of abrupt right angle turns that appeal. And you soon realize that you should have taken a tip from Theseus and unwound a ball of thread in order to return from this maze.

Unlike Theseus, you have no minotaur to slay in these labyrinths, only delights to savor. And the bewilderment adds to the magic. If a museum exists to capture your spirit and remove you from the outside world, then these Smithsonian mazes succeed very well.

If you *really* want to be bewildered, you should venture into the staff section of the Museum of Natural History. Armed with an appointment to see Dr. So-and-So, you take an elevator to the third floor, circle the

From the collections of birds' eggs

rotunda high above the African elephant until you have reached the right door, then enter. No matter which door you choose, you are faced with an almost identical situation: long rows of white steel lockers

Fur storage vault

forming corridors that seem to stretch beyond the curve of the earth. There are fat cabinets and short lockers and tall lockers and cabinets stacked two high and three high and four high.

Labels on the outsides of these cases, say things like "Gryllidae" (that's crickets, son) and "Romaleinae" and (as a much appreciated change) "Hawaiian Lava Tube Cave Crickets." You're in Entomology, is where you are. And each of those cases holds drawers—maybe 12 drawers, maybe eight, maybe a myriad. And each of those drawers holds crickets, or whatever—a great many of them in each drawer.

Two drawers of bird skins

You return to the rotunda (where there are a whole lot more drawers with bits of mammals in them) and go on to the next major door. If it doesn't lead into a private office with

a man in it who looks up bemusedly from his study of sea birds, it will lead you into another cabinet-lined corridor filled with vertebrate zoology or perhaps anthropology or archaeology. And each case is chock full of drawers in which reside hundreds, no thousands, perhaps even

Boxes of beetles

hundreds of thousands of specimens dealing with the subject.

If you follow a corridor all the way and then, instead of returning to the rotunda, take a door into the wings of this huge building, you will encounter still more drawer-filled cabinets and you will also become good and lost. Finally some ornithologist up to his armpits in drawers will look at you sharply and you will realize that this is the fourth time you've passed him, and you will admit that you have slipped into an unwanted

orbit, and he will tell you that you are in the bird wing (hah!) and whom did you wish to see?

You will answer Dr. So-and-So is whom I wish to see, Sir, and he will shake his head abstractedly and go back to poring over the tiny cotton-stuffed skin of a *Loxia curvirostra*, which ordinary people call a cross-

Ornithologist and Secretary S. Dillon Ripley studies bird skins.

bill. There are a lot of little stuffed crossbill skins in that drawer and there are a lot of drawers in that locker and there are lockers as far as the eye can see in any direction.

You wade through them, back through more doors and corridors, to the anthropology section, and here all the cases of drawers are

111

crammed with bones—old bones, big bones, tiny bones, well-preserved bones, kind-of-shot bones. Thousands, tens of thousands of bones.

And so it goes in the Museum of Natural History. Just as the visitors

At work in the fossil collection

downstairs are drawn through their maze of displays, the scientists and researchers upstairs dwell in the midst of a maze of specimens. A very few of these specimens find their way into the exhibits below, exhibits carefully designed to tell people an exciting story about the earth and all its creatures and elements—rocks and lava and chemicals—from the

great blue whale to the Hope Diamond. The exhibits that tell this story are assembled and given meaning by the people upstairs, making use of their drawers full of crickets and mouse skulls and crustaceans and bits of flint and fossils and perhaps the skull of a Sioux warrior or a bronze lamp from an archaeological dig.

A Smithsonian scientist examines a mineral specimen.

Of course the work upstairs goes a lot further than that. A museum does not need 24,000,000 entomological specimens in drawers in order to select a few good ones to show off downstairs. It does need them for the new discoveries and additions to knowledge that the upstairs people are working at while you and I gape at the exhibitions.

Vast collections have always proved useful in research, for every specimen that substantiates a theory helps turn the theory into a new fact. Only drawers full of bird specimens allow an ornithologist to make true measurements, take notes on feather patterns and other technical details. To an ornithologist, a bird in the hand is obviously worth two in the book.

Scientists in a Venezuelan cloud forest film the behavior of the woodcreeper.

The Museum of Natural History has by far the Smithsonian's greatest number of specimens. But other museums, too, have their hidden collections. At the Museum of History and Technology I have seen drawers and drawers of political memorabilia. At the Hirshhorn I have seen huge sliding racks filled with prints, walling the inside of a vast basement storage area. The Cooper-Hewitt in New York City, one of the newest of our museums, has a collection of more than 100,000 objects representing the decorative arts and available

Myriad specimens in the vertebrate paleontology laboratory

to research students. Even the National Air and Space Museum has block-long cases of air- and space-craft models which are used for reference and not seen by the general public.

The Smithsonian Institution has something like 70,000,000 objects in all its collections. A tiny proportion are on display—yet you know it would take you a couple of 40-hour weeks to look at all that is exhibited in every building. The rest is in drawers or racks or cases. It's obvious that if a star ever did fall on Alabama it would go straight into a Smithsonian drawer.

by Edwards Park

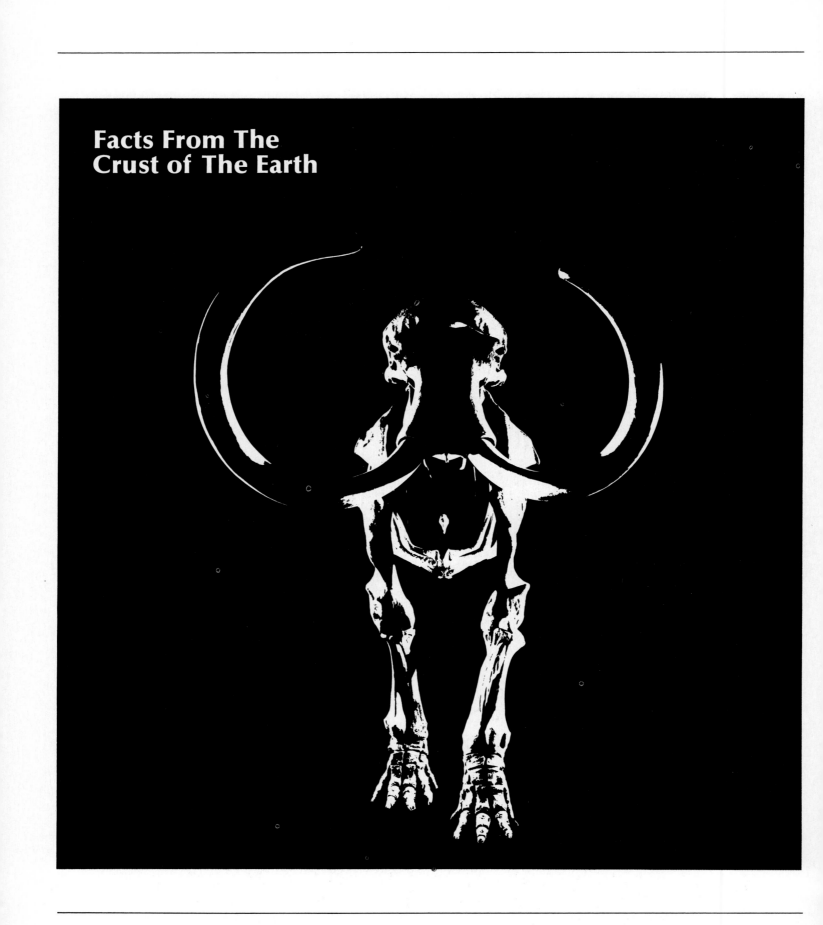

Facts From The
Crust of The Earth

ests since its earliest years. While first Secretary of the Smithsonian Joseph Henry was lukewarm about fossil collections, such illustrious Americans as Cotton Mather, Benjamin Franklin, and Thomas Jefferson had ventured opinions on the nature and origin of the bones, shells, tree trunks, and other fossilized remains that weathered out of cliffs or were turned up by farmers' plows. When Joseph Henry brought Spencer Fullerton Baird to the Smithsonian in 1850 to be Assistant Secretary in charge of Natural History, Baird arrived with several thousand fossils in addition to his immense collection of contemporary life forms.

Baird's passion for collections and genius for organization and funding were tolerated and appreciated by Henry. These early years of the institution, the 1850s, were also the years of some of the great exploring expeditions of the vast geographical area now called the United States.

Fielding Bradford Meek and Ferdinand Hayden went out in 1858 to examine the geology of Kansas, in the process establishing the existence of Permian rock formations in North America for the first time by collecting fossils like those found in Permian strata in Europe. Meek became, in 1858, the first full-time paleontologist at the Smithsonian. Like many of the early scholars at the Smithsonian, Meek

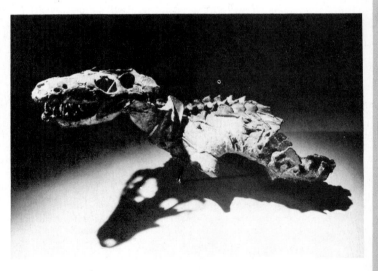

Skeletons from ages past, a sabertoothed cat circles a ground sloth (above). During Ice Ages, woolly mammoths (left) roamed all continents but Australia and Antarctica. *Thrinaxodon*, a 25-inch mammal-like reptile (right), lived in Africa, India, Antarctica 200 million years ago.

Gold rushes. The latter half of the 19th century was full of them—Sutter's Mill, Alaska, Ballarat, just to name a few. Thousands, even hundreds of thousands of men and women thrilled to the glitter of quick riches. But who has ever heard of or cared about Bone Cabin, Como Bluff, or the Judith River, Canyon City, Tendaguru, the Great Karoo, or Haddonfield, New Jersey? Paleontologists have, because the latter half of the 19th century was also the era of the Great Dinosaur Rush.

Paleontology—the study of bygone plant and animal forms—has been one of the Smithsonian's principal inter-

received no pay; however, he had free room and board in the Castle, in a room in which he lived alone from 1861 to 1876 when he died of tuberculosis. After his death it was said of Meek that he had "described invertebrate fossils of almost every phylum from all geologic periods."

Much of Meek's greatest work involved the analysis and description of fossil specimens collected by Hayden's U.S. Geological and Geographical Survey of the Territories.

Hayden's survey was a precursor of the U.S. Geological Survey (still in existence). With John Wesley Powell (leader of the first scientific expedition down the Colorado River) at its head, the U.S. Geological Survey was to find itself intertwined with the Smithsonian, even to the present day.

William Stimpson, naturalist for another survey, the U.S. North Pacific Exploring and Surveying Expedition, came to the Smithsonian in 1856 as the head of invertebrate zoology. Stimpson spent nine years at the Smithsonian describing the 5,000 specimens, including many fossils, collected during his survey. In the meantime, his lively personality led the other "Bairdian" field collectors to refer to his place of residence as the "Stimpsonian Institution." In one cryptic letter in 1858 to Hayden, then in Kansas with Meek, Stimpson enjoined him to "be virtuous among the Cheyenne and see that Meek dont get a ____." History is left to fill in the blank.

Naturalist William H. Dall, perhaps the greatest of Alaska's explorers, was another Geological Surveyor with a longtime Smithsonian connection. The association between the Smithsonian and the Geological Survey proved

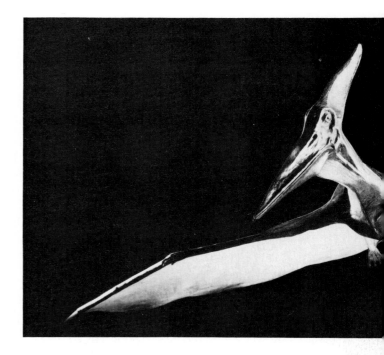

Ten-foot-long *Thescelosaurus neglectus* (above) lived in Wyoming during the late Cretaceous; its bipedal posture is characteristic of small, active dinosaurs. Above right: restoration of 12-foot-wingspan *Pteranodon ingens*, probably the best flier of the aerial reptiles. At right: *Antrodemus valens*, a 25-foot Jurassic flesh eater.

beneficial to both parties. The institution contributed laboratory and office space and instruments to survey scientists, and in return received many specimens. Of particular importance was the Othniel Charles Marsh collection of dinosaur specimens. Marsh, with Edward Drinker Cope (one of the Great Dinosaur Rush competitors), had been funded by the Survey and Yale University. After his death in 1899, the Smithsonian and Yale split his incomparable collection. Most of the dinosaurs presently on exhibit in the Dinosaur Hall of the Museum of Natural History—*Diplodocus, Stegosaurus, Triceratops, Gorgosaurus,* and

others—were taken out of the earth by Marsh's collectors in the 19th century.

Also from the survey the Smithsonian drew its fourth secretary, paleontologist Charles Doolittle Walcott. Secretary from 1907 until his death in 1927, Walcott spent part of nearly every year of his long stewardship of the Smithsonian in the field, collecting fossils from the Cambrian period of about 570 to 500 million years ago (see page 38).

As the Depression years were followed by the war years, Smithsonian and survey field workers added to the already immense National Museum collections of fossils. The

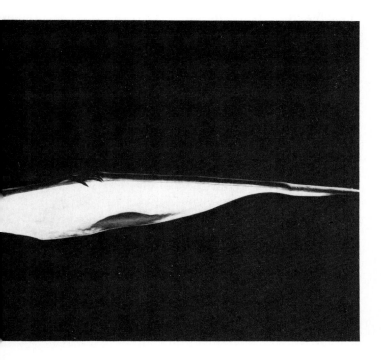

Smithsonian to this day has no rival in its assemblages of North American fossils.

And what of today? The last decade has seen what is often described as a revolution in paleobiology (paleontology with an emphasis on the life modes of ancient life forms). Yes, and no, say the curators. Paleobotanist Leo J. Hickey has traced the ancestry of many modern flowering plants as far back as 110-120 million years ago by studying both modern plants and the fossil impressions left by the leaves in the muds and clays of ancient rivers, swamps, and coastal plains. Concentrating on the vein patterns of the

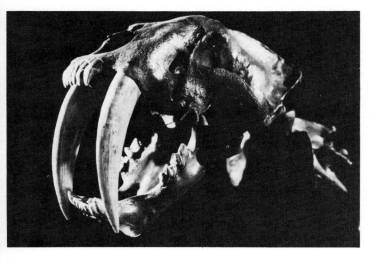

leaves, Dr. Hickey has established the evolutionary sequence of some of the flowering plants (today the dominant floral forms on earth). Until very recently, the evolution of the flowering plants was poorly understood, since many were mistakenly identified by the original collectors.

How about the newly notorious "hot-blooded dinosaurs?" Not a new idea at all, says vertebrate paleontologist Nicholas Hotton. The idea has been bruited about since the turn of the century. Hot blood aside, are dinosaurs really extinct? As they were when they ruled the

Carnivore and herbivore from different ages: the Pleistocene sabertoothed cat (below, left) had long teeth for stabbing thick-skinned prey; the plant-eating *Camptosaurus nanus* (below), from the late Jurassic, was a dinosaur no larger than a turkey.

117

earth, almost certainly. But in recent years, some paleontologists, Dr. Hotton among them, have revived another old concept, pointing out the similarities between birds and some small dinosaurs and intimating that birds may be the direct descendants of those ancient reptiles.

Most intriguing, the Natural History Museum's extensive collections of early reptile fossils have been used to compare specimens found in Antarctica with those known to have lived in southern Africa perhaps 200 million years ago. The similarity of these fossils is yet another piece of evidence that continents once joined together have drifted apart. Studies of the ancient distribution of such creatures as brachiopods, ostracods, and foraminifera also support the almost incontrovertible evidence of continental drift.

The curators still love their collections. Dr. G. Arthur Cooper, Curator Emeritus in the Department of Paleobiology, reminds the visitor that during the half-a-billion years since animals began their great efflorescence on the earth, literally millions of species have come and gone, to be known only through collections of their fossils. Dr. Ellis Yochelson, a Geological Survey paleobiologist, adds: "a paleontologist without a collection is like an atomic physicist without a cyclotron."

Nineteenth-century paleontologist Charles H. Sternberg undoubtedly summed up the attitude of his colleagues then and now when he wrote: "At the age of seventeen . . . I made up my mind what part I should play in life, and determined that whatever it might cost me in privation, danger, and solitude, I would make it my business to collect facts from the crust of the earth."

by Alexis Doster III

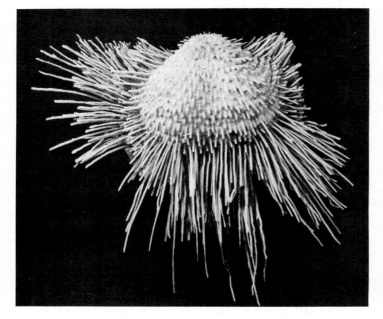

Waagenoconcha abichi (Waagen), an extinct three-inch brachiopod, lived in seas that covered West Pakistan 250 million years ago.

Eruption of Kilauea Volcano, Hawaii, 1969, symbolizes the great subterranean forces driving continental movements.

Understanding Life

by Edward S. Ayensu

Every year more than five million people walk through the exhibit halls of the National Museum of Natural History. Few visitors realize that, in addition to the dinosaurs and diamonds, the museum houses one of the world's largest "natural computers," the organized collections. In 20 acres of floor space, in cabinet after cabinet lining a maze of halls behind the scenes, rest 50 million specimens from the realms of anthropology, botany, and zoology. The chief task of the museum's scientific staff—its curators—is to place all these specimens into the categories of a data retrieval system invented some 225 years ago by a Swedish naturalist named Carolus Linnaeus.

Called systematic biology, or taxonomy, this is quiet, unspectacular work that earns few headlines. But since the museum's inception under Secretary Spencer F. Baird, systematics has been its first priority. The basic information derived from the identification and classification of natural history collections is regarded as the cornerstone for the acquisition of biological knowledge.

Taxonomy's binomial nomenclature—those two Latin names which have been given by *Homo sapiens* to all known living things and which seem forbidding to many laymen—provide a scientist with a great deal of information about an organism: its relationship to similar organisms and its place in the evolutionary scheme of things.

For some of the Smithsonian's major natural history holdings—such as 26,000 human skulls—modern computers have been hooked up, as it were, to the natural computer to speed up this retrieval process. Apart from Smithsonian scientists, the computerized information is used by other museums, governmental agencies, and universities in this country and abroad.

Retrieving information is one thing; programming the computer is another. There are an estimated 10 million species of plants and animals on the earth—and untold numbers have lived out their evolutionary histories and become extinct. So taxonomists, of which there are relatively few, will probably always be far behind the creative diversity of nature. Some three million species have so far

Edward S. Ayensu of the Museum of Natural History's Department of Botany, formerly its chairman, is author of numerous publications, as well as of a forthcoming book on orchids of the world. A citizen of Ghana, he also served during moon shots as the voice of NASA in Africa.

been catalogued. The process is slow, painstaking. To determine that a certain animal belongs in a certain genus and is a member of a certain species, the taxonomist needs to compare almost everything about the new animal to the features of its look-alike relatives.

Simply put, the ultimate goal of the botanical and zoological classification undertaken by Smithsonian biologists is to unravel the extremely complicated and

Probing a preserved and dyed fish skeleton, Dr. Victor Springer observes details of bony structure. He seeks clues to environmental adaptations of the species, and the species' relationship to similar fish.

fragmented evolutionary history of life—a story that spans perhaps three billion years—and provide a systematic framework for understanding the flora and fauna of today's world.

Given the sheer numerical burden of species past and present, and given the relatively small number of qualified taxonomists and institutions that pursue this area of inquiry, the task is awesome. On days when yet another shipment of specimens from some remote corner of the world comes in, the systematist may feel like Sisyphus.

If you were to ask each of the Smithsonian's 200 systematic biologists why he does it you would get 200 different answers. But all of them would, if analyzed, come down to the word "curiosity"—the very human drive that lies behind all basic research, all pure science. In a society dominated by mission-oriented, problem-solving research, the Smithsonian remains one of the few centers where the free-ranging curiosity of trained minds is allowed full play.

And as for our overburdened Sisyphus, more often than not he creates his own burden. The systematist's work involves more than sitting in a laboratory poring over specimens. His kind of research includes extensive field studies and the collection of specimens. Throughout the institution's history, its scientists have taken every opportunity for scientific exploration here and abroad. Smithsonian field work literally spans the globe.

What actually propels a Smithsonian anthropologist to devote his adult life to studying the ecology of aboriginal cultures in the South American tropics? What motivates an entomologist observing the feeding behavior of beetles, or an invertebrate zoologist pondering for years the locomotion of snails, or the vertebrate zoologist trekking through the wilds of Africa to map the distribution of small mammals, or the ornithologist following migrating birds from one continent to another, or a botanist devoting years of study to the mating, feeding, and seed-dispersal habits of fruit-eating bats?

To critics all these activities may seem irrelevant, even silly, a waste of public and private funds and therefore inappropriate. But the simple truth is that the human race must pursue such interests in order to comprehend the biological forces that control our very existence (including the existence of the critics). The often unappreciated fact is that major scientific breakthroughs in biology, medicine, and other fields frequently have their origins in unspectacular basic research efforts.

Scientific discoveries that have changed everyone's life have been made possible simply by the random curiosity of a few dedicated people whose ultimate goal was to understand certain natural phenomena. Sir Arthur Fleming was not looking for penicillin when he studied molds. From the platform of taxonomy, a specialist may turn up any number of unexpected questions and answers.

For more than 500 million years, the rivers, lakes, and oceans of the world have teemed with microscopic creatures called ostracods that look rather like mollusks such as clams but which are in fact crustaceans, more closely related to shrimps. The untrained eye would be hard put to distinguish one kind of ostracod from another. But biologists have determined how sensitive these creatures are to changes in temperature, depth, and salinity of the waters they inhabit. Indeed, the structural changes brought about by environmental conditions are so specific that some fossil ostracods are known as "guide fossils" and are useful in dating rocks. By comparing present-day ostracods with fossilized ones obtained from the bed of the Mediterranean Sea and from salt and gypsum quarries mined since Roman times, Smithsonian specialists have been able to trace periods—stretching back 15 million years—when the Mediterranean opened

Researcher of skeletal remains, physical anthropologist Lawrence Angel reads human bones like a book. Above, Dr. Angel has recreated a man's appearance in life by careful examination of his skull.

and closed, when it cooled, and when it almost dried up. These astounding changes are part of the larger pattern of the drifting of continents and plate tectonics, a process which goes on today literally beneath our feet.

Scientists also use fossil plants as a wedge to open up new vistas in man's quest for knowledge. In some recent instances, paleobotanical studies enabled plant scientists to claim as their own some territory that zoologists have considered their preserve: coral reefs. These reefs are generally assumed to be the constructions of minute animals which make up the large coral colonies so familiar to the diver in tropical seas. But Smithsonian research in the Caribbean has revealed that the energy to maintain the complex reef system is primarily provided by plants and that there are, in fact, many reefs built not by corals, but by a hard rocklike plant—coralline algae. With a texture and appearance similar to a pink plaster of paris, the corallines are not easily recognizable as living organisms, let alone plants, for they manufacture calcium carbonate within their cell walls. During the past 5,000 years, growing layer by thin layer, the algae have built structures as great as 30 feet in thickness and more than 100 feet wide on the outer ramparts of many wave-torn reefs in the Caribbean.

That the transfer of part of a major geological presence from the animal kingdom to the plant kingdom did not make headlines is, of course, beyond the understanding of the taxonomist. No doubt there will be arguments about it, but whatever war it triggers will be fought in the polite pages of scientific journals. In due course it will be resolved, high school textbooks will be rewritten, and we will have learned something altogether new, unexpected, and who knows how useful.

The Smithsonian's collection of mammals is one of the largest in the world. Numbering more than half a million, the specimens are preserved in the form of skins, skulls, skeletons, and fluid-preserved material. A collection of this scope affords better definition of the anatomical variation found in species as well as a better understanding of animal habitats. The major research thrust has centered around biogeographical surveys—the mapping of mammal populations. In Africa, for example, Smithsonian mammalogists have collected small mammals from most of the ecological zones. With the aid of computers they have assembled the details of gross anatomy, geographic distribution, relative abundance, and ecological preferences. In cooperation with other specialists, they have gained vital information on external parasites, and viral and rickettsial organisms which threaten either man or his domestic animals. This basic information is necessary if better measures are to be taken to protect public health. For example, Smithsonian mammalogists have participated in the identification and screening of rodents that are carriers of the highly infectious and deadly Lassa fever—a viral disease discovered in Nigeria in 1969.

Whether the specialty is birds, echinoderms, insects, or worms, the basic taxonomic work done by systematists leads not just to a more orderly comprehension of our companions on earth but often to practical and beneficial effects on human progress and health.

One of the world's most widespread diseases, for example, is schistosomiasis—more widespread now because of human activities, specifically dam-building. Dams create standing water and therein, in the tropics, certain kinds of snails thrive, serving as hosts to the early stages of a kind of parasitic worm which as adults, loose in the water, infest people who use the water for washing or irrigation. The use of the Smithsonian's information on snails and worms (and insects, which may serve as a biological control mechanism) is part of a world-wide effort to reduce the effects of this ravaging disease.

Disease is one thing; health is another. Why some people live longer than others is a public health mystery that engages the minds of many medical and scientific researchers these days. Physical anthropologists at the Smithsonian, pursuing their own lines of inquiry, follow some promising leads. The study of bone biology from past human populations provides clues as to diseases prevalent at various times throughout history. One Smithsonian anthropologist is currently engaged in studies of a pre-17th-century burial site near Vilcabamba, Ecuador, where the average life span reaches past 60, with many persons living well into their 90s. Do these people possess a superior genetic make-up or is their environment healthier? Answers to such questions may fill in needed details in our emerging comprehension of the nature of human longevity.

The United States National Herbarium, located in the Museum of Natural History, contains more than four million plant specimens, making it one of the world's leading centers of systematic plant studies. Though worldwide in scope, the herbarium is especially strong in plants of the Western Hemisphere and the Pacific.

An estimated 400,000 plant species survive in the world and of these only a fraction of the microscopic forms have been identified and classified. The number of plants of potential economic importance—as sources of food or medicines or horticultural subjects—is unknown, and the collection and naming of plant species gains an obvious value as scientists screen all the world's flora.

Immediate practical benefits can also arise from the application of data gathered during pure research. For example, one Smithsonian botanist was engaged in classifying the members of the pineapple family in the South American tropics and ended up helping to solve a public health problem, namely malaria. What do pineapples and malaria have in common? Mosquitoes, it turns out. The pineapple plant is constructed in such a way that it stores water in an open cup. These leafy "water tanks" serve as ideal breeding spots for the mosquitoes which transmit the malaria protozoan to man. Armed with knowledge of the distribution of different aerial pineapple varieties, public health in several South American communities was improved by spraying the pineapple population to prevent mosquitoes from multiplying.

Over the years, Smithsonian botanists have specialized in another plant group that on the surface seems commonplace: grasses. To most people grass is that mixed

Smithsonian researchers recently sent out word of a worldwide flowering of *Ma-dake* bamboo (above). After blooming, whole forests die back. Warnings helped countries prepare for shortages of the excellent building material. Scholars alerted South Americans to spray bromeliads whose leaf tanks (below) harbor disease-carrying mosquito larvae.

blessing that is pretty to look at but needs a great deal of care on weekends. However, it must not be forgotten that, as expressed in Isaiah, "all flesh *is* grass." To grazing animals, grasses have always been a substantial part of the diet. And for countless years, the human race has depended upon its own domesticated grasses: rice, wheat, barley, rye, oats, sorghum, millet, corn, sugar cane, and bamboo.

In recent years, grass studies have centered on the biology of bamboo, notably the Japanese *Ma-dake* bamboo, a species that was imported to this country in the last century. A particularly interesting fact about this species is that it flowers only at very long intervals—each clump wherever in the world it may be, all at the same time. And when the flowers die, so do the shoots, falling back to the earth before life is renewed from fresh sprouts.

Just how much of this bamboo exists in the United States and precisely the timing of the flowering cycle were unknown until the early 1970s when a mass flowering was predicted. In response to the call of *Smithsonian* magazine and the institution's Environmental Alert Network, more than 1,000 Smithsonian Associates, students, and gardeners sent specimens to the Department of Botany, greatly increasing our knowledge of this plant's distribution. The flowering cycle, we now know, is exactly 120 years.

As for that less exotic plot of grass—the lawn—a Smithsonian scientist has made an exhaustive analysis of this ecosystem, determining the total energy budget of a lawn, the interactions of its plant and animal inhabitants, and its response to upkeep: it turns out that the same plot of ground planted to edible vegetables would bring about a slight—but only slight—energy gain.

Energy budgets. Ecosystems. Ecology. These are relatively new, dynamic terms in the lexicon of biology. And biological research at the Smithsonian took a dynamic turn itself when in the 1960s Secretary S. Dillon Ripley began to stress that problems facing contemporary societies require an increase in the multidisciplinary approach to research. He believed that the collective knowledge of the museum's compartmentalized specialties could be focused and integrated to provide wholly new vistas in biological understanding. While the institution continues its emphasis on taxonomy, the multidisciplinary approach has brought a more flexible attitude and a more urbane outlook to Smithsonian research.

The changes can be seen at two levels—those of the individual and of the team. Today one finds a Smithsonian botanist examining the interactions of desert plants and insects with their environment from the standpoint of

123

pollination ecology and energy flow. On the other hand, zoologists specializing in bees and other pollinating insects are becoming experts in certain plant forms.

As for the team approach, terrestrial, aquatic, and marine ecosystems in a host of regions have been subjected to intense probing by interdisciplinary groups of Smithsonian researchers in league with colleagues from other institutions. The majority of these team studies have been in those lush and little-understood biological systems of the earth, the tropics.

When the Panama Canal was created, it flooded a large area in 1914 that came to be called Gatun Lake and created a 4,000-acre island that lies only a few hundred yards from the ship channel. Since 1923 the island, known as Barro Colorado, has been a tropical biological preserve with more than 70 mammal species, 300 bird species, and some 2,000 kinds of flowering plants. From its earliest days under the National Research Council the island has been a researcher's Eden, attracting to its shores many of the luminaries of biological science. In 1946 the Smithsonian took over its management, and it became the Smithsonian

Tropical Research Institute. With a small resident staff it plays host to scientists from around the world. It is fair to say that no island of similar size has ever been the subject of such thorough scrutiny.

No one visiting the tropics fails to be impressed with the teeming variety of plants and animals to be found. Surely, one tends to assume, so rich an environment must be relatively stable—that is, able to recover easily from almost any natural or man-caused insult. Barro Colorado has served as an ideal laboratory in which such assumptions can be

Smithsonian scientists conduct intensive ecological research on two tropical islands—Barro Colorado (details shown on this page), and at Carrie Bow Cay in the Caribbean (opposite). The former, in the Panama Canal's Gatun Lake, holds such varied life forms as howler monkeys, red passion flowers (below), and the vine snake (left). Findings from basic research here can help conserve forest resources.

questioned and the answer—surprising to many—is that tropical ecosystems are actually fragile. Because of seed-dispersal characteristics and the isolated, scarce occurrence of individuals of the primary tree species, and because of the relatively delicate layer of topsoil, among other factors, the tropical rain forest is incapable of regenerating on the large tracts of land which man has severed from it for intensive agriculture around the world.

On Barro Colorado research is directed to achieving a complete environmental understanding. To this end, the climate and the fluctuations in populations of plants and animals are meticulously monitored. The structure of communities is assessed, and in some cases the health of individual animals tested and catalogued.

There are, for example, some 2,000 mantled howler monkeys living in the green canopy of Barro Colorado's dank rain forest. Successive groups of researchers have looked into nearly every facet of their lives: what they eat at various times of the year (and how much energy they use to get it), their social life, the meaning of their deafening howls, and how they move around in the trees. Because the howlers are an endangered species, much of the research is designed to achieve better insight into their management. The monkeys are captured, marked, and measured. Even tooth casts and blood samples are taken, this last because the population is known to be susceptible to yellow fever. In 1949 a yellow fever attack nearly extinguished the island's monkey population. Current studies of the howler's population size, gene frequency, and community structure will give Smithsonian biologists enough data, it is hoped, to learn more about the effect of any future outbreak of yellow fever and, for that matter, to tell how to protect other wild primates from disease.

Because they are relatively discrete laboratories of evolution, islands have attracted much of the Smithsonian's research attention. Besides Barro Colorado, other islands under intense study are Aldabra in the Indian Ocean, home of giant tortoises and a number of other endangered species; Ecuador's Galapagos Islands, the crib of Darwinian evolution; Dominica in the Caribbean; the Phoenix Islands in the Pacific. From these studies, information is accumulating which, among other things, will help environmental scientists manage and plan the other "islands" among us—natural refuges and parks set aside for the preservation of wild creatures. Given the natural rates

Tiny Carrie Bow Cay attracts attention of the world's scientists. Smithsonian scholars dive here to study marine life of the New World's largest barrier reef. It lies off Belize in the western Caribbean.

of extinction and the needs of various species for space, how big should a refuge be to ensure the survival of a species? Long-term studies of island ecology are providing mathematical principles for making such determinations.

Other research programs have focused, among other places, on Nepal's Chitawan National Park, where the behavior of tigers is being studied in an effort to increase this majestic animal's chance of survival. On Carrie Bow Cay in Belize (British Honduras), Smithsonian biologists and geologists are studying the population dynamics, community structure, and plant and animal associations of the second largest barrier reef in the world. In these places and others, Smithsonian researchers and their local counterparts, using team and individual approaches, have not only made significant contributions to basic knowledge but also have encouraged and enabled the sound management of fragile and irreplaceable habitats.

Yet another focal point for ecological research is the Chesapeake Bay Center for Environmental Studies, 2,600 acres with 14 miles of shoreline, along the Rhode River complex, a sub-estuary of Chesapeake Bay. The center's programs integrate ecosystem research with land-use planning and this is combined with a public-awareness program that includes courses for local children in environmental needs.

Of special interest is the center's Forest Ecology Program for which eight study sites were chosen, ranging from Hog Island, undisturbed for centuries, to areas that were cultivated until the 1940s. Comparative analysis will enable Smithsonian scientists to determine more precisely the factors that control the succession of species in forest communities, information that is a basic ingredient for predicting and controlling man's impact on temperate forest lands. The data may also find practical application in the understanding of tropical forest ecosystems.

Strong emphasis is also placed on marine biology. Since 1971 Smithsonian scientists at the Fort Pierce Bureau, located between Fort Pierce and Vero Beach, Florida, have been probing the life forms of the sea. Using a 130-foot floating laboratory, they, along with colleagues from other organizations, collect base-line data on the diversity of marine organisms—from worms and crustacea to fish. The waters around this part of Florida are subject to continuous pollution, and a major thrust of the work at Fort Pierce is to determine the sources of the pollution and the extent to which it affects the creatures of the sea. The Smithsonian maintains two oceanographic sorting centers, in Tunisia and in Washington, D.C. Technicians have collected plant and animal specimens from all of the oceans, processed them and distributed them to institutions and laboratories throughout the world. In all, 60 million specimens have been made available for marine research.

Unique among the Smithsonian's complex of biological research operations is the Radiation Biology Laboratory located a few miles north of the Mall, in Rockville, Maryland. The laboratory dates back to 1929 when Secretary Charles G. Abbot established the Division of Radiation and Or-

ganisms within the institution's Astrophysical Observatory. Now an independent bureau, the laboratory's research still focuses on the measurement of solar radiation and its influence on various biological systems, but with sophisticated techniques and fields of knowledge that have blossomed in the past 50 years. Biochemists and biophysicists are analyzing the phenomenon of photosynthesis, the process by which plants use sunlight to produce carbohydrates in their chlorophyll-containing tissues—the process upon which life on this planet depends and one which remains imperfectly understood.

An organization that feels responsible for classifying the plants and animals of the world is often the first to realize when a species is endangered. Throughout its history, the Smithsonian Institution has been particularly interested in the conservation of the world's biological resources. In recent years, and especially since Secretary Ripley took office, world-wide monitoring of plants and animals has become a significant area of emphasis. Work on endangered species of birds has been featured prominently. Similarly, the National Zoological Park is deep into the study of animal reproduction, particularly of endangered species of birds and mammals (see pages 128-139).

In 1973, the Congress of the United States requested that the Smithsonian produce the first comprehensive review of the threatened and endangered plants native to this country. Working with colleagues from other institutions and using the herbarium's extensive collections, as well as others, botanists at the Smithsonian found that 2,000 plant species, about 10 percent of the flora of the continental United States, need protection if they are to survive the pressure of human encroachment on their habitats. Half of the flora of Hawaii was found to be similarly imperiled.

Owing to the breadth and depth of the natural history collections, Smithsonian biologists have been able to serve as impartial arbiters in delicate issues involving public policy. A few years ago, the level of mercury in fish was a matter of national concern. After several charges and counter-charges, Smithsonian biologists were called to express their views. The answer, that no conclusive charges could be levelled against today's use of the waters, was obtained after analyzing specimens from the fish collection at the institution, amassed over a century. Similarly, the Smithsonian birds egg collection played an important role during the controversy over DDT. Several conservationists had complained that the number of bird species in certain areas was declining because of the indiscriminate spraying of DDT to kill insects on which the birds feed. Rather than the destruction of their insect food, it was found that the more serious effect of DDT on bird populations was to weaken egg shells. Birds that had been contaminated with DDT laid eggs with rather thin shells that could not provide a solid protective shield for the embryo. Using the egg collection, it was possible to prove conclusively that shells with no DDT in them were much thicker than those with traces of it.

Another example of the importance of the Smithsonian's biological collections concerns the effects of air pollutants on lichens—a unique group of plants consisting of fungi and algae living together in a symbiotic association. From the beginning of recorded interest in lichens up to the present day, specimens of these organisms from the United States and elsewhere have been collected, identified, and stored at the Smithsonian, resulting in one of the largest collections in the world. Although the sensitivity of lichens to the environment has been known for years, it only recently became obvious that lichen species can be used as biological monitors. The historical series of collections is proving to be indispensable for accurately locating the destination of heavy metals and substances such as sulphur dioxide from a chemical plant. Since lichens are extremely sensitive to such pollutants, one can determine the distance air pollutants travel by checking for the presence of lichens on trees and buildings closest to a chemical plant, and comparing the results to those at a distance.

In every case, biological research at the Smithsonian emphasizes the systematic classification of plants and animals, their adaptation to the environment, and their utility

Researchers at Carrie Bow Cay examine living organisms only moments out of the sea. Back at the Smithsonian in Washington, others custom build big salt water aquariums to house living specimens from the Cay.

to man. Such studies, undertaken with a sense of historical perspective that only our vast collections can provide, cannot be underestimated. For they affect the very existence and welfare of humanity.

The Greening of the National Zoo

The director of the National Zoological Park (NZP) quietly disappeared for a week in April of 1972. He made a round trip to China. And on the return, two giant pandas accompanied him. From the arrival of these rarest of zoo creatures, a gift of the people of the People's Republic of China, panda-monium reigned.

For many people, the Year of the Pandas marked the beginning of a new era for the National Zoo. Dr. Theodore Reed, Director, is wary of this generalization, for he knows the whole story. He compares the zoo's varied operations

Famed pair of giant pandas from China steal the show at the Smithsonian's National Zoological Park. The female's name, Ling-Ling, means "tinkling bell" and the male's, Hsing-Hsing, means "twinkling star."

Lifer behind bars will soon be sprung. The cage comes down to give Nikumba, a male gorilla, and other great apes a new enclosure with plenty of room to roam.

to the many facets of a Tiffany-cut diamond. As he says, "Nobody can see all the sides of the zoo at one time."

But after World War II, enough of its sides were apparent to make people realize the zoo was in trouble. NZP received few funds for modernization, animals in small cages lived too close together for good health, buildings needed

Masai giraffes—natural zoo headliners—stand out above the crowd of African animals. Long necks enable giraffes in the wild to munch leaves high in trees. At the zoo their hay racks hang near the ceiling. Indian blue peacock preens during mating display.

repair, the research program needed a boost. A new plan for the zoo was originated and funded in the 1960s. By the 1970s it had evolved into the "Master Plan," a name uttered with reverence around the zoo campus.

The Bird House was completely renovated and the Great Flight Cage was built and stocked well before the famous pandas, Ling-Ling and Hsing-Hsing, came to town. Such delicate hoofed stock as dorcas gazelles and the oryx lived in a new building. Bongos and white rhinoceroses lived in another new building, now inhabited by the pandas.

Bright and royal eye of the king vulture of South America looks out for carrion. Below, the African black rhinoceros has worn its horns down by rubbing them against objects in the enclosure.

Bewhiskered sea lion—a new pool in its yard—will delight visitors. Below: Prehensile tailed skink can hang by its tail and smell with its tongue—which carries scent particles to a sensory organ in its mouth.

At the same time, out there waiting in the wings, stood a little group of zoo activists. They called themselves the Friends of the National Zoo, or FONZ. They looked hard for ways to help the zoo realize its master plan. Its numbers reveal the success of FONZ, and reflect the magnitude of change at NZP. In 1972, barely 1,500 supporters belonged to FONZ. By 1976, FONZ numbered 18,000. Among other things, FONZ volunteers assist researchers to maintain pregnancy watches, even at night.

On the zoo campus, the new Lion Hill was finished, replete with soil and sod. The new Administration Building,

Jamaican anole—chartreuse lizard of Caribbean islands— blends in with bright forest foliage. Pet shops often sell New World anoles.

say, a garden of the animals.

Seldom do visitors realize that large zoos are little cities unto themselves. The National Zoo's 30-man police force provides round-the-clock security every day and night of the year. The zoo's maintenance force must react quickly. For instance, if a tear occurs in the mesh of the Great Flight Cage, valuable birds can escape, and probably will. The zoo's Graphics Shop constructs the signs for the new Totems, or guideposts.

Food service for the animals is phenomenal. Each day a big hippo eats three-quarters of a bale of hay, three gallons

131

Above: Cattle egrets like these invade the earth. From the Old World they have spread to both North and South America. Right: Dama gazelle stands poised on slender legs and tiny hoofs. Herds of damas wander African deserts.

to be inconspicuous, got its own hill, too. Only the highest windows peek out. Trees planted in the sodded sides provide even more camouflage. A convincing man-made mountainside—with cliffs and a cave—rises to house the polar bears. A glockenspiel, with bells from the Netherlands, marks the time with tunes and moving animal figures. Everywhere new plantings help create, as the Arabs

of grain, three gallons of alfalfa pellets, 32 pounds of hydroponically grown grass, and eight pounds of carrots.

You can just imagine what all the animals in the zoo must eat in a week—but you don't have to. Moses Benson, chief of the zoo's commissary, has the figures at his finger tips.

This is a week's grocery shopping list: the animals consume 85 bales of timothy hay, 60 bales of alfalfa, and 2,500 pounds of assorted pellets. Vegetables include 125 pounds of fresh peas, 750 of apples, 350 of bananas, 250 of cabbage, 550 of carrots, 450 of kale, 450 of oranges, 25 of onions, 450 of sweet potatoes, 10 of tomatoes, with 250 ears of sweet corn in season, and a bushel of parsley. Each giant panda eats 20 pounds of bamboo a day, a total of seven tons a year.

From the butchery, the animals receive 450 pounds of horse meat a week, 3,000 white mice, 2,000 earthworms for the kiwis, and 28,000 crickets sent in cardboard egg cartons from the producer, the Flucker Cricket Farm of Baton Rouge, Louisiana. In the small mammal house the incessant chirp of crickets rings clear, punctuated from time to time by the fierce twitter of a tiny beast pouncing on its song-filled prey.

Gorillas do not live by bananas alone. They demand entertainment. And each day they watch several hours of television. Naturally, their keepers choose only those programs fit for their impressionable charges. Like kids of

Popular polar bear inhabits a spacious new enclosure that blends in with cliffs of Rock Creek Park, a shady retreat in Washington, D.C. Below: Zoo-born, these white Bengal tigers never roamed free. One that did was the first of their line, Mohan, a male captured in India in 1951. Today, all white tigers live and reproduce in zoos.

"Sesame Street" age, the gorillas groove on commercials. They enjoy the soap opera "As the World Turns." And intense interest was displayed during the National Geographic Special, "Search for the Great Apes."

Keepers and trainers work closest to the animals and sometimes develop a sixth sense about them. An odor, a sound, or even an unusual silence instantly tips them off to sickness or other difficulties. Throughout the day, the

keepers, vets, and scientists analyze health problems and seek cures. For instance:

"This baby has diarrhea," Al Perry the elephant trainer, tells a supervisor. He refers to little Shanthi, a pachyderm newly arrived from Sri Lanka.

"I've thought about giving the poor thing a few peanut butter sandwiches," Mr. Perry continues. All the while,

Keeper Arthur Cooper takes a kittenish friend for a walk. The yellow Bengal tiger cub, Marvin, was named for the Director of the National Portrait Gallery, Marvin S. Sadik.

Seeing such incidents, people often ask about the feelings, the emotions, of animals. Dr. Christen Wemmer, of the Smithsonian's Conservation and Research Center, provides a thought-provoking answer. "Animals newly arrived from the wild may feel as human refugees do—lost and pretty hopeless."

Smokey Bear and a young visitor to the zoo get acquainted. The original black bear named Smokey came to the National Zoo in 1950 after Forest Rangers rescued him from a fire in New Mexico. Right: Newly hatched corn snake slithers out of hand.

Shanthi keeps moving, and poking the tip of her trunk into the man's pockets.

"The trouble could be in her diet," Mr. Perry adds, "but it might also be because she is so miserable—being so new around here—with all the big, unfamiliar elephants."

At this time, Mr. Samuel Samaranayake—who accompanied Shanthi from Sri Lanka—climbs into the elephant enclosure. Shanthi seems to perk up, and she moves in to snuggle up close to the two men, the most important human beings in her life.

Fresh fruit and vegetables—tenderly chopped by keepers—add to the wealth of loving care lavished on animals at the National Zoo.

Sometimes animals appear to know how keepers are feeling, perhaps most when the human friend is sad over a death in the family, or in the zoo family.

Fawn of endangered Père David's deer gets a lift to the zoo hospital for a look at its injured leg, in the cast. Right: Keeper Leroy Robertson shares a hug and some good-natured horseplay with an Asian elephant.

Curley Harper, a keeper at NZP, has a word to add about the intelligence of the panda: "Any animal that can invent so many games for itself is not dumb."

Whatever animals may or may not feel, people certainly open their hearts to them. Smokey Bear was one of those beloved animals at NZP. The original Smokey died, but there is a new one now. And like Lassie, there will always be another to carry on the tradition and to soak up all that affection.

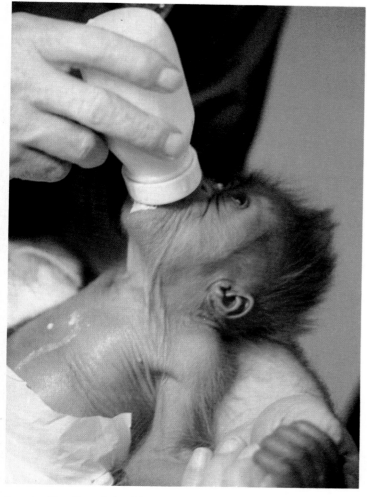

Born looking like a little old man, a baby orangutan eagerly takes milk from a bottle. Zoo programs help such endangered primates survive.

Dr. John Eisenberg, the zoo's Resident Scientist, outlines the new strategy for breeding rare animals in captivity: "We are preparing a series of species profiles. Each of these brings together all that mankind knows of an animal, and emphasizes those factors relating to its reproduction. Such profiles usually give us the clues we need to make the

Rare golden marmosets, monkeys that resemble toy lions, multiplied at the National Zoo only after scientists learned to simulate their South American habitat.

animals comfortable and secure enough to reproduce.

"Zoos may have their shortcomings, but increasingly we possess the priceless ability to conserve live genetic material. Yet extinctions will occur in our time, as they have throughout the ages. We'll make mistakes. But we'll also win victories for wildlife now, before it is too late."

Friends to the end: Pygmy hippos chew the fat over their moat. In their case, researchers helped the threatened species feel comfortable enough to breed.

Like the Cheshire cat in Alice's Wonderland, the charming lesser pandas continually perch on the limbs of trees and smile. They are the only close relatives of Chinese giant pandas.

Few zoo visitors are aware of the intensive scientific work going on behind the scenes. Away from the display area, veterinarians and researchers ply their quiet professions in a new zoo hospital and research center. Records of

birth and growth behavior for breeding in captivity can help researchers save endangered species. Due to such work at NZP, a little South American monkey, the golden marmoset, is making a comeback.

The scientific approach also worked with lesser, or red, pandas. These are tree-climbing relations of the big black and white pandas. Until their little population explosion at NZP, few zoos had succeeded in breeding them. One part of the formula for success is to provide the female with at least three secure nests. Without them she will abandon her young.

Nobody really knows why NZP has such breeding success with its pigmy hippos. Adults weigh about 500 pounds, and the young resemble English bulldogs in both size and appearance. Pigmy hippos are hairless and black and shiny, as if a keeper had applied shoe polish and a lot of elbow grease.

Endangered symbol, the bald eagle, benefits from breeding research at the zoo's "farm," the Conservation and Research Center in rural Virginia. Above: Crab-eating fox receives first aid for its injured tail.

With the dramatic decline of creatures in the wild, zoos must grow their own animals or trade or buy from other zoos. And for many species, NZP's 165 acres is too small to sustain an ambitious breeding effort.

In 1973, the zoo acquired 3,150 acres of rolling hillsides in Front Royal, Virginia. It's 20 times bigger than the NZP itself, and here wild breeding stock can wander in great paddocks.

Of course, rare animals are the pride of the zoo. Among those nurtured at the new Conservation and Research

Center at Front Royal are Père David's deer, muntjacs or Asian barking deer, South Asian civets called binturongs, zebras, tree kangaroos, shaggy two-humped Bactrian camels, and the onager or wild ass. A new bird hatchery,

At the station in Virginia, a scimitar-horned oryx grazes a Blue Ridge Mountain meadow with its young. Researchers painlessly fasten a sun-powered radio transmitter to a local turkey vulture. To study its movements, scientists home in on the signal. Angry onager, a wild jackass, bursts out of its transport enclosure.

brooding cages, and large outdoor enclosures should be completed by 1980.

As an added benefit, hay grown at the Center contains just the trace elements needed by many zoo creatures. Rather than buy such fodder from out West, NZP is able to harvest it here, only 75 miles away.

Lots and lots of zoo babies is just what NZP wants. For Ling-Ling and Hsing-Hsing, panda immortality must come in the form of cubs. And during mating season, interest is very keen around the Nation's Capital. Ling-Ling is expected to be in heat each spring and autumn. Should mating occur, birth may follow anywhere from 118 to 168 days later. The babies will be hairless and weigh some five ounces—about the same as a newborn kitten, or a stick of butter.

Ling-Ling and Hsing-Hsing, patterns for so many cuddly teddy bears, are already bigger and far stronger than most professional football fullbacks. And by the way, panda fur is as coarse as tweed.

Scientists know so little about pandas that there is no way to be sure if there will be a family in their future. But should cubs appear, they will begin life in practically a brand new zoo, one emerging right now. It's greening, and blossoming, and growing right up through the old NZP. And a prouder spot you'll not easily find.

by Joe Goodwin

Oryx herd grazes in a field of grass. Spacious surroundings help them reproduce and rear the young. Above: Bamboo chomper, the giant panda, may yet surprise the world with babies bred in captivity.

Owls in the Attic

No one knows exactly when the first live animals and birds came to the Smithsonian Institution, but they have inhabited the premises on the Mall at one time or another for more than 125 years.

The earliest on record were donated to the Smithsonian's museum by government surveys, exploring parties, and a few by individuals. Secretary Joseph Henry noted in 1855 that a substantial number of living animals had been added to the collections, some of them of great rarity. The most conspicuous of these was a two-and-one-half-year-old grizzly bear, weighing five or six hundred pounds. Other early arrivals were a pair of roseate spoonbills, an American antelope, two wild cats, a Virginia deer, and very large numbers of live serpents. Henry reported that since the institution was unable to provide suitable accommodations for the larger animals and birds, Dr. Charles Henry Nichols, the superintendent of the recently established United States Insane Asylum (now St. Elizabeth's Hospital), had cheerfully agreed to receive any specimens sent to him, and that they would be given every attention required. Henry added, "as a source of harmless amusement and mental diversion to the patients of an insane asylum, a collection of living animals has no equal, and it is much to be desired that the number at the Washington asylum may be materially increased."

As the collections of animal and bird skins and skeletons steadily increased, taxidermists were employed to mount them for museum exhibits. Many of the living animals that arrived were retained temporarily to serve as their models. Occasionally a staff member became personally attached to one of the live models and made it his pet, providing a cage for it on the premises. The number of inhabited cages spread around the rotunda of the Arts and Industries Building and its kept animals increased until official action had to be taken to regulate the practice. Separate housing for them was needed.

With part of the funds appropriated for the New Orleans Exposition in 1884, a steam-heated, two-story frame building was constructed between the Arts and Industries Building and the present Hirshhorn Museum and Sculpture Garden to accommodate the larger animals. Additional impetus for this popular

menagerie on the Mall came from the national concern over the rapid disappearance of various endangered species. William T. Hornaday, chief taxidermist, was determined to bring attention through museum exhibits to the buffalo and to other birds and beasts threatened with extinction. In 1886, with the U.S. Army, he set out with a party of assistants to tour the West in search of buffalo for his purpose. In addition to making a collection of buffalo skins, he succeeded in bringing back a live buffalo calf, which became a major attraction on the Mall for the all too brief period of its life—it died two months later.

In the summer of 1887 the First Lady, Mrs. Grover Cleveland, received the gift of an attractive spotted fawn from a friend in northern New York. Attempts to maintain the fragile newcomer on the White House grounds proved to be impractical, and she offered it to the Smithsonian. It was promptly accepted. Mrs. Cleveland often drove down to the Mall with her friends to visit the fawn and see the other animals. Several months later President Cleveland was presented with a fine, large eagle by an admirer from Tennessee. Pleased

with his unusual gift, the President soon found that eagles were even less adaptable to White House living than fawns, and it too was transferred to Hornaday's care. Both additions brought yet another dimension of public interest to the menagerie.

The burgeoning embarrassment of live riches soon outgrew the two-story building constructed for the purpose, and Hornaday was forced to commandeer additional space in a long, low wooden shed situated between the Smithsonian and the Arts and Industries Building. A bear pit was added at the Western end for the black bears, while a large cage inside housed a cinnamon bear. Adjoining it was a "glass tent" for rodents and a larger cage for birds of prey, which included eagles, vultures, and owls. As other gifts were received, additional cages were hastily constructed and installed wherever space would permit. Soon the wildlife filled the shed and ousted the other activities for which it was originally used.

Hornaday's ambition to bring public attention to the plight of the buffalo was supported in April 1888 by the gift of a four-year-old bull and a three-year-old cow from a Nebraska cattle ranch. A staff member was dispatched to bring them back, a mission triumphantly accomplished on May 10th. In anticipation of their arrival, and also to provide for four deer already in the collection, a small barn and several fenced enclosures were erected at the south end of the ellipse between the Smithsonian and the Arts and Industries Building. Thus dry quarters and cool shade were provided, as well as the space required for storage of equipment and feed. With this physical enlargement, the wildlife activity began to compete seriously with the other concerns of the Smithsonian. In order to administer the operation, the Department of Living Animals was created on May 9, 1888, with Hornaday and two assistants as staff.

Within a short time a small herd of buffalo arrived as a gift from a wealthy donor in Detroit, followed by the well publicized donation of a magnificent wapiti or elk from "Buffalo Bill" Cody. On November 3, 1890, *The Washington Post* proudly announced the birth of a baby female buffalo calf to the original pair of buffalo, and reported that the event was proclaimed to the Mall by a sustained chorus of cries and lowing calls from the herd. Visitors peered over the fences to see the tiny brown and yellow fluffy calf, which measured just 24 inches in height at birth.

While the public thronged the menagerie to observe and be amused by the antics of the birds and beasts in captivity, their own behavior was less than amusing, according to newspaper accounts. Occasionally visitors brought dogs deliberately to harass the imprisoned denizens, sometimes to extremes. One fine antelope was driven to such a frenzy by a large mastiff that he killed himself by repeatedly butting his head against his enclosure. In June 1889 *The Evening Star* reported that some visitors entertained themselves and their friends by spitting tobacco juice into the eyes of the captive monkeys and how the latter responded to their torture with cries and belligerent behavior. It became necessary to arrest offenders and take them to the local police station, where, however, they were released upon rendering collateral of five dollars.

Harassment of the animals by visitors occasionally led to more serious results. The press reported that a buffalo cow escaped from her pen and sauntered over to a group of West Virginian farmers who had come to Washington for the day. Confident that they knew all that was to be known about handling cows, the stalwart farmers attempted to drive the vagrant animal back from the public area into its enclosure again. Having once tasted freedom, the buffalo cow was not about to follow instructions. Cornered at last, the queen of the plains charged the assembled farmers, scattering them before her, some into the nearby trees and over railings, while some even attempted to climb the walls of the Smithsonian Building. Peace was restored only after an assistant keeper arrived on the scene with a pitchfork and readily returned the buffalo to the enclosure, where she immediately resumed her grazing as if nothing had happened.

A habitual escapee from the menagerie was one of the three black bears in the pit. Having discovered an outlet, he frequently climbed to the roof of the menagerie building. There he would walk back and forth along the ridgepole while astounded visitors gaped and ran to summon the keepers. The latter would shrug their shoulders unconcernedly, for the bear always returned to the pit of his own volition after his outing.

The motley wildlife on the Mall grew with weekly additions. Name it, and chances were that there was at least one example on view—Angora goats, Rocky Mountain sheep, woodchucks, hedgehogs, African porcupines, ring-tailed monkeys, turkey buzzards, carrier pigeons, hawks and eagles, opossums, a Mexican peccary, an ocelot, a jaguar (named Jack), a Mexican spider monkey, buffalo, elk, assorted lizards, alligators, snakes, and turtles.

Since the Civil War, the topmost tower of the old Smithsonian Building had been inhabited by families of barn owls. They lived independently in the lofty reaches above scholars and visitors, surviving on rodents and sparrows captured on the Mall, and they were recognized as an established part of the Smithsonian scene.

Barn owls had also been a prominent feature of Hornaday's menagerie in the late nineteenth century; he mated a single owl donated to the Department of Live Animals with one (or another) of a pair of owls which had been taken from the Smithsonian Building's tower for that purpose. Eventually the menagerie had nine barn owls, which were accustomed to sitting side by side observing the visitors with unblinking severity.

Meanwhile the feathered tower guard continued to keep a lonely vigil in their lofty eyrie atop the Smithsonian Building for almost a century. As late as 1945 the editor of *The Scientific Monthly,* then housed in the building, reported that owls came to his window in "the Brownstone Tower" as he called it, and he noted seeing them flying about the tower at dusk and of hearing them chatter.

By the mid-1950s the ever-increasing weight of owlish deposit in the towers caused one of the floors to founder, leading to an extensive program of repair work accompanied by a cleansing of the Augean stables. The constant presence of workmen and the noise of construction in their domain caused the resident owls to summarily depart the premises and seek another eyrie. The openings in the fifth story of the tower were accordingly boarded up against the advent of potential owlish squatters, and fully 15 years passed before the institution was to invite the owls to return. The coverings over the fifth story openings in the tower were removed once more, and a pair of barn owls were home grown and groomed at the National Zoo to become the tower's first residents in the new era. It was not a simple operation, as attested in a remarkable document entitled "S. I. Barn Owl Re-Establishment Research Project" which had been carefully prepared by the bird unit of the National Zoological Park. Detailed specifications were provided for every eventuality. For example, it noted that owls reared at the zoo for stocking the tower "will be given preliminary training in catching live food" before being transferred to their new quarters. To prevent homesickness and to add a touch of reality to the scene "a quantity of barn owl pellets, feathers and droppings will be provided by the National Zoological Park to give the loft that 'homey look.' "

With every possible emergency provided for, one chilly February morning in 1974 various officials gathered, shivering respectfully at the base of the tallest Smithsonian tower to observe as a wooden cage housing the pair of barn owls—named Alex and Athena—was tenderly conveyed up the endless length of ladder to the trapdoor in the floor of the fifth story, and there given the freedom of the loft. To ensure that the resettlement program would succeed, it was necessary to keep the birds confined to their quarters by means of wire screening for several months before they could be allowed to forage for their own food.

Some months passed in apparent tranquility, and it was decreed that the owl family had become officially settled, and would remain. In the spring, shortly after their arrival, they had given birth to six owlets, which in the course of time had grown and flown away. Assuming that the parents had become permanent fixtures, egress was provided through an open vent to enable them to come and go as they wished in search of their own food. They went—and did not return. First, Alex made his escape, abandoning his mate somewhat summarily. At some undetermined time later Athena also departed, presumably in the wake of her mate, and the tower loft once more was left vacant.

The Smithsonian, however, refuses to accept this disappointment as an end to the project. Another pair of young barn owls, named Increase and Diffusion, are ensconced in the tower, and have produced offspring. Tradition will be preserved.

by Silvio A. Bedini

143

PART FIVE

Images of Man

A mask of the Kwakiutl Indians emerges from a ceremonial dance in the Pacific Northwest. Wondrous artifacts like this one fill Smithsonian halls, yet an understanding of the human behind the tangible object is and always has been the Smithsonian's goal. Thus the seen and the unseen—both real—comprise the image of man.

Music somehow guides and echoes the moving spirit of human life. So why not waltz through memorable musical events at the Smithsonian?

Life—seen through the eyes of Smithsonian folklorists—becomes folklife. Our cherished customs were celebrated most notably at the Washington, D.C. Bicentennial event, the Festival of American Folklife. If you missed the event in '76, live it now, page 150.

A deep concern for Native Americans—Indians and Eskimos—lies at the heart of the Smithsonian. Ruth O. Selig's essay recounts more than a century of careful scholarship in this increasingly important field.

Early Smithsonian explorers often concentrated on Indian tribes and lands. Scholars also went out to distant corners as far apart as Afghanistan and Argentina. Between yesteryear and today, man can explore more than a century and a quarter of anthropological and archeological studies.

In closing, meet cultural historian Richard Ahlborn. He studies an era that began more than 375 years ago in what is now New Mexico. His quest for the roots of that art-rich American-culture reminds us that images of the past build for the nation's future.

Do I Hear A Waltz?

Years ago a blind piano player of remarkable talent named Alec Templeton performed at the old Rainbow Room in New York and cut at least one album of his "Musical Impressions." In this he played and sang and imitated and generally romped his way through operas and musical situations, singing all the parts of a phoney Wagnerian passage in phoney German—things like that. One of his sides was called "A Trip Through a Music Conservatory" wherein he takes you down a cor-

German violin by Jacobus Stainer, late 17th century

ridor past door after door from which come sounds of everything from scale practicing to lieder singing. The music fades from one room as you pass and builds up, discordantly, as you approach the next. Wonderfully clever.

The Smithsonian Institution doesn't have a Music Conservatory. There is no single building on the Mall where visitors can hear everything from plainsong to punk rock. There is, however, a Division of Musical Instruments with an enormous and varied collection that touches the great ages and achievements of instrument makers and performers. The keyboard collection alone contains 244 instruments: pianos, plucked string keyboards, harpsichords, virginals and spinets,

clavicytheria, clavichords, organs, and other miscellany. Talk about storage space! There are 19 grand pianos in that one wing of The Museum of History and Technology.

These instruments are used primarily by the Smithsonian Chamber Players.

English serpent
by Cramer and Key,
c. 1805-1807

The Players travel around the country, playing Handel and Bach and Mozart and other composers whose works were contemporary with the division's instruments. They also play occasionally at special doings around the Smithsonian—affairs like the "American Music and Ballroom Dance, 1840-1860," a thundering success in period costume at the Renwick Gallery not so long ago.

Oboe da caccia (curved), mid-18th century, and German flute by Heinrich Grenser, late 18th century

But at the Smithsonian one does not have to rely on occasional concerts to hear music. At various places and times across the Mall, the sounds come and go, music of every variety, thanks mostly to the Division of Performing Arts. Thanks also to the di-

Viennese contrabass saxhorn
by August Beyde, mid-19th century

rectors and curators who welcome music in their domains when it's available and sometimes go searching for it when it's missing.

The result is that on a normal spring day—the time of year when music is most apparent at the Smithsonian—you *can* hear something not unlike Alec Templeton's marvelous

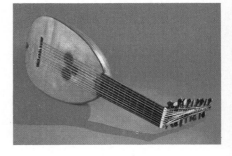

Italian lute with later
alterations, 16th century

cacophony of styles and periods and instruments and tunes. You step out of, say, the Museum of Natural History, where you have heard the music of amplified cicadas and other small beasties in the Insect Zoo, and

German orchestral kettledrums, probably 1770-1775

no sooner do you reach the portico overlooking the Mall than you hear the strumming and sawing and singing of some Bluegrass group that has gathered beside Uncle Beazley, the fiberglass *Triceratops.* No sooner are you into the mood for Bluegrass than your course takes you within earshot of the carousel outside the Arts and Industries Building. And as it wheels endlessly around, a tinkling, thump-

Parisian harmonium by M. Kasriel, 1850

ing little march comes from its intestines. Children orbiting serenely aboard horses and pigs and zebras

(and especially the horse Winkie, the perpetual, inexplicable favorite) seem charmed by the sound; passersby find themselves marching to the carousel's haunting rhythms.

You enter the "1876" exhibit in the Arts and Industries Building, and the thump-tinkle is overwhelmed by the

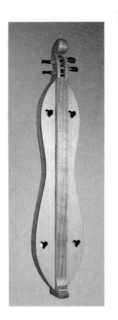

Winchester, Kentucky, plucked dulcimer by Homer Ledford, 1973

thunderous chords of the Welte Orchestrion on a balcony above the rotunda, blasting out Offenbach waltzes, or the overture to *The Mikado,* or a lilting piece of Strauss.

English bass viola da gamba by Barak Norman, 1718

The perforated paper roll unwinds across its electrically driven bellows, the wooden pipes tweetle, the brass horns blare, the snare drum rattles, the bass drum whumps, and every now and then a little metal finger, activated by the proper perforation in the paper, darts sideways and tings the triangle.

Even if you work in the building as I do, it's hard to pass the rotunda while this is going on. You join the throng by the fountain, gaping up at

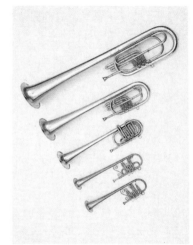

Family of saxhorns, J. Howard Foote (donor), New York City, 1880s

the old machine, swamped by its great voice and the pictures it evokes: Austrian cavalry officers and their ladies dipping through a waltz or can-can girls turning their backs and flipping up their little skirts fetchingly at the proper moment. And with the rest, you clap when the roll runs out, and you toss a nickel into the fountain for luck.

Often, when the orchestrion finishes its "gig," a Steinway in the "1876" exhibit comes to life with period songs played by a docent in period costume, and sometimes, unforgettably, a few visitors pause beside it and sing along with it. Once I heard a Stephen Foster song picked up by a woman with a glorious trained voice; when she was finished, the entire

Chamber players at the Smithsonian perform on violin, harpsichord, and viola da gamba

building and all its visitors were silent for a long moment.

Up the Mall, near the Museum of History and Technology, there is a good chance of finding some kind of performance at a noontime in April or May. A jazz group, perhaps, or a student rock band, or one of the ver-

One of many "Good News Singers," Waukegan, Illinois, performs at the Smithsonian

satile groups that erupt from the armed forces—the Army Blues or the Navy's Commodores, for example, at home with everything from the big band sound to hard rock.

There are also scheduled concerts held in the institution's several auditoriums. A Hoagy Carmichael evening at the Baird Auditorium in the

Hyde School members of "America's Spirit," from Bath, Maine, perform a musical historical play

A performer makes music at the Spring Celebration in April, 1977

Natural History Building caught my eye on one crowded calender. And finally, there is the National Gallery Orchestra which performs at intervals in the courtyard of that building.

Sometimes a traveling group gains permission to put on an impromptu

performance at the Smithsonian. I remember one March day when I was listening to a serious discussion in the Leonard Carmichael Auditorium at the Museum of History and Technology and became aware of a rather pleasant disturbance, the

The musician above performs in the 1977 Spring Celebration

sound of choral music coming from somewhere in the building. I welcomed the excuse to leave, and slipped away to follow the sound. It was the Earlham College Chamber Singers and Musicians from Richmond, Indiana. The director had asked the Smithsonian authorities if there was a place in the museum where the group could rehearse for that night's concert at the Kennedy Center.

Dizzy Gillespie, one of the greatest trumpeters, appeared at the Smithsonian in 1975

"You bet," said the authorities. "You'll go on exhibit, right by the Foucault Pendulum that giant brass plumb that swings back and forth from the roof of the building. The visitors will love it."

And of course they did, and so did the Smithsonian authorities, and so did the Earlham College Chamber Singers and Musicians, trying out their madrigals and lieder and anthems. And so did I.

Another time, at the same place, I paused to listen to a brass band of the 1850s performing early American marches on instruments of that period; long, bell-mouthed horns and nuggety little trumpets and things like that. The music was fascinating. You could picture it being played from village bandstands in

With vigor and precision, the U.S. Navy's "Commodores" delight listeners on the Mall

another America to celebrate Millard Fillmore's election. It was a perfect foil for the We the People display, nearby, where I had an appointment.

I walked away from the band, finally, and the oompahs and tweets faded as I turned a couple of corners in We the People—and there was

more music coming from the political campaign exhibit. "Hurrah for Blaine and Logan!" shouted one song, and another pointed out firmly that Hayes and Wheeler were sure to win because "they're brave, they're honest and true" and that would have some positive effect on "the red, white and

Close-up of a student-performer in "America's Spirit" reflects keen participation

blue!" Rousing songs, unamplified speeches shouted from those same village bandstands, torchlight parades down Main Street.

A musician performs intently at the Smithsonian in April, 1977

I left that huge building that afternoon by way of A Nation of Nations which takes up a large part of the west end of the Museum of History and Technology. Here, too, was a constant building and fading of songs

as I passed the exhibits of the influences that shaped our country. Tinkly ragtime piano gave way to Sir Harry Lauder who, in turn, bowed out to a colonial folksong. Music was everywhere, just as it has always been and is now in America. The sound of it enormously enhanced the exhibits.

Sometimes it's the surprise of hearing music that seems most effective. In the National Portrait Gallery you move through the long corridors, absorbed by the variety of art included in this nominally restrictive museum—the Hall of Presidents, a rare collection of miniatures, a special exhibit that tells you something

A student-performer provides music at the Spring Celebration (1977) sponsored by the Division of Performing Arts

you didn't know about a historic figure. And then, at the central junction of corridor and stairway you come on five young musicians adjusting their chairs and music stands and preparing for a brief lunchtime concert. It's not a big deal, no invitations or notices. The music is simply there, if you want to pause and listen. A very nice surprise.

That's the way it tends to be at the institution—a matter of awakening, whether by the sight of an object or by the sound that fittingly accompanies it. Music is delightfully and inextricably part of the Smithsonian's method of discovery.

by Edwards Park

Finding Roots on the Mall

On the wide Mall that stretches from the Capitol to the Lincoln Memorial, many a Yankee has sampled a Mississippi fishfry . . . youngsters have plucked up courage to join real Indians in tribal dances . . . dancers from the city have astonished watchers with kicks as high as the Washington Monument.

Such wondrous, people-to-people exchanges have taken place at the Smithsonian's Festivals of American Folklife. The tenth festival occurred at the time of the Bicentennial celebration, and it blossomed into an extraordinary affair. Five thousand performers and craftspeople from 50 states and 38 foreign countries delighted more than three million spectators. When the dust settled, it was clear America had really been seen and heard; the festival had helped fulfill the nation's post-Vietnam, post-Watergate yearning for self-confidence and hope. It was a healing—experienced by those who came, and spread by them throughout the land.

Spirits soar as D.C. Repertory Company dancers kick high. They celebrate black culture in America.

Indoor audience soaks up an Italian-American puppet show. Festival visitors often renewed old-country ties.

Though the annual festival played during three summer months in 1976, it claimed only a three-day July weekend when it began in 1967. Several different themes were highlighted in those early years: Regional Americans, African Diaspora, Native Americans, Old Ways in the New World, and Working Americans. Organizers at the Smithsonian and the National Park Service found that a way to bind it all together was to wrap those star-spangled subjects around a solid core of grass-roots musical events.

Music hath charm, no doubt, but workers and craftspersons often stole the show. Visitors found it enthralling to watch artisans at work—the products so deeply satisfying, whether hooked rugs or woven baskets or caned rockers.

An innovative concept that raised some intellectual eyebrows, the festival idea could never have worked without the Smithsonian's wide-ranging scholars—the folklorists—who discovered fresh talent in unexpected places. To give a bang-up beginning to the first festival, they started New Orleans jazz bands parading in one direction while a Bohemian hammer dulcimer band from East Texas marched in another. And balladeers, banjo pickers, and craftsmen studded the landscape. As the news spread of the good sounds and colorful handicraft skills, nearly 300,000 visitors turned their steps toward the Mall. Clearly, something special was happening at the festival and it was authentically American right down to its toes.

The word "folklife" denotes that special something. It involves the intimate culture that abides with families and gives flavor to old home places. Clans, regional groups,

A *charro*, or Southwestern cowboy with Mexican roots, jumps rope the hard way—inside his lariat loop. Right: folk dancer from Senegal, a nation of West Africa, glows with vitality and pride. Many U.S. blacks could trace their roots to his land.

Skilled hands and a hook tease yarn into fluffy crochet (top left). Wood-strip basketry begins (right). Stitchery pictures grow, and with a Mexican-American touch. Frilly, flowery shapes emerge from precisely snipped sheet metal.

performers who came to a festival from their own home country. People shook hands and chatted with performers; they dabbed their eyes when the music waxed homey and opened them to catch fast tricks of guitar pluckers, zither strummers, and bongo thumpers.

Kids dug sand, threw hay, climbed aboard a real railroad caboose. They met Eskimoes, patted—very carefully—the horses of park policemen, and one year pulled a primitive, rope-rigged ferry across the reflecting pool on the Mall.

153

A scrimshander from Maryland, Lee Meyer, carves ivory to create scrimshaw, a craft handed down from old-time whaling men.

minorities, and even majorities cherish it; fiddlers, potters, country cooks, and city vendors express it. "You can take the boy out of the country, but you can't take the country out of the boy"—or the girl, for that matter. So they tell us, and with reason: the inner goodness and inherent strength of ordinary people are living national treasures often undervalued in a history that focuses on the prominent. We are all part of the great natural, national saga; let's call it folklife.

"We believe folklife is the source of the creative energies of each person and each group in the United States," says Secretary Ripley. "The Smithsonian is a conservation organization, and it seems to us that conservation extends to human cultural practices. We look to the festivals as demonstrations of cultural roots that are too often ignored. It's a matter of soul and ethnic lore."

At the various festivals, whites could share in the spirit and the pride of blacks. Anybody could feel Polish and proud of it, or steadfastly Greek. The taproots of our national experience do indeed reach back into the old countries. Ethnic audiences responded with special huzzahs to

One tent drew families as if by magnetism: here families could tape-record stories of their own customs, their personal folklife.

Dirt-farmers, sheepherders, and blacksmiths planted, herded, or hammered at various displays and stalls up and down the Mall. Mules, visitors soon learned, are essentially folksy animals, swathed in legend and lore. Jack Hawthorne, a mule skinner who came to the festival from

Arkansas basket maker weaves split-oak strips around and between uprights, also of oak. His springy baskets protect breakables.

Pulling and singing in unison, sailing men heave on a windjammer line. Rhythmical songs, sea chanties, help weld the working men into a team. Another kind of lineman (right) perches atop a telephone pole. Each occupation spawns special folklore.

Missouri, where people take mules very seriously, added a new fillip to these creatures' briar-eating reputation. "During the Civil War," as Jack told the story, "a Missouri mule even ate up a wagon."

A mule trader borrowed a mounted park policeman's horse and showed how to tell an animal's age from its teeth. He came from Mississippi, as did weavers, a blacksmith, and a catfish-fry cook.

Kentucky whittler Edgar Tolson delighted visitors with his biblical and rural scenes, each composed of several wooden figures. Black artisans of South Carolina bound

Myra Adams of Arkansas cooks up corn soup. She also showed how to bake cornbread in a cast-iron skillet. The hot bread is both staple and soul food for many blacks and white people in the south.

Embroidery figures almost dance before the eyes. The folk artist who stitched them runs a country store in Belzoni, Miss.

Mr. Tatsusabora Kato depicts the face of a Japanese folk hero. His canvas is a kite, one he made by hand using traditional methods.

strands of sea grass with strips of palmetto to make fragrant, striped baskets. Their skill has its roots in Africa, before slavery in this country. But not all festival products could be carried in the hand: trainmen set up a real caboose on the Mall and welcomed visitors aboard, regaling them with the lore of the railroads; workers constructed a manhole, with down-deep demonstrations of how to splice telephone cables.

Though he may have come to the Mall for tall tales or fancy fiddlin', many a visitor to a summertime festival set aside a few minutes for another kind of visit. People would walk beyond the joyous tumult to stand quietly inside the colonnades of the nearby Lincoln Memorial. People studied the great man's face; searched those sightless eyes of stone. Lincoln's expression suggests many things to many people, but in his face most visitors find compassion, humility, and a compelling faith in all our people, whatever their ancestry and traditions. Notably similar feelings have emerged from the festivals of American folklife. And in the end, these feelings have outshone the fun of the events themselves.

Could he but peer down from his memorial along the Mall during one of these festivals, Mr. Lincoln would surely rejoice; the Union that he bound together is still holding firm.

by Joe Goodwin

The Indian Legacy

by Ruth Osterweis Selig

At the 1876 Centennial Exposition in Philadelphia, the Smithsonian Institution and the Bureau of Indian Affairs mounted a joint display of the ethnology and archeology of the United States. The Assistant Secretary and Director of the National Museum, Spencer F. Baird, thought the exhibit particularly important since it would probably be the last of its kind. "By the Bicentennial," he explained, "the Indians will have entirely merged into the general population." Baird would indeed have been surprised to return to the 1976 folklife celebrations on the Mall. There he would have seen Native Americans demonstrating through traditional crafts, dances, and ceremonies that Indian cultures are not only alive today but resurgent. During the folklife festival many Indians also came to the National Museum of Natural History to examine photographs, artifacts, and archival documents relating to their own past.

Scholars interested in American Indian cultures know well the massive record of Indian languages, literature, philosophy, arts, and history preserved through the Smithsonian archival records, publication series, and artifact collections. Although the Smithsonian's North American Indian collections are not the largest in the world, they are unique in being so well catalogued and described. From the institution's beginnings, interested students, including Indians, have come to study these collections. In this decade, when tribal museums have grown from 15 to 80, Indians have come to the Smithsonian in increasing numbers to trace personal and tribal histories and to participate in museum training programs. The trip to Washington can provide deeply moving, personal experiences—such as for one woman, rediscovering 259 Sioux legends. George Abrams, member of the Seneca Nation of Indians and director of the new Seneca-Iroquois National Museum in Salamanca, New York, located many photographs to help him amass for his people the "greatest collection of Seneca photographs in the world."

George Abrams's people, the Iroquois, have had a continuous relationship with Smithsonian anthropology, almost from the very beginning of the institution. One of the earliest Smithsonian anthropologists (or ethnologists as

Ruth Osterweis Selig, museum specialist with the Smithsonian's Department of Anthropology, has taught anthropology at various secondary schools, George Washington University, and has designed and taught anthropology courses for teachers.

they were then called) was the Iroquois J. B. N. Hewitt, who joined the Smithsonian staff in 1886 and ultimately left nearly 8,000 manuscript pages and 10,000 file cards on Iroquois languages and cultures. Asked about the significance of the Smithsonian artifact and manuscript collections, George Abrams explained, "If the early ethnologists like Hewitt had not collected these materials, they would have been lost forever. Now they are part of Indian heritage for all time, but also the heritage of all peoples from which to learn about Indian culture."

Thus, at the same time that other branches of the U.S. Government were destroying or radically changing many

Delegates to Washington, the Indians above were individually painted by Charles Bird King in 1822. Though the portraits were lost in the Smithsonian fire of 1865, this combined work fortunately survived.

North American Indian cultures, the Smithsonian was preserving a unique record. To understand how this happened one must go back to the very beginnings of the institution, to two men inextricably identified with the Smithsonian and with the study of North American Indians: Joseph Henry and John Wesley Powell.

When the Smithsonian regents first met on September 7, 1846, Secretary Henry presented a plan for Smithsonian investigation of North American Indians given him by his good friend, the eminent historian, Henry Rowe Schoolcraft. Schoolcraft recommended that the institution support linguistic research, archeological investigation, and the collection of Indian artifacts. Schoolcraft had spent many years traveling through Indian country, noting the destructive effects of the rapidly moving westward frontier. These were the years of Congressional removal of Indian tribes, Indian migrations from the East, land cessions east and west. Indian delegations visited Washington and, in many cases, had their portraits painted for the War Department's Indian Gallery, usually by Charles Bird King.

Keenly aware of the need for greater understanding of Indian cultures on the part of the government, Schoolcraft urged both Congress and Secretary Henry to appropriate money for research. Congress agreed, selecting him to conduct a large scale inquiry for the Indian Bureau. The Smithsonian regents also responded favorably, allotting funds to encourage study and procure collections to "illustrate the physical history, manners, and customs of the American aborigines."

Secretary Henry was pleased. He would encourage Smithsonian correspondents throughout the country to respond to Schoolcraft's circulars, requesting accurate and detailed observations about Indian languages and customs. In this way Henry could give impetus to the fledgling science of ethnology, which had always had particular interest for him since it provided a common ground between the humanities and the sciences. By 1877, when Henry would declare anthropology the "most popular branch of science," he could look back with pride to the institution's beginnings when it gave special attention to the study of "antiquities, philology, and other branches of the new and interesting department of knowledge called ethnology."

In fact, Henry had published an archeological monograph as the first volume in his great Smithsonian series, at a time when only Harvard, Yale, and the Smithsonian were providing funds for basic research and publication.

Diffusion of knowledge by publication was (and remains to this day) an important aspect of Smithsonian anthropology. The accumulation of study collections added another dimension to the growing resources relating to the North American Indians. The 1846 act establishing the Smithsonian placed under its charge the government's natural history collections including material from the Wilkes Expedition, 1838-42 (see p. 164). In the following decade, surveying parties sent out by the U.S. Interior and War Departments brought back large numbers of specimens to join the collection housed in the Patent Office Building, and later in the Castle.

"Collections" meant not only artifacts but also written reports. Though a single ethnologist could not visit every Indian tribe, the questions and instructions to the correspondents, the explorers, the Army Medical Corps field officers, and others provided a kind of extension course in ethnographic observation and collection. In 1877, for example, Secretary Spencer Baird arranged for Edward W.

Nelson, a weather observer in Alaska (page 165), to make ethnographic observations and collections from the hitherto largely untouched Bering Sea Eskimos. In five years' time, Nelson amassed for the National Museum one of its great treasures, the world's largest and finest collection of Bering Strait Eskimo materials. So well documented as to origin, method of manufacture, and use were these materials that they are still studied and exhibited today.

The record catalogs of the collections joined other manuscripts describing Indian cultures and languages. Learning of the growing accumulation of linguistic manuscripts, John Wesley Powell, then director of the U.S. Geological

At the 1972 Folklife Festival, Rose Gonzalez of San Ildefonso Pueblo, New Mexico, demonstrated the making and decorating of pottery—and thus the survival of a vital American culture.

and Geographical Survey of the Rocky Mountain Region, offered to consolidate them with his own linguistic materials and to publish the whole in a series he was organizing through the Interior Department. In accordance with Henry's long standing policy of not "expending funds on anything which can be done as well by other means," the manuscripts were turned over to Major Powell. With that transfer, the future of Smithsonian North American ethnology was probably sealed.

In the 1870s Powell had directed numerous government surveys, always having his men collect ethnographic and linguistic data among Indian cultures as well as geological specimens. Powell was a committed anthropologist as well as a geologist; above all else, however, he was a superb administrator and bureaucratic manipulator. At the end of the decade Powell organized the Bureau of Ethnology which was placed under the Smithsonian Institution, its name finally changing to the Bureau of American Ethnology (B.A.E.). Although Secretary Baird viewed the bureau as a Smithsonian unit, Powell, the bureau director, viewed it as his own. He explained why. "The Bureau of Ethnology is an institution created by myself and whatever its success has been achieved through my labors." Major Powell was not a modest man; he was formidable, capable, driving, and charismatic. During his reign, he managed to shape not only the B.A.E. but the beginnings of American anthropology.

For Powell, language held the key to culture. He therefore sought to master and classify the linguistic diversity of the North American continent. He wanted to identify the vast number of tribes and dialects, make population estimates, record the history of Indian land cessions. To organize the work, Powell conceived of three large projects: one, a linguistic classification and mapping of the entire tribal population of North America; two, a "synonymy" or dictionary of all tribal names; and three, a history of treaty relations. To work on these projects, Powell brought in trusted friends he had worked with in his survey days. Tireless, dedicated, card file men, they were scholars, devoting their lives to bibliographies, dictionaries, grammars, and massive descriptive monographs, always striving for utter definitiveness.

One of these, James C. Pilling, hoped for nothing less than to publish separate, complete, bibliographies on all the 58 Indian language stocks which Powell had recognized. When Pilling died at 49, he had published 10 volumes listing all known published and manuscript sources for these respective languages. Pilling's accomplishment was monumental, for he was dealing with about 300 mutually unintelligible Indian languages.

Of Powell's three projects, the linguistic classification and map appeared first in 1891, the history of treaty relations in 1899. The "synonymy" or dictionary of tribal names fared less well. Otis T. Mason had begun it as a personal card catalog of tribal names to aid the National Museum collections. When the B.A.E. was established in 1879, Mason turned his card file over to Powell who saw its potential as a classification tool and encouraged his staff to work on it.

The project languished in the 1890s although James Mooney worked on it for a time. Mooney, a former newspaperman, had first come to the Bureau from Indiana to see Powell and show him his own 3,000-item list of Indian tribes. Recognizing a fellow list maker, Powell hired him on the spot. Mooney stayed with the B.A.E. for 36 years, becoming one of its most illustrious field ethnographers, working primarily among the Cherokee of North Carolina, (from whom he collected myths, and numerous manuscripts written in Cherokee in the Sequoyah syllabary) and among the Plains Indians. Mooney was also one of the hard-working contributors to the synonymy, or tribal list, which was laying out the whole field of North American Indian studies. The project, begun by Mason, used by Powell and Pilling, and worked on by Mooney, evolved into a massive collaborative effort, eventually becoming the great cyclopedia issued during 1907-1910 as the famous B.A.E. *Bulletin 30*, the *Handbook of American Indians North of Mexico*, edited by Frederick Webb Hodge.

The Powell classification thus led to the *Handbook*. It had another result that was equally lasting. In 1893, when Otis T. Mason planned the American Indian Exhibition for the Chicago Columbian Exposition, he began organizing the exhibition around Powell's recently published linguistic map. For several months Mason struggled with the problem, which proved enormous since some of the most prominent linguistic stocks, such as Algonquian, spread over very diverse geographical areas. Eventually he decided to organize exhibits by "culture area" rather than language, grouping the Indians and Eskimos into 18 regions with discrete natural resources and material cultures. This conception—the influence of environment upon American Indian life—became a permanent theoretical advance in anthropology.

The 1893 exhibits also included a new display format developed under the direction of artist-anthropologist William H. Holmes: the use of life-sized costumed figures involved in typical tribal activities. This new approach began to replace the earlier displays of artifacts alone, arranged by type rather than by tribe. The earlier exhibits—row upon row of display cases of artifacts—reflected the intense interest among museum anthropologists in classification and comparative technology. Through a series of pioneering studies published in the 1880s and 1890s such as Walter Hough's on fire-making and William H. Holmes's on pottery, Smithsonian anthropologists had described Indian artifacts on the basis of manufacture, form, and function.

The transition in exhibit approach, from a comparative to an in-depth "culture area" approach, reflected new interests not only among the museum scientists in charge of all collections and exhibits, but also among staff members in the Bureau of American Ethnology. Under Powell, there had always been two approaches to the study of the American Indians. The majority of men like Pilling spent their time in offices collating the synthesizing the data accumulating since the days of Secretary Henry. But some, like James Mooney, traveled for long periods of time learning a few cultures in detail. By the 1920s anthropologists, under the influence of Franz Boas of Columbia University, were committing themselves to extended field experiences, learning the languages and studying all aspects of the cultures they visited. This marked a second stage of Smithsonian anthropology, although the sequence was not a smooth chronological one. Though James Mooney did extended fieldwork of the new sort in the 1890s, the real pioneer field ethnographer, Frank Cushing, had worked even earlier.

Frank Hamilton Cushing, "boy genius" of the bureau, was born in 1857, weighing only a pound and a half. Always frail, with few friends, Cushing spent most of his boyhood alone, reading—especially about Indians. His professors thought him bright and encouraged him to write scientific papers at a young age. When Spencer Baird brought Cushing to the museum at the age of 22, he had already published a paper in the *Smithsonian Annual Reports*.

In 1879 the young anthropologist was sent to the Southwest with the Stevenson Collecting Expedition. Colonel

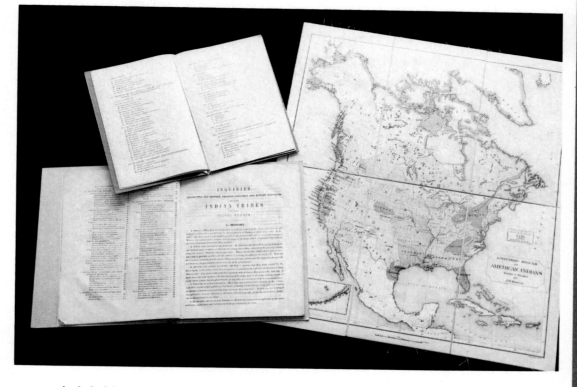

James Stevenson and his wife, Matilda Coxe Stevenson, went often to the Southwest. They never stayed long, being interested in collecting massive amounts of objects and information quickly. In one year's expedition they collected 8,500 objects, mostly pottery. Their field methods, which at times included using the wealth and the assumed

Beside John Wesley Powell's pioneering map of North American language families lie ethnological questionnaires prepared by H. R. Schoolcraft and Otis Mason in 1875 for the use of Smithsonian field correspondents.

power of the army and government, endeared them neither to the Indians nor to Frank Cushing. The Cushing-Stevenson enmity was unfortunate; the one time they did collaborate—during the 1881 field season at Zuni—the Smithsonian was provided with one of this period's best documented Southwestern collections.

Powell at this stage needed the talents of both the Stevensons and Cushing, for he had two quite separate interests in the Southwest: collecting objects and delving into the Indians' closely guarded religious life. Powell had visited the Pueblo communities years before and realized that it would be impossible for anyone to gain real knowledge of the culture without total immersion in the tribal life, in particular the religious life. In 1880 Powell visited

Stevenson and Cushing at Zuni, New Mexico, seeking to convince Cushing to stay on alone. Cushing hesitated. No American had ever undertaken such a mission. Whether Powell convinced Cushing or simply ordered the Stevensons to go is unclear. What is clear is that the Stevensons went off without leaving Cushing any provisions whatsoever. When Cushing discovered himself not only alone, but with "no coffee, sugar, flour—nothing," he felt completely abandoned, like a "doomed exile." Thereupon the Zuni governor invited him to move in with his family. "If

you do as we tell you," the governor told him, "you shall be rich, for you shall have fathers and mothers, brothers and sisters, and the best food in the world."

Cushing immersed himself in Zuni life. He adopted Zuni dress, ate the food, spoke the language. In the next five years, he returned east only once, and then only to show his own culture to some Zuni friends, taking them to Washington and Boston. In Washington Cushing attended a local scientific society meeting, where John Wesley Powell, seeing him dressed in his Zuni clothes, loudly ordered him "to go home and get dressed." During another evening, Cushing called on the noted B.A.E. anthropologist and Indian advocate, Alice Fletcher and her Omaha Indian colleague, Francis La Flesche; together they talked into the night, comparing Zuni and Omaha customs. Cushing soon returned to the pueblo, where he gained greater and greater access to ceremonial life, finally becoming initiated into the sacred Priesthood of the Bow. Cushing had penetrated Zuni culture at last.

Years later when "Tilly" Stevenson saw a photograph of Cushing she scribbled on the back: "Frank Hamilton Cushing in his fantastic dress worn while among the Zuni Indians. This man was the biggest fool and charlatan I ever knew. He even put his hair up in curl papers every night! How could a man walk weighted down with so much toggery?"

Tilly Stevenson, like Frank Cushing, had come to know the Zuni, but it is doubtful if she ever came to understand them any better than she appreciated Cushing. The vast amount of material she collected is still valuable, but she never gained the Indians' trust as he had by isolating himself from his society, willing to immerse himself completely in theirs. Always striving to understand and record traditional Zuni culture, Cushing combined an enormous sympathy and skillful objectivity which made him the pioneer field ethnologist of American anthropology.

When Cushing died at 43, his colleagues gathered in Washington to pay him tribute. Among those who spoke was his friend, Alice Fletcher, now 72 years old. Fletcher spoke of Cushing's imaginative sensitivity and his ability to understand the inner thoughts of the Indians, perhaps because to him, as to them, everything was alive, and the "unseen was the real." When Fletcher spoke of Cushing's "unconscious sympathy," she could have been describing herself. Like Cushing, her concern for the Indians' welfare and her empathy with their deeply religious nature had won her their continuing respect. Along with her adopted son and collaborator, Francis La Flesche, she left a rich record of Omaha life and religion in her published works, unpublished manuscript papers, and photographs.

Long before Alice Fletcher ever visited any Indian com-

Above left: Canadian Iroquois visitors to the Smithsonian were photographed in 1901 with ethnologist J. N. B. Hewitt (back, second right), who was himself a Tuscarora Iroquois. Among the anthropological documents collected by the Smithsonian: the 1889 portrait below of a Cheyenne U.S. Army scout and his family at Fort Keogh, Montana.

munities, she worked for Indian causes, lending money for Indians to buy individual pieces or allotments of land. Then in 1881, at the age of 40, she asked an experienced frontiersman to take her west to visit the Indians. Reluctant to take the small, seemingly frail woman on such a journey, Thomas Tibbles told her she could never endure its hardships. He rarely underestimated the foul weather, bad food, or difficult terrain, but he did underestimate Alice Fletcher's determination. Together with Tibbles and his Indian wife, Bright Eyes La Flesche, Fletcher travelled extensively, visiting Omaha, Winnebago, and Sioux Indians.

While Fletcher was studying the Omaha, Bright Eyes' brother Francis was in Washington working for the Indian Bureau. He was soon to join the B.A.E. staff, meet Alice Fletcher, and embark on a remarkable personal and professional collaboration which culminated in the Fletcher-La Flesche classic, *The Omaha Tribe*, a detailed, in-depth study of the Omaha Indian culture.

Francis La Flesche knew his cultural heritage firsthand; he, like his sister, had been born in a reservation teepee, child of the last chief of the Omaha tribe. Francis attended a Presbyterian mission school on the reservation, then the National University Law School in Washington before coming to the B.A.E. as a staff ethnologist.

Today many field notes by the great Smithsonian fieldworkers are housed in the National Anthropological Archives—for example, the materials of Mooney, Fletcher, and La Flesche. By the 1930s the early office work of Powell and Pilling, of Hough and Holmes, had given way to the field research which resulted in so many classic archeological and ethnographic studies of North American Indian cultures. These studies were published through the Smithsonian series and distributed to libraries and scientific societies the world over. In addition, many of these field studies resulted in photographic reports, today included among the archive's collection of 90,000 photographs, most taken between 1860 and 1930. Among the archival materials is the remarkable John P. Harrington linguistic collection: 1,000 boxes with approximately a million and a half pages of field notes. These notes include vocabularies, dictionaries, grammars, linguistic notes, as well as ethnographic, historical, and biographical information.

Like Mooney, who collected lists of anything that interested him, Harrington was obsessed with collecting. Much of his life, Harrington averaged 18 hours a day recording and annotating ethnological data, often from Indian tribes' last native speakers. He committed his life to recording these languages, recognizing the tragedy that a whole language—sometimes even a culture—died when its last surviving speaker died. Totally immersed in his

work, nothing else was important to Harrington, not his wife who left him nor his child who grew up without him. His colleagues apparently liked him but rarely saw him, for he preferred fieldwork to office work, collecting to publishing. From about 1906 until 1960, Harrington continued to work until his Parkinson's disease became too serious. Finally, unable to care for himself, he moved into the hospital, where his daughter found him and took him home for his few remaining months. After more than 50 years of work, Harrington died, leaving behind him an incredible

". . . so much toggery," said fellow field collector Tilly Stevenson of Frank Cushing's photograph in Zuni dress. The young Smithsonian anthropologist had adopted this pose for a portrait by Thomas Eakins.

record of North American Indian languages.

When one asks older Smithsonian anthropologists to name the unusual men and women from earlier days, two men invariably are mentioned: Harrington of course, and Ales Hrdlicka (pronounced Alesh Hurdlichka). The two were contemporaries, but in most ways, they could not have been more different. Harrington was gentle, shy, modest, selfless. Hrdlicka was neither gentle nor modest. Yet there was even a greater difference: Harrington concentrated on collecting, Hrdlicka on publishing.

Hrdlicka was as prolific as he was arrogant. His publications, numbering more than 300 separate items, set forth the bases for the measurement and description of varied human populations. He founded the *American Journal of Physical Anthropology* and through its pages defined and developed the entire field. He wrote a paper himself on almost every imaginable subject relating to physical anthropology. To public inquiries, he had one standing answer. "Refer the inquirer," he told his secretary, "to my paper on that subject."

Hrdlicka came to the Smithsonian in 1903, moving into the "new museum" in 1911. There he built the Division of Physical Anthropology to a pre-eminent position through his growing collections, library, staff, and publications program. Among his many opinions he held none more strongly than his belief that no human had set foot in America prior to the end of the glacial period between about 5,000 and 10,000 years ago. Before the discovery in the 1940s of the carbon-14 dating technique, there was no way to pinpoint dates. Hence much debate centered on the antiquity of man in America. Hrdlicka insisted, as is generally true, that skeletal remains in America were indistinguishable from those of modern Indians; he attacked others' so-called discoveries of "ancient man," and maintained that the geological evidence of ancient deposits of extinct animals associated with artifacts was inconclusive.

He was wrong, of course. Today, although there is still disagreement among scientists, all agree that the first arrivals certainly were here by 14,000 years ago and may have come as early as 25,000 years ago. But Hrdlicka's extreme stand and the prestige he placed behind it had a salutary effect, serving as a challenge to others to prove conclusively a contrary position. The ambitious archeologist had to show that the association of human bones and artifacts with extinct animal bones was direct and primary, not accidental or intrusive from later burials.

To meet Hrdlicka's challenge, paleontologists, geologists, and others were called in to examine new archeological finds, and by the 1930s more acceptable evidence of early man in America emerged. A major turning point came in 1926 when the first man-made fluted point was found in clear, direct association with extinct bison bones. An American Indian hunter had indeed once roamed the plains along with herds of extinct bison. One of the leading authorities on the emerging picture was Smithsonian archeologist Frank H. H. Roberts, Jr., whose work helped show that the early Paleo-Indians had hunted big game with weapons, tool kits, and social organizations very different from those of succeeding cultures. These successors in turn, were shown to be very different from the cultures known after 1492, which Powell and his contemporaries wrongly assumed had been essentially static for centuries before the European conquests of America. The detailed chronological developments documented by Smithsonian archeologists for the Plains, the Southwest, and the Arctic coasts demonstrated that the traditional ethnographic cultures described by the early Smithsonian correspondents and ethnologists were not the survivors of unchanging, ancient cultures. Instead, they represented the results of much change, experimentation, and growth.

In the 1930s and 40s archeology became increasingly scientific and professional as the detailed time and space frameworks were worked out for the various sections of the country. Not only archeology, but anthropology as a whole was undergoing change, becoming a larger and more professionalized discipline, with numerous universities establishing graduate programs to train anthropologists for both field and library research. In 1928 when Matthew W. Stirling was the first college trained anthropologist to become chief of the B.A.E., a new era had arrived. Stirling inherited a staff that included the bureau's first Ph.D., John R. Swanton, one of the B.A.E.'s brightest stars, who devoted his life to organizing knowledge of Southeastern Indian cultures. He published hundreds of pieces combining the results of his own fieldwork with information he found in the 400-year-long English, French, and Spanish documentary records, pioneering the ethnohistorical approach so important in North American anthropology today.

The tradition of North American Indian research and publication continues as part of the Smithsonian's anthropological programs which also cover many other areas. Important research continues on Paleo-Indian, Arctic, and Plains archeology, on the study of Indian art, technologies, languages, and tribal histories. In addition, the Smithsonian is preparing a new 20-volume encyclopedia, the *Handbook of North American Indians,* which will provide coverage of scholarly knowledge of the history and cultures of all North American Indians and Eskimos from the earliest prehistoric times up to the present. Begun in the late 1960s with the first volume scheduled to appear in 1977, the *Handbook* should become the standard reference work in the field.

The Smithsonian's work with the American Indian is a long tradition, its legacy enormously rich. The history of

At an ecumenical Indian religious conference in the Canadian Rockies, for which a Smithsonian anthropologist acted as historian, a city-bred Mohawk youth ponders his roots in the embers of a dawn campfire.

this relationship reveals not only the Indian cultures recorded, but the changing interests of American anthropology and American Indians as well. For example, during the depression, interest in the museum's collections among Indians was aroused as federal programs designed to stimulate Indian economy and tribal pride brought Indians to the Smithsonian to study the collections. Reinterpretation of traditional forms emerged in newly flourishing Indian art.

Today, interest among Indians in the Smithsonian has again surged, with Indians arriving for the folklife festivals,

the Archival Training Program, and the more general museum training program for American Indians who want to protect, study, and exhibit material culture in tribal museums. In addition, as American Indians become convinced of the need to protect their tribal records, there is also growing awareness and appreciation among all Americans of Indian cultures. With Indian identity and distinctness intact, with Indians the fastest growing minority in America, the record created by Joseph Henry and John Wesley Powell at the Smithsonian is here for all to use. It exists as a legacy for every American.

Pages from the Field

Among the leading American patrons of science in the 1850s were Joseph Henry and the Smithsonian. "With scarcely an exception, every expedition of any magnitude has received. . . aid from the Smithsonian," reported Spencer Baird, Assistant Secretary in 1852. Government-sponsored exploration parties went out not only to the unknown reaches of the western United States but also to other parts of the world like the Amazon Valley and the Bering Sea. In return for outfitting the expeditions with equipment, training the explorers to make observations and collections, and helping to prepare their reports, the Smithsonian was rewarded with the expedition's specimens.

Today's scientists (their skills and attitudes honed by the experiences of a profession that has matured to adulthood in the past century) may find the accounts of many earlier explorers—most of them necessarily amateurs—naive, even embarrassing. Yet these were the pioneers, and subsequent knowledge has to one degree or another rested upon their shoulders.

Wilkes Among the Fijis

The hairdos, grudges, and royal prerogatives of the Fiji Islanders fascinated Charles Wilkes, the young naval officer whose 1838-1842 expeditions to the southern Pacific and Antarctica produced a startling wealth of objects for curious Americans to behold. His anthropological specimens were first displayed in the Patent Office, then transferred to the Smithsonian Castle in 1857. In his official report, *The Narrative of the United States Exploring Expedition*, Wilkes devoted particular attention to the "Feejees," among whom he had wandered with some trepidation.

Before proceeding to the narration of the operations of the squadron in the Feejee Group, it would appear expedient to give some account of the people who inhabit the islands of which it is composed.

Our information, in relation to the almost unknown race which occupies the Feejee Group, was obtained from personal observation, from the statements of the natives themselves, and from white residents.

The Feejeans are extremely changeable in their disposition. They are fond of joking, indulge in laughter, and will at one moment appear to give themselves up to merriment, from which they in an instant pass to demon-like anger, which they evince by looks which cannot be misunderstood by those who are the subjects of it, and particularly if in the power of the enraged native. Their anger seldom finds vent in words, but has the character of sullenness. A chief, when offended, seldom speaks a word, but puts sticks in the ground, to keep the cause of his anger constantly in his recollection. The objects of it now understand that it is time to appease him by propitiatory offerings, if they would avoid the bad consequences. When these have been tendered to the satisfaction of the offended dignitary, he pulls up the sticks as a signal that he is pacified.

In the process of dressing the hair, it is well anointed with oil, mixed with a carbonaceous black, until it is completely saturated. The barber then takes the hair-pin, which is a long and slender rod, made of tortoise-shell or bone, and proceeds to twitch almost every separate hair. This causes it to frizzle and stand erect. The bush of hair is then trimmed smooth, by singeing

Vendovi, a Fijian chief, wore the characteristic turban-like headdress.

Charles Wilkes sketched his ship Vincennes, *one of six in the squadron, in Antarctic ice to illustrate the party's official narrative.*

it, until it has the appearance of an immense wig. When this has been finished, a piece of tapa, so fine as to resemble tissue-paper, is wound in light folds around it, to protect the hair from dew or dust. This covering, which has the look of a turban, is called sala, and none but chiefs are allowed to wear it; any attempt to assume this head-dress by a kai-si, or common person, would immediately be punished with death. The sala, when taken care of, will last three weeks or a month, and the hair is not dressed except when it is removed; but the high chiefs and dandies seldom allow a day to pass without changing the sala, and having their hair put in order.

Gifts from Japan

The Department of Anthropology's first artifact, bearing the catalog number "one" and entered on March 9, 1859, was a swatch of red silk brought back from Japan by Commodore Matthew Perry. To the Smithsonian he passed along almost every imperial gift accumulated on his celebrated mission that opened the door to United States–Japan trade. He also returned with numerous scientific specimens of interest to scientists. As the Commodore concluded treaty negotiations, he entertained Japanese officials aboard ship, and described the festivities in his personal journal.

27 March 1854
. . .I spared no pains in providing most bountifully for this numerous party, being desirous of giving them some idea of American hospitality in comparison with their portions of fish soup. My Paris cook labored for a week, night and day, in

Commodore Perry entertained the Japanese with wine, food, and song at a ceremonial repast on board the ship Powatan.

getting up a variety of ornamental dishes which would have done credit to Delmonico of New York. I had always intended to have given this dinner if the negotiations had taken a favorable turn, and had therefore retained alive a bullock, sheep and many kinds of poultry. These with hams, tongues, and numerous preserved fish, vegetables, and fruit furnished an abundant feast, not only for the Japanese, but for all the officers of the squadron, who were invited to join the party, the better to entertain the Japanese guests. Of course there was plenty of champagne and other wines with a good supply of punch for the upper table, and in the cabin almost every description of delicate wines for the commissioners with liqueurs, which they seemed to prefer, especially maraschino.

The chief commissioner Hayashi ate and drank sparingly though tasting of almost everything, but the others proved themselves good trenchermen, Matsuzaki getting gloriously drunk, and the other three quite mellow.

. . .The party on deck was very uproarious, the Japanese taking the lead in proposing toasts and cheering à l'Anglaise at the top of their lungs whilst two bands stationed nearby added to the din.

. . .Previous to the dinner hour the commissioners with their attendants visited the Macedonian and saw the crew of that ship at general exercise and also witnessed the movements of the engines of Powhatan, put in motion purposely for their examination. They were saluted by Macedonian, Mississippi, and Saratoga, and after retiring from the table were entertained on deck with the performances of the very excellent corps of Ethiopians belonging to Powhatan. Even the gravity of Hayashi could not withstand the hilarity which this most amusing exhibition excited. He and his coadjutors laughed as merrily as ever the spectators at Christy's Minstrels musical show have done. At sunset they all left the ship with quite as much wine as they could well bear. Matsuzaki threw his arms about my neck and repeated in Japanese as interpreted into English: "Nippon and America, all the same heart," and in his drunken embrace crushed my new epaulettes.

Japanese caricature of American guests at the official banquet

U.S. Marines assay the brawn of a Japanese sumo wrestler.

An Eskimo Sauna

A determined and intense naturalist, Edward Nelson traveled to Alaska as a young man and spent four years (1877-81) in the North. He mapped the territory, photographed Eskimos wherever he went, and offered to purchase any article they possessed—altogether forming a collection of 10,000 specimens. He also compiled several Eskimo vocabularies. As a Smithsonian research associate, Nelson published his findings in a lengthy report *The Eskimo About Bering Strait.*

This handsome clan of Kinugumiut Eskimos at Port Clarence, Alaska, agreed to a portrait by Edward Nelson about 1880.

On October 3, 1878, I arrived at Kigiktanik in a large kaiak with two paddle men. As we drew near the village one of the men welcomed us by firing his gun in the air, and then ran down to help us land, after which he led the way to his house. The room was partly filled with bags of seal oil and other food supplies, and the remaining space was soon occupied by a dozen or more villagers, who came to see us and were regaled with the tea that was left after I had finished my supper, and soon after my blankets were taken to the kashim, where I retired.

A small knot of Eskimo were gathered in the middle of the room around a blanket spread on the floor, and were deeply interested in a game of poker, the stakes being musket caps, which were used for chips. Scattered about on the floor and

Nelson compiled an Eskimo-English dictionary of 422 pages now reposited in the National Anthropological Archives.

sleeping benches were a number of men and boys in varying stages of nudity, which was entirely justified by the oppressive heat arising from the bodies of the people congregated in the tightly closed room. Two small seal-oil lamps, consisting of saucer-shape clay dishes of oil with moss wicks, threw a dim light on the smoke-blackened interior. In a short time the planks were taken up from over the fire pit, and a roaring fire was built for a sweat bath. The men and boys brought in their urine tubs and wore loonskin caps on their heads. Each one had a respirator made of fine wood shavings woven into a pad to hold in the teeth to cover the lips and nostrils, without which it would not have been possible for them to breathe in the stifling heat. When the wood had burned down to a bed of coals the cover was replaced over the smoke hole in the roof, and when the men had perspired enough they bathed and then went out to take a cold water douche.

Traveler in Tibet

The first Tibetan collection was brought to the United States, if not to the West, by diplomat-explorer-scientist William Woodville Rockhill. In 1888, when Tibet was closed to foreigners, he entered the country dressed as a native speaking the language he had learned under the tutelage of a Tibetan monk, and succeeded in moving about freely with two supply carts, mules and a Chinese servant. In 1891-92 he made a second journey to the country under the auspices of the Smithsonian. This excerpt was taken from his published diary *Journey Through Mongolia and Tibet:*

Rockhill pauses in front of a camel train in Peking during his journey through China and Tibet for the Smithsonian.

September 5.—To-day has been employed, as have been all other days I have passed in Tibetan towns or villages, receiving . . . men and women, showing and explaining to them the various foreign things I carry with me, asking occasionally a question and endeavoring to elicit information without exciting suspicion. It is horribly tedious and a sad strain on one's patience, but a part of my work.

The interpreter for Chinese of the Ta lama came to see me

early this morning and asked me in his master's name to leave the town this afternoon, as he feared that the lamas would again get drunk and might stir up a row. I naturally refused and said I did not care if they did, that I was under Chinese protection, and the Shou-pei and his men would have to take care of me as I intended immediately informing the Major of what he had just told me.

There was a big crowd of lamas and towns-people, both men and women, in the kung-kuan the whole day long, and the Hsien-sheng and I exerted ourselves to the utmost to make friends with them, and fortunately succeeded fairly well; they all went away saying that we were good friends, and that they hoped I would come back again. Trade was not brisk, for the people had nothing of any value or interest to sell me; one man brought me a couple of pecks of yadro, *a small bulbous root called* chih-mu yao *by the Chinese, but I had no use for it; another brought a knife, and a third some wooden cups, but no one could supply me with the things I really wanted, a kettle, a felt hat and a pair of boots. . . .*

Goitres are very common here, but I have not seen any very large ones. Syphilitic diseases also appear to be very prevalent. I noticed two men to-day with very heavy beards, and another man had a great deal of hair on his chest, arms and legs. He is the only one of the kind I have seen in Tibet. The women are much undersized, and the tallest man I have remarked here was only five feet, ten inches.

Most of the Chinese here know some of the French missionaries whom they have met at Bat'ang or farther east, and all speak most kindly and respectfully of them. One man told me that he had traveled some fifteen years ago with a father whom he called Hsiao-yeh. I cannot imagine what his European name can have been. . .

I also heard that Captain Bower* crossed the Om Ch'u on the ice right in front of Ch'amdo, which he was not allowed to enter and where he nearly had a fight. He then went to Meng-pu and Pungde, from which point he followed the same road I have been traveling along. He stopped at Draya for a day and visited the lamasery on the hill and its curiosities, among which a skull of gold especially deserved attention. I suppose it is a libation bowl.

*Bower does not appear to have left his lodgings while in Draya. This is another one of the senseless lies told me. I leave it in my diary for it helps one to understand how many difficulties a traveler in these countries has to contend with when he wants to get any question straightened out.

The Ainos of Yezo

Anthropologist, chemistry professor, musician, editor, and writer are but some of the titles that befit Romyn Hitchcock, Smithsonian curator of Foods and Textile Industries from 1883 to 1886. Hitchcock went to the Orient to teach English at the Japanese government school at Osaka, and he remained there many years for research. He devoted particular attention to the sparse remaining inhabitants from an earlier race, now known as the Ainus, on Japan's northernmost major island, Hokkaido, and on its smaller off-lying neighbor, Yezo. His report *The Ainos of Yezo* was published by the Smithsonian in 1890.

An Ainu man and woman at Sharik, Yezo, standing before the door of a straw house, were photographed by Hitchcock in 1888.

The Ainos are small in stature, although rather larger than the Japanese. They are more strongly built, and doubtless endowed with greater powers of endurance. In color they are rather brown than yellow, but scarcely darker than the Japanese. On this point, however, it is difficult to speak with confidence, for they do not bathe or wash, and the natural color of the skin is not often seen. The hair and beard, which are thick and bushy, are allowed to grow to full length, and they are never combed or brushed. Consequently an Aino at home presents a very uncouth appearance. Nevertheless, it is evident enough that most of them would be fine-looking men if they could be induced to bathe, comb their hair, and put on good clothes. Although ignorant and superstitious, they do not look like savages or barbarians. Their manners are gentle, their voices soft and pleasing. . .

Probably few who read these lines have ever seen the lower stages of human savagery and barbarism, still less have they an adequate conception of the physical and moral condition, or of the manner of life, which characterizes the lower types of human existence. The American Indian is a picturesque character as we think of him roaming over plains and through forests, hunting the buffalo and other wild animals, sleeping peacefully in his wigwam, and enjoying the fruits of a luxuriant soil. But come nearer, and we find that the hunt is for food and raiment, the wigwam is close and smoky, the fruits of the earth are nuts, and acorns, and roots, and grubs dug out of the ground. To know how miserably a savage lives, one must see him in his house.

A century ago the Ainos were living in the age of stone. They are beyond it now only because they have obtained knives from the Japanese. The stone arrowheads, which one may pick up almost anywhere, even in the plowed fields of Hako-date, have given way to heads of bamboo or iron. At Yeterof I purchased a stone implement for cutting, which could not have been very old. They have no writings, no records of their past, no aspirations. Their language is still a puzzle, their traditions and myths are scarcely known except to a few students. They are incapable of advancement. After a century of contact with the Japanese, they have learned no arts, adopted no improvements. The hunter today shoots the bear with poisoned arrow from a bow as primitive as early man himself, although the Japanese are famous for their archery and weapons.

Thick, black hair is characteristic of the Japanese Ainus. Hitchcock studied prototypes in the coastal village of Abashiri.

Religion In China

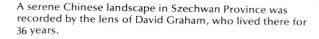

A serene Chinese landscape in Szechwan Province was recorded by the lens of David Graham, who lived there for 36 years.

In 1911 David Crockett Graham and his wife boarded the steamship *Siberia* at San Francisco with a number of missionaries bound for West China. Word arrived enroute that China was in the throes of revolution, so they settled in Shanghai to study the Chinese language. When the chaos abated the Grahams traveled to Szechwan Province, where they lived and worked until 1948. Graham was a scholar of religions, zoological collector for the Smithsonian, and photographer. He wrote two reports: *Religion in Szechuan Province, China in 1928,* and *Folk Religion in Southwest China* in 1961. This excerpt is from the latter work.

In Shanghai in 1911, and many times later in Szechwan and Sikang, I had an interesting experience. When I tried to take a picture of natives with whom I was not acquainted, they would run away as fast as they could as though their lives were in danger. The explanation given me by natives and by missionaries was that it is believed by many orientals that by taking one's picture you capture his soul, or at least a vital part of it, and that it enables you to shorten his life by several years, to injure him in other ways, or even to cause his death. Many times when I was taking a picture the bystanders have said, ''He is going to take you to a foreign country.'' They meant not just the person's picture, but a vital part of the person himself. This goes a long way toward explaining image worship in China. It is assumed and believed that if one has the picture or the image of a person or a deity, the soul, mind, or personality of the one who is pictured or imaged is present. Generally the people regard it as a great advantage to see the image of the god whom they are worshipping. This assures them that the deity is actually present and is paying attention to the worshiper, his acts, and his prayers.

A Chinese god and his two wives appear in a Taoist temple near Suifu, Szechwan. His lips are smeared with opium.

One day I had a long discussion with some boatmen about gods. Finally one boatman said, "You Christians worship a god all right, but it has no body. We make images of the gods so that we can see them and know what the gods are like." The common people feel that there must be something visible and tangible so that the mind is reached through the senses, in order that they may realize the likeness and actual presence of a god. The image is thought of as his body.

"Rain and mosquitoes" in Southeast Asia

Sumatra, Thailand, Borneo—even the Himalayas, East Africa, Haiti—all corners of the world called to William Louis Abbott, one of America's great field naturalists. From the thousands of specimens he presented to the Smithsonian from 1880 to 1916 came a particularly rich collection of birds and mammals from Southeast Asia. Although financially independent and not a staff member, he was accorded the honorary title of associate in zoology. Abbott corresponded with the curator of anthropology, Otis T. Mason, as follows:

Abbott visited a Suiban village on Sipura Island off the west coast of Sumatra to collect mammals and ethnological material.

Singapore   *Sept. 18, 1902*
I am sending you a quantity of Jakun material, Sumpitans, Baskets, traps, with Photos and measurements, and a bark canoe. This last is a very primitive specimen of naval architecture. There is a spring spear trap (for tiger and pig), rather a small one. It is nothing but some sticks, but there are detailed plans of it, and you might try setting it up out doors upon the ground, driving the sticks into the ground.

Straits of Malacca,   *Oct. 25, 1903*
I am on my way north after another trip to the Mergui archipelago. I suppose I should be going to west coast of Sumatra as that seems to be the most productive place hereabouts, but am so thoroughly tired of the continual rain and mosquitos near the equator that I want a rest in a decent, dry climate and it will be dead dry in Burmah until next May.

"The natives have done pretty well trapping for me," wrote Abbott in 1906. Above, two he encountered in the Pagi Islands.

I left Singapore 5 days ago, having shipped off 17 cases to Smithsonian, containing the results of the last cruise in the Rhio archipelago. There was not much for your department, the most interesting things were two wooden images which I discovered in a cave on the shore of Pulo Sang Car, or False Durian Island. They were evidently made by Orang Mantong, a village of these being nearby.

Straits of Malacca,   *Mar. 30, 1904*
Now in your printed instruction which you kindly sent me, it is stated that large objects such as canoes are not particularly wanted owing to space occupied, etc. Now, no model will properly show a canoe and the fuller the Museum is crammed, the more hope of getting money out of Congress for a new place.

Singapore   *Sept. 28, 1904*
. . . As to our working hard—The great difficulty usually is to find enough to do. So much time is lost between the cruises and so much time is spent getting from place to place in a sailing vessel. I don't think I spend more than 190 days a year in actual collecting. However, the intervals come in handy sometimes as it gives the numerous cuts and scratches on my hands time to heal up. You see the arsenic gets into the cuts and makes them slow healing. Besides, I am generally more or less poisoned with arsenic, showed by slight attacks of acute eczema and running of the eyes and nose.

The Aleutian and Commander Islands

The world renowned anthropologist, Ales Hrdlicka, by his own wish entered America as a literally penniless boy from Czechoslovakia, having thrown his last 15 cents into New York harbor from the ship. He went to work at 13, studying English and business in his spare time. Medicine became his first profession, followed by anthropological science. In 1898 he began to lead yearly expeditions to faraway places where he unearthed and studied skeletons of prehistoric men and the higher primates. He founded the Smithsonian's Division of Physical Anthropology in 1903 and remained its curator until his death in 1943. The following extracts are from the journal of his last expedition. Still searching for the roots of man in America, he went to the Aleutian and Commander Islands, possible remnants of a land bridge that once linked Asia with North America.

Before noon leave for Commander Bay, Bering Island. Reach first a bay about 3-4 miles above it—a native house, but no one at home—met in a boat later, had been fishing and sealing. An elevated part along a nice small river looking exactly like a site in Aleutian Islands, with rich vegetation—but nothing except a few shallow depressions that may have once been native dwellings—certainly not ancient. Rich vegetation extends over much of the valley—evidently due just to the rich soil, as at Old Harbor. All this richer than in any of our Aleutians.

Hrdlicka (right) with two Coast Guardsmen in the Aleutians.

Almost 200 years after Russian explorer Vitus Bering died, Hrdlicka visited his grave on desolate Bering Island.

Walk to Commander's Bay—just a wide cove, backed by a broad green valley. Windy here, through a depression in the hills. A fast fair-sized stream of crystal-clear water runs through the valley, which is covered by rich rank vegetation. A short distance above the cove they show us what they believe to be the keel of Bering's ship—looks old enough, heavy wood and hand-made spikes—but may be from some other wreck. On a grassy low bluff short distance up the valley on its right side, stands Bering's Cross, site of the Commander's death from scurvy and burial, with a depression not far off of the semisubterranean hut of his crew. A tragic-historic spot, of a direct interest to us Americans, too, for it was on his return from a voyage on which he and his companion Cirikov discovered Alaska that, ill already, Bering reached this place and here succumbed.

This present cross is not the original one but a recent replacement. It is large, made with care, and bears an appropriate inscription. The green bluff on which it stands is above the reach of any tide or waves and is altogether a fit resting place for the great Captain. Somewhere in the fan-shaped lower flat are said to be still some of the Bering's small cannon, but these were not located by us. A historic and pleasing, even though once tragic spot, which we were loath to leave. . . .

Head-Hunters of Ecuador

Crossing the South American continent by foot and canoe, dwelling among head-hunting Indians of the Upper Amazon and Stone Age tribes of New Guinea, and uncovering the important Olmec civilization in Mexico were all in a day's work for Matthew Stirling, a lifelong Smithsonian anthropologist and archeologist. Stirling joined the Smithsonian staff in 1921, a year out of the University of California; he went on to become chief of the Bureau of American Ethnology. An excerpt from his report *Historical and Ethnological Material on Jivaro Indians* of 1936 describes the head-shrinking process of the tribe in Ecuador.

They march back bearing the heads with them until at a distance where they are presumably safe from pursuit. Here a camp and a temporary shelter is erected, usually on a sand bar in the river, and the preparation of the tsantsas is begun. This process requires approximately 20 hours; 12 hours for the preparation of the heads and 8 hours for smoking them. As soon as the camp has been made the heads are taken from the baskets and the leaf wrappings are removed. A slit is made vertically in the back of the neck and each head is skinned as a skin is removed entire from a rabbit. Then any meat adhering to the inside is scraped off and a fine piece of Chambira fiber is used to fasten the eyelids shut. The skin is then reversed so that it is in its original position, the head forming a sack with the neck as the opening. Three pins of chonta wood are thrust through the lips so as to hold the mouth closed evenly and string is wrapped over them on the outside so as to insure the lips remaining in position during the succeeding operations.

. . . A large earthenware pot is then half filled with water. In this is placed the juice from a parasitic vine called chinchipi. *This mixture is brought to the point of boiling and the head placed in it for two hours. The astringent qualities of the chinchipi, according to the Jivaros, prevent the hair from falling out. At the end of this time the head, reduced to about one-third of its original size, is fished from the pot. It is well cooked, the skin very thick and of a rubbery consistency and pale yellow in color. As a rule, nothing is done to the eyes, although sometimes a large red-and-black seed is placed under each lid to bulge them out slightly. At this time, when*

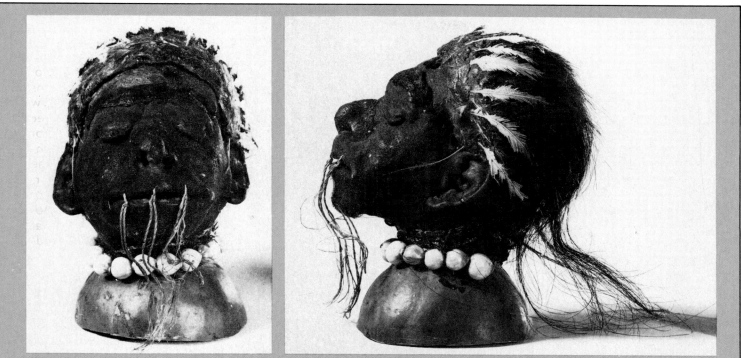

A warrior with the misfortune to be captured in battle, or perhaps who stole his attacker's wife, is known as No. 397,131 on the Smithsonian shelf. In 1930, Stirling purchased this shrunken head (shown half size) in Quayaquil, Ecuador for $20.

the head has cooled sufficiently to handle, the slit up the back of the neck is neatly sewed up.

. . . Stones are placed in the fire so as to be thoroughly heated when the head is taken from the pot. The operator then holds the head in the palm of one hand with the neck up and, picking up the largest of the heated stones with the aid of a pair of sticks, he drops it into the cavity inside the head. He then begins rotating the head rapidly in his hand so that the stone rolls around continuously inside the cavity. The hot rock gives off a sizzling sound as it contacts the wet skin and a smell like that of burnt leather.

. . . The operator picks up . . . (a) small stone with his free hand and with it smooths out the features, keeping them as nearly as possible in a natural position. As soon as the rock inside has cooled somewhat it is removed and another freshly heated one substituted, smaller rocks being used as the head continues to shrink and harden from the drying-out process. During this procedure the external smoothing of the features is continued. This goes on for 2 or 3 hours, when the head has become reduced to a minimum. From time to time hair is plucked from the head and eyebrows and eyelashes so as to keep the hair in proportion to the other features.

As a final process, hot sand is used in place of the heated stones, the head being about half filled at each application; this penetrates into crevices and completes the desiccation of any niches within the head. About evening the shrinking process is completed. The reduction of the features makes the fine facial hairs or down very prominent. At this stage the operator singes off most of this fuzz with an improvised torch, being careful not to damage the eyebrows and eyelashes.

Frequently the base of the neck is sewed around with fiber. This being done, the crown of the head is perforated and a loop of string is passed through and attached to a small transverse piece of chonta wood on the inside. By this the head is hung from a rack about 3 feet above the fire. Here it remains all night over a smudge, being heated and smoked. . .

The smoke changes the color of the heads from yellow to black, and the final drying process makes them very hard.

As a last procedure, the heads are polished with a piece of cloth, much as one would shine a shoe.

by Judy Harkison

Rediscovering Old New Mexico

Los Alamos, home of the atomic and hydrogen bombs, stands on a mesa in northern New Mexico. A monument to our modern age, it rises above a region that in some ways still slumbers in the Middle Ages.

Hardly a century after Columbus made his landfall in the New World, Spain planted a colony in northern New Mexico. Over the years farmers laid out fields and orchards. Herders brought sheep. And somehow, here

Scholarly explorer, Richard Ahlborn assembles a figure of Death in her cart.

in the upper valley of the Rio Grande, time nearly stood still for the Spanish frontiersmen and their descendants.

Richard Ahlborn, a cultural historian, specializes in the traditional patterns

Child's saddle . . . man's spurs, both reflect deluxe craftsmanship available only to wealthy men of the Spanish Southwest.

of Spanish life in what is now the U.S. Southwest. His studies complement the Smithsonian's long-term research into the customs of the Indian peoples who also live in northern New Mexico. For when the first Spanish settlers came, they moved in

alongside the Indians, often living in pueblos. These adobe buildings bore a close resemblance to the buildings being introduced as part of the Hispanic heritage of the new settlers.

Roman Catholic padres came too, and raised adobe mission churches in the Indian pueblos and in newly established Spanish villages. Sun-dried adobe bricks also formed fortified walls and towers and civil buildings for Spanish soldiers and officials.

Apolonio Martinez shaped this recent work of religious folk art, "Flight Into Egypt."

My personal discovery of the Southwest's Hispanic culture began in the reference collections of the National Museum of History and Technology. Here, Richard Ahlborn introduced me to a figure personifying death. *La Muerte* represents an essential element in New Mexico's Hispanic past . . . and present (left).

"In the Spanish tradition, Death is always a woman," Ahlborn explained as he adjusted "Doña Sebastiana's" bow and arrow and made sure she sat securely in her wooden cart.

Each Good Friday she rides her *carreta de la muerte,* or "death cart." Village men belonging to a religious brotherhood, the *Hermanos de Luz,* or "Brothers of Light" bring Death in her cart out of their meetinghouse, or *morada.* Outdoors, Death rides in the Way-of-the-Cross processional to Calvary, a local graveyard. The *hermanos* are also known by the common term *Penitentes*, a word which many of New Mexico's Hispanic people consider pejorative. The term *penitente* refers to flagellant practices and the selection of one "brother" to undergo the agonies of Christ, *El Cristo.*

An example of uniquely New Mexican folk art, this *retablo* of St. Anthony harks back to padres of yesteryear.

"In the past, perhaps some of the brotherhood nailed the *Cristo* penitent to the cross," Ahlborn added. "But more often ropes held him, as we can see from a few rare old photographs.

"For the brothers, to share but a little of the pain that Christ experienced was, and is, a vital part of a cycle celebrating his ultimate victory over death.

"Unfortunately, a bad press has blown the penitential activities of the brotherhood far out of proportion to their year-around community services. Their social services include care for the sick, consolation for those bereft, and assistance to the needy. The brotherhood provides a focus for village and ethnic identity."

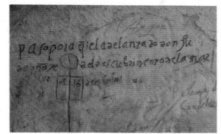

Conquistador Don Juan de Oñate carved his name on Inscription Rock in 1605.

Later, in the museum collection room, Richard Ahlborn and I unwrapped special protective paper from flagellation scourges braided from yucca fiber. A nearby glass cabinet held a small coffin with a latticework cover that housed a jointed, wooden carving of the crucified and

A wayside cross represents the steadfast faith of Hispanic New Mexicans.

interred Christ, *El Santo entierro.* His wounds are stylized, but gory.

Somehow, the whips, death cart, and other penitential devices seemed out of character, at least to my sensibilities. For around us, also resting on shelves, were the most gentle sort of artworks from the same community of hands that produced the items of painfully intense piety.

175

Kachinas—dolls for teaching children the tribal religion—represent life forces still revered by the Pueblo Indians.

Most delightful to my eyes were the *retablos,* crisply executed holy pictures painted on wooden tablets with thongs to hang on the walls of homes. The handmade *retablos* portrayed the favorite saints or *santos,* members of the Holy Family, or the Holy Trinity. Such items of religious purpose were an important focal point of inspiration and consolation in the daily struggle for survival on the frontier.

Those who made and used the holy pictures were a tough, rural people, wedded to their faith and their fields. A relatively few *santeros* crafted the *retablos,* and statues—*bultos*—for Hispanic communities of New Mexico, beginning in the late 1700s. The images differed from their models, commercially printed and imported devotional art from Europe. The New Mexican artists established a strong, local style, fully deserving the term folk art.

"When work and worship were done," Ahlborn continued, "villagers did—and still do—have fun. You should see the Hispanic people dressed up for fiesta. There is nothing like the gaiety of these local events. Old and young share a sense of excitement and belonging."

While padres sought to win the Indians to the Christian faith, the secular community worked to draw the native Americans into an economic structure not of their own making.

"Ordinary settlers," Ahlborn explained, "were the vast majority of the small Spanish population, only a few thousand by 1800. They worked hard to make do with what they had, and yearned for a few of life's graces. Life was not comfortable.

"Their houses—all with earthen floors—were furnished with Indian

"By the early 1800s, a better-off house might also contain a shelf or cupboard, a few wooden utensils, and a single silver heirloom. Much of the real value of property lay in the land, fruit trees, crops, and domestic animals."

Village shrine holds religious art—like this cross—of the "Brothers of Light."

In addition to shortages in the physical world, the colonists were hampered in their spiritual needs by a lack of priests (in New Mexico, the brown-robed Franciscans). In time, that scarcity shaped communal life in the nearly forgotten outpost of the northern wilderness.

Also in the early 1800s, the religious brotherhood (modeled partly on the Third Order of St. Francis) began to appear. The *Hermanidad* was especially important in the outlying settlements that watched for Indian attack and waited for the infrequent visits of priests to administer Church sacraments.

Spaniards, Anglos, and Indians signed cliffs of El Morro National Monument.

I also learned from Ahlborn that Don Juan de Oñate was the first conquistador who had the "privilege" of trying to settle Spaniards in New Mexico. He arrived in 1598, accompanied by priests, his military force, and several hundred colonists with their Indian retainers.

textiles and pottery, as well as distinctively Spanish weaving and furniture—usually a stool or two, and a leather or pine chest. Iron and copper tools were few and highly prized.

And when Mexico completed her break with Spain (1821), the colony on the Rio Grande was left with less contact with the Latin world and even fewer priests than before. Immediately, Americans—usually Protestants—started coming down the Santa Fe Trail urging along wagons filled with manufactured goods. After the Civil War, railroads came, following the United States headlong rush for Manifest Destiny. In the face of such changes, many Hispanic New

Over the years more Hispanic people have come to terms with the economic and educational requirements of Anglo-American culture. But acceptance of Anglo standards by Hispanic New Mexicans remains uncertain. Perhaps to be expected, many veterans who came home from the Viet Nam war joined the *Hermanos de Luz*. These men, who had faced daily hardship in civilian life, came to know mechanized death in Asia. At home, they seem to find consolation and support in communal responsibility for penance and public service.

As in the past, both peoples are somewhat aloof, mixing but not mingling. And now it is the Anglo's turn to work out a life-style within the culturally diverse region.

What will be the destiny of these three intertwined peoples—all strengthening their ties with the past while enjoying a share of the future?

Whatever happens, Smithsonian scientists and historians, like Richard Ahlborn, will observe and document

A village devotional center houses a richly decorated altar.

Many localities possess such old figures of Christ on the cross. Crucifixes play a central part in Good Friday processions.

Mexicans held ever more tightly to their heritage from the colonial past.

Many grew poorer, unable to join the new life-style as long as they depended on primitive tools and a medieval economy. Few historians can deny that Spanish New Mexicans—like the Indians—suffered injustice at the hands of Anglo judges, politicians, and merchants. (As used by the old order in New Mexico, Anglo means anybody not Indian or Spanish.)

The Americans who came to New Mexico in the late 1800s often ridiculed the *hermanos* and by implication their cultural values. But many Anglos are broadening their outlook—no doubt about it. Thousands of people from all over come to live near Albuquerque, Santa Fe, and Taos. It often happens that travelers to the state first find delight, then significant values in both Indian and Hispanic cultures.

the continuing human experience in the Southwest, as well as in other parts of the United States.

by Joe Goodwin

PART SIX

The Artist's Eye

Opening night at the new Hirshhorn Museum and Sculpture Garden brought forth 2,500 citizens who came to gaze at 800 works on display and to admire how the artist's eye reflects their respective worlds (following story). According to Secretary Ripley, that opening night was "one of three outstanding cultural events connected with Washington in this century."

The other two events had to do with the Smithsonian's Freer Gallery and the National Gallery of Art, both of whose inaugurations are heralded in the central essay of this section, written by Joshua C. Taylor. The essay also discusses the Smithsonian's other museums and galleries, all of which house a total of 150,000 works of art.

As another example of the extraordinary events that illuminate the affairs of the Smithsonian art museums, Marvin Sadik was asked to comment on the acquisition of a particularly outstanding portrait (page 184). In addition, correspondents Judy Harkison and Joe Goodwin delved into the files of the Archives of American Art and the realms of the Smithsonian's folk art repositories to produce essays on these institutional topics.

179

It's Modern Art and You'll Like It

Whenever I'm back home, the old city room gang likes to get on my back. Not about the stuff I'm filing—nobody's challenged me yet as the fastest wordsmith in the South—but about how turned on I get describing some paintings I've seen in Washington. Last time, Ed Shipley—he's my editor—even had a guy in the pressroom set up a phony headline: ART BUG BITES WASHINGTON REPORTER; CONDITION SERIOUS.

That headline's ridiculous, of course; I wasn't bitten by any kind of art bug. What really happened was that I got hooked by a museum, and I'm not the only one in Washington who's suffered from that particular form of Potomac fever.

The museum that did me in was the Hirshhorn, or—to be more precise (as any reporter should be)—the Hirshhorn Museum and Sculpture Garden of the Smithsonian Institution. It got to me about three months after the paper first sent me to Washington.

Politics and politicians were my thing then, as they still are, and in my best three-martini fantasy I could see myself closing some nationally televised press conference with an authoritative: "Thank you, Mr. President." Or discovering another Wayne Hays. That kind of thing doesn't happen right away, of course, and I had to start with the usual coleslaw of ribbon-cuttings, swearings-in, or—on an exceptionally good day—an interview with some Capitol Hill Solon who had something to say.

That was how I first got to the Hirshhorn. The museum was having a ceremony on its entrance plaza where the First Lady was to dedicate an Alexander Calder sculpture made specially to be touched by the blind. She finished on schedule. So, with plenty of time left to file my copy, I thought I'd hang around a bit and maybe pick up some background or spot some other big game. The Calder sculpture was a wild, bright flamingo color where the late afternoon sunlight hit it, and a deep, deep red where there were shadows. After what the First Lady had said about blind people, I couldn't help thinking how lucky I was to have the eyes to see it.

Over the next few weeks, I found myself occasionally remembering

Photographs by Betsy K. Frampton

that sculpture. And one morning when I was near the Hirshhorn again—Ed Shipley had wired me to stop looking for Calhoun's ghost or whatever I was doing in the Capitol corridors and to go out and talk with some real live protesters on the Mall—I thought I'd take another look at the Calder. I got a shock; it looked completely different. Different reds, different shadows, different shapes.

"Hey—you don't think they could be switching sculptures on us?" I asked myself. Maybe there was some kind of story here. So I marched inside the museum to see if they had a press guy and in a few minutes was being introduced to Sid Lawrence who said he'd be glad to help. When I asked him whether it was a different sculpture, and what in the world they had done with the old one, he looked puzzled for a moment, then laughed. "The sun moved," he said.

"What?"

"The sun moved. That's one of the things about sculpture. The way it changes as the sun moves around. It's alive that way. It's one of the things a sculptor thinks about."

Sid—who is a good friend of mine now—asked if I had time to look at some other things that would show what he meant. We took an escalator to the second floor—a big circle, with two rings of galleries. When we got there, the inner ring was lit with sunlight and filled with sculpture. Some were by sculptors I more or less knew: Daumier, Degas, Rodin, Renoir. In the outer ring were paintings; except for a few by Ben Shahn and Jackson Pollock and Edward Hopper, they were mostly by artists I didn't know about then. Sid pointed out some Daumier bronze caricatures of politicians that he thought would interest me—and they fascinated me. Then he went off to take a phone call.

I meant to stay just a few minutes, but there's something about a circular building that pulls you around. Before I knew it, another hour had ticked off. And I really had to shake it to reach the end of the Mall before those protestors blew away.

The whole thing might have ended there if your favorite senator and mine hadn't made his annual speech on the Senate floor about civic duty.

might be spared by the besieging English army. A sacrifice like that is big news forever.

What was just as interesting, though, was what Mr. Lerner was telling me about Rodin: of the 11 years the artist worked to finish the Burghers, of his courage in the face of opposition, of his integrity and imagination. He had been asked to make a monument to the past; instead he had created this profoundly moving statement about his own belief in mankind and the human spirit. It was to the future he wanted the Burghers to speak.

That got to me: "courage," "integrity," "imagination," "struggle." When I thought about those, I thought about politics and government, presidents and generals, the rough-and-tumble world I worked in. But to talk that way about art and artists? That was another idea. If I'd thought about art at all—and the fact is that I never much had—I thought it was something else. I didn't know exactly what: making pretty pictures, maybe, or painting something cheerful to hang on the wall, or just indulging yourself with pleasing patterns or shapes. As far as I'd always been concerned, I was in one place and art was someplace else. We might meet now and then, but that was all.

In it he mentioned the Burghers of Calais. And because the senator always presumes to know a little more than anyone else, I thought I'd track that reference down and find out what he was talking about. Somewhere I remembered that Rodin had made a sculpture about the Burghers; Rodin rang a Hirshhorn bell, and so I called Sid. He said that yes indeed the Hirshhorn owned a cast of the work, it was in the Sculpture Garden right next to Jefferson Drive. He also said I must have a natural nose for a story: Abram Lerner, Director of the museum, was just then collecting material for something he was writing about the Burghers.

Immediately I made an appointment to meet Mr. Lerner in the Garden.

We talked for a long time, first about the Burghers and then about Rodin. The part about the Burghers was ter-

rific. I could see the scene as if it had been on page one: that summer morning in 1347 when the six leading men of the town marched out through the gate, their necks hung with ropes, to offer themselves as sacrifices so their fellow citizens

Had I missed something? Were "art" and "real life" linked in a way I didn't know? Were the qualities that made it possible for an artist to paint what had never been painted before connected with the qualities that made some old-time senator work for what he believed in, whether it was popular or not? There was a lot I needed to find out. Mr. Lerner saw my puzzlement. And when I told him what was going on in my head, he said: "Let's walk through the museum."

We did, and that's when the museum finally hooked me. With his encouragement, I began to see things in a new way. We looked at a painting by Mondrian and he talked about the intense convictions that lay below the artist's seemingly cool geometric style. He showed me a sculpture by Picasso in which junk (really, just junk) had been transformed by the artist's vision into the witty representation of a woman with a baby carriage. There was a strange painting by Dali in which the image of death kept slipping slyly into the midst of life. And I saw a woman painted by de Kooning where his feelings tumbled across the canvas in a way that words—not even from a great wordsmith like me—could never do.

To my astonishment, I skipped my softball game the following Saturday. I wanted to go through the museum alone. That's not as good as having a guide (later I learned the Hirshhorn has docents who guide people everyday but Sunday), but I saw more than I'd ever seen before. And it's gone on from there: I've bought books, gone to other museums, even signed up for a contemporary art course at George Washington University. Of course I'll never be able to write about art like a professional; politics is still my beat. But I feel as if I have a new dimension—or maybe another lens for looking at the world.

When Ed Shipley last came up to Washington, I took him to the Hirshhorn. I think he finally understood a little bit of why I get so excited about the new way I'm looking at things. He still kids me, of course, but he did allow as to how what he calls "this art stuff" doesn't hurt the way my copy reads. In fact, possibly it helps. Maybe that's why he changed my assignment—I'm on the road now, covering the President. It feels good.

by Stephen E. Weil

183

A Singular Acquisition

Once-in-a-lifetime experiences sometimes shock, sometimes delight their victims. When they hit institutions, however, the reaction tends to be more controlled. Yet one extraordinary event—the acquisition of a superb American portrait (opposite) by the National Portrait Gallery—so stimulated the Gallery's Director, Marvin Sadik, that he abandoned institutional reserve and produced an appropriate effusion, as follows:

Of all self-portraits by American artists, none is more brilliant than the famous rondel painted by John Singleton Copley. This stunning work of art, which might fairly be considered the cornerstone of its genre, has by great good fortune recently been acquired by the National Portrait Gallery. It will be added to our 2,500-item collection of historical paintings, sculpture, prints, and photographs.

The acquisition of this portrait was made possible by a matching grant from The Morris and Gwendolyn Cafritz Foundation. It joins more than two dozen other self-portraits in the collection of the National Portrait Gallery. The earliest of these self-portraits, which antedates the Copley by more than a decade, is by Matthew Pratt, painted when he was a student of Benjamin West in London. Later examples include self-portraits by Eastman Johnson, Mary Cassatt (page 202), Charles Sheeler, and the photographer Edward Curtis, as well as by two Americans better known for their achievements in other arts, George Gershwin (page 93), and e.e. cummings.

The Copley painting is datable to the early years of the artist's career in England, where he had gone, not to escape the Revolution, but to ascend "the summit of that Mighty Mountain where the Everlasting Laurels grow."

John Singleton Copley's famous portraits of Midshipman Brine and Mrs. Rogers (above) were painted in 1782 and about 1784, respectively. His circular self-portrait (opposite), measuring some 18 inches in diameter, dates from about 1780 when the artist—born and trained in America—was just commencing his career in England.

A few days in London, however, were sufficient to make him conclude that, after all, "the works of the great Masters are but Pictures." And later in the year, during a brief sojourn in Italy, Copley would write his wife Sukey, still in Boston, "I know the extent of the arts, to what length they have been carried, and I feel more confidence in what I do myself than I did before I came." Having painted both Tories and rebels in America as the commissions for portraits presented themselves, Copley was also successful in London throughout the period during which the colonies and the mother country were at war.

The portrait shows Copley as he was described at the time, "very thin, pale . . . prominent eyebrows, small eyes, which, after fatigue, seemed a day's march in his head." It is painted in a style less hard-edged than that typical of his American portraits, and more freely, even audaciously, brushed upon the canvas—as if the gravity of his American style had taken wing, and Copley's dream of Art, so long pent up within him, had found release in a new and grander vision of mankind and the world.

Although the early literature of American art history disdained Copley's English period as inferior to his native achievement, it is now justly recognized as superlative in its own right and indeed in the vanguard of early nineteenth century Romanticism. Here, then, is the creator of *Midshipman Augustus Brine* and *Mrs. Daniel Denison Rogers,* of *Watson and the Shark* and *The Death of Major Pierson*—masterworks among the great portraits and history paintings of western art.

by Marvin Sadik

Discovery of American Art

by Joshua C. Taylor

American art can no longer be taken lightly nor is its worth a matter of public doubt. A quick look at the market would be enough to reassure anyone who needs palpable proof.

American 19th-century paintings by little-known artists that only a few years ago had no market at all now sell for substantial prices, and for some works American collectors now have to compete with knowledgeable foreign purchasers. Museums which made no apology some time back for quietly selling off inherited American paintings and sculpture now find it impossible to mount a representative exhibition of certain contemporary American artists without borrowing works from abroad.

But American art is "in" in more ways than just in the market. A whole new evaluation of American art is both symptom and catalyst for a changing attitude towards art in general, towards both art of the past and art of the present. Not only does it mark a change in patterns of collecting; it is evidence as well of a new approach to history that has far reaching effects, and not only for professional historians.

Some extent of this change can be seen in the nature and growth of the Smithsonian's commitment to art. From the time of its founding in 1846, the Smithsonian included art in the range of its studies. But by late in the century most of the works it owned were accommodated rather casually in the halls of the original building, often suspended over cases holding scientific material. By 1975 a remarkable change had occurred: six distinct Smithsonian museums were now dedicated to art (not counting the National Gallery of Art), and all except the Freer Gallery had been opened in the preceeding 10 years. Furthermore, not only were significant parts of the collections of the new museums American, but the Archives of American Art had joined the Smithsonian organization, and research and publication in the area of American art had become a notable activity. Although the beginning was slow, the expansion was rapid.

The international acclaim accorded the vital post-World War II artists in New York provided the confidence and curiosity for a new appraisal of the art that had come before. Such a stimulus was necessary, sadly enough, because the art of America's past had persistently been pushed aside in an effort to adapt to the taste of others rather than to assess what was produced at home. In spite of boasting about native genius, few peoples have been so hesitant as Americans in admitting pleasure in their own art. University departments of the history of art have paid far more attention to the art of the most remote civilizations than to that of America, and it is a rare institution that has judged the subject of sufficient importance to merit the attention of a major professor.

Art had to be brought about by deliberate effort in this country; it was not the perpetuation of a tradition. The artist had to win his way, often in the face of a suspicious or—worse—apathetic society. At the very time young artists in Europe felt themselves free to oppose academies and social institutions, artists in America were creating academic societies as a means for their own defense. They had to continuously explain to themselves and to the public what art was about—and they have been doing it ever since. Art in America went through many phases in this process of self-education; it was first very English, then very Italian, German, and finally French, and at one point adopted the stance of anti-art. Ironically, this latter "art as non-art" was the view that had the first broad appeal.

Dangling from the Castle's walls, the Smithsonian's paintings yielded primary attention in the 19th century to scientific exhibit cases (opposite). Only gradually did the institution perceive the peculiar cultural and artistic values of such American works as "Squire Jack Porter" (above), painted by Frank Blackwell Mayer in 1858.

The anti-art movement in American art took place chiefly during the 1840s and 50s (the very years in which the Smith-

Director of the National Collection of Fine Arts, Joshua C. Taylor is author of America as Art which was nominated for a 1976 National Book Award. His academic specialties are 19th- and 20th-century artistic theory and American and Italian painting of the last 200 years.

decadent civilization, yet it provided a basis as old as the oldest traditions in art. To paint wild nature unchanged was both morally uplifting and American. Such was considered, moreover, a democratic art since each man could judge it on the basis of his own knowledge of nature, untrammeled by education or accepted notions of aesthetic refinement.

The confusion of words such as "nature" with "national" points up one of the difficulties that has always beset the study of American art. If to represent nature was a manifestation of a national characteristic, to do otherwise could easily be looked upon as foreign, as less American.

Even more confusing when talking of the actual goals and content of American art are certain other inheritances from the 19th century. No period before it was quite so concerned with self-analysis as the 19th century, a period which seems not to have stopped at 1900. Looking at the past as a series of synthe-

sonian Institution was beginning to function), and had a lasting effect in assessments of art in America. The premise, sustained by the writings of the English critic John Ruskin and to a degree by the writings of Ralph Waldo Emerson, held that nature was the great teacher and inspiration of man, and that the greatest art was that which, in a self-negating way, directed attention to the beauties of nature itself, to the handiwork of God, not of the artist. Although blessed with few works of art by which to train its artists in traditional methods, America abounded in nature, and it is not surprising that a theory basing moral instruction on nature rather than on the works of past geniuses should find favor here. Furthermore, America's nature was new, insofar as European eyes were concerned, untouched by

sized cultures, each with a rise and fall and a clearly definable artistic style, the thoughtful 19th-century man asked himself what the definitions of his own culture were. He devised a vocabulary for supporting his notions of what he thought he was or wanted to be—romantic, classic, militant realist, etc.—and historians ever since have dutifully taken his words as accurate statement of fact, using them sometimes as the diagnoses for which the historians were responsible for finding the symptoms.

Unfortunately for those wishing to study American art, the historical scheme that finally emerged for the 19th century was based exclusively on European art, more often than not on French art. By the 1920s the history of art was rendered in exclusive forms as stylized as the art of the

time. Not surprisingly there was much that had happened in art of the United States (as well as in the art of many other countries) that did not fit this tidy organization of realism, impressionism, symbolism, and so forth. For a very long time, regrettably, the failure to match this historical model in all its particulars was looked upon as a deficiency of American art.

Connoisseurs tried to find American equivalents to Delacroix, Courbet, or Monet and were distressed to find that their candidates were simply not comparable; as in many such situations, differences were judged to be defects of quality, not variations in intent. The critics often failed to note that artists might share techniques, yet differ fundamentally in their goals. The sentiment in a painting by Weir or Childe Hassam is there not because they failed to understand Monet but because they believed in the evocation of mood.

Naturally, as a result of this meddling with the shape of history, the names of relatively few early American artists survived to be recorded in 20th-century text books, and the reputations of American artists were not rated highly in the minds of collectors and "people who know."

Throughout the 19th century, collectors in the United States bought much more heavily in European art than in American. Furthermore, when the first large-scale museums were founded in the 1870s, their primary goal was to make the whole range of European art, schematically organized, available to a wide public in order to elevate public taste and remedy the appalling failure of American artists to become recognized members of tradition's parade.

The great collections that were assembled toward the end of the 19th century made, and still make, an enormous contribution to the art and culture of the United States. But living artists require more than spiritual support. There were exceptions among collectors, to be sure, those who wholeheartedly supported contemporary American artists, and there were some historians who persisted in noting that American art had a past of its own. Until well into the 20th century, however, they were working against the grain.

It was to some of these highly individual collectors working against the grain that the Smithsonian owes much of its initial expansion in the arts. Although the superb depictions of Indians painted by George Catlin in the 1830s were given to the institution in 1879, they were, significantly, then looked upon as ethnological documents rather than as works of art—and this was true also of the earlier Indian portraits by Charles Bird King and the paintings lent by John Mix Stanley (almost all of which were destroyed in the Smithsonian fire of 1865). A varied group of paintings, sculptures, and prints accumulated, but not until 1903 was a sizable collection of works of art bequeathed to the nation—art recognized as art. It was turned over to the Smithsonian in 1906 on the determination that the Smithsonian's art collection was now to be considered the Na-

" . . . a man named Freer from Detroit came through here," reported Secretary Abbot in 1905. That visit culminated in the millionaire's gift of the Freer Gallery of Art (opposite). A fastidious bachelor with Vandyke beard and fine eye for art, Charles Lang Freer had rounded out his collection by journeys to Egypt (below) and the Far East.

tional Gallery of Art. Characteristically, in this collection (left by Harriet Lane Johnston, the niece of President Buchanan) only nine of the 31 works were by Americans.

But by the beginning of the century, collecting habits were changing. Although Charles L. Freer was chiefly concerned with Oriental art, he did not separate that special attachment from what he found appealing in certain di-

rections in the art of some of his American contemporaries. He was a close friend and supporter of James Abbott McNeill Whistler and friend and patron of many American artists whose works manifest the sensuous refinement that Freer admired in Eastern art. As a result, the collection that he gave to the Smithsonian in 1906 included—besides the comprehensive collection of Oriental objects which make the Freer one of the most important museums of Oriental art in the world—a choice representation of a particularly refined and elegant phase of contemporary American painting. By the time that Charles A. Platt's beautifully detailed building on the Mall was ready for the collection in 1923, it included over 1,000 American paintings, prints, drawings, and sculptures from the period of Freer's lifetime.

Another collector, John Gellatly, a younger contemporary of Freer's, also saw contemporary American art as compatible with past cultures and maintained that it was the equal to what the past had produced at its highest moments. To prove his point he acquired an extraordinary range of paintings and decorative arts from ancient Egypt, Greece, and China, ivories and other intricate objects from medieval Europe, and European paintings and decorative arts from the Renaissance through the 18th century—including a dazzling collection of Renaissance jewelry—all to be placed beside his Albert Pinkham Ryders (he settled on 17), Thomas Dewings, Abbott Thayers, and others. In 1929 he presented the entire collection to the Smithsonian for its National Gallery.

William T. Evans, unlike Freer and Gellatly, was quite willing to accept the art of his contemporary fellow Americans without associations with the art historical past. A major promoter of American artists, he began his extensive gift to the Smithsonian in 1906; the gift included a perceptively chosen representation of American painting at the turn of the century. So almost in spite of itself, by the late 1920s the Smithsonian was the satisfied possessor of an extensive collection of American art of the late 19th and the early 20th century. But what to do about it? It was not yet seemly for scholars to devote their time to such studies. Photography and the graphic arts had moved into the range of Smithsonian interests as technologies, and there they largely remain (the National Museum of History and Technology has an extensive collection of photographs and European and American prints). The place for the scholar in art was still doubtful.

With the proud name of the National Gallery of Art, the Smithsonian collection was moved to a wing of the newly constructed Natural History Building in 1910, there to remain for well over 50 years. Although it had a full-time di-

189

rector in 1920 (the painter-anthropologist William H. Holmes), was overseen by a dutiful advisory commission of established notables in art, and continued to amass works, the collection prompted no one to ask penetrating questions about American art, past or present.

Meanwhile, much was changing in the art world of America. Artists were becoming much more active on their own behalf, organizing independent exhibitions, gaining wide recognition through painting and sculpture in public buildings, and taking part in discussions of art in education. By the 1920s the history of art, even American art, was becoming an established discipline in American universities. Had the building designed by Mr. Platt for the then National Gallery of Art in 1925 been built on the Mall as planned, additional emphasis might have been given to museum studies in American art. But the gathering collections had to wait some years more for attention.

During the depression of the 1930s the artist took on a new role in American society. It probably came as a surprise to some people that there were now so many artists, and that like others they were deprived of their normal means of support. For the first time the U.S. Government became the major patron and through its various art projects made the artist a conspicuous person in his community. Welcome or not, the American artist was a local reality. This prominence became all the more obvious when a totally new National Gallery of Art was chartered in 1937 as the magnificent gift of Andrew Mellon. The Mellon National Gallery was not to admit the works of living artists. Rather, it followed the traditions of the great museums founded in the 1870s by presenting great works by past masters for the expansion and enrichment of American culture. American artists were not wholly pleased. Although they were dazzled and proud to have such superb works as part of their artistic environment and were prepared to draw inspiration from them, they were also concerned about their own place in the cultural world.

Again the Smithsonian collection—called from 1937 the National Collection of Fine Arts—almost became a significant force. It was proposed as the basis of a new museum on the Mall which would continue government patronage of living artists as well as show the work of the past. It would also undertake programs to foster an understanding of art throughout the country. Unfortunately, the handsome modern building designed by the Saarinens for the project remained just a beautiful design.

Building upon the belief and energy generated in the grim years of the 1930s and the years of World War II, American artists began to come into their own at the war's end. To its astonishment, New York found itself the international center for contemporary art. This had never happened before. Also drawing on interests discovered during the 1930s, critics and historians began to look with a new eye at America's past. Exhibitions were mounted on artists of the recent past—Ryder, Blakelock, Eakins. And then, little by little, interest moved backward to rediscover 19th-century landscape painting and less well known portraitists of the 18th century. In 1954 the Archives of American Art was founded in Detroit based on the assumption that all documentation on American art was worth preserving—that American art was a subject that merited study in depth.

It was also in the 1950s that the Smithsonian began to take note once again of the fact that it had a collection. Wedged into every available cranny in the Natural History Building were several thousand American works, just the kind that were being "rediscovered." So the venerable old Patent Office building was saved from destruction to house them as well as a new collection to be formed of American portraits.

By the time the National Collection of Fine Arts (NCFA) opened to the public in the refurbished Patent Office Building in May 1968, it could present an amazing panorama of American accomplishment in art, and there was much more in the collection yet to be rediscovered and shown. For the first time, also, the museum had funds to acquire paintings to make the presentation more comprehensive. Furthermore, with the gift of the S. C. Johnson and Son Collection (over 100 American paintings of the 1960s) and other accessions, it was possible to bring the collection up to the present, to pull together the past with the ongoing work of American artists.

Once started, the Smithsonian's active support of art moved quickly. The National Portrait Gallery opened in the old Patent Office Building in October 1968; in January 1972 the building constructed by William Corcoran for his first museum, now named for its architect James Renwick, opened as the NCFA's gallery for American craft and design; and in October 1974 the extraordinary collection of sculpture and modern painting presented to the nation by Joseph H. Hirshhorn opened in its spectacular new building and sculpture garden on the Mall.

Joseph H. Hirshhorn presented a collection of some 6,000 paintings and sculptures to the nation in 1966—to which he later added considerably more—ranging in date,

Helen Frankenthaler, student of Jackson Pollock and practitioner of the non-traditional technique of applying paint as stain on canvas, painted *Small's Paradise*, acrylic on canvas, in 1964.

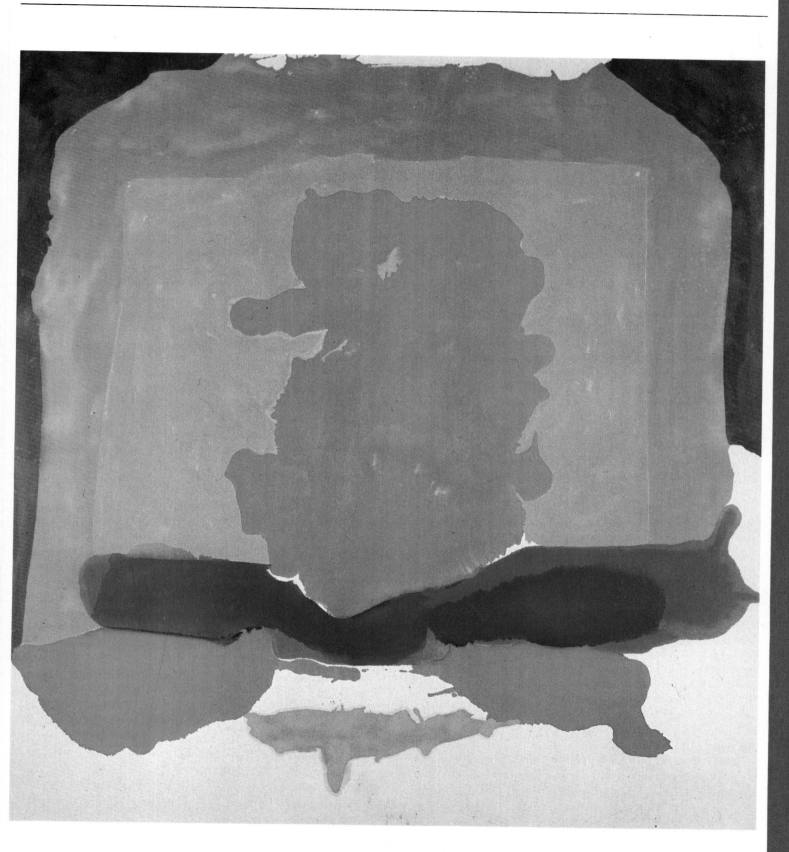

with few exceptions, from the 19th century to the present. The selection of sculpture is particularly rich and inclusive, both in European and American works, and the paintings add enormously to the Smithsonian's presentation of American art from the mid-19th century to the present. As one moves from the earlier part of the century it is notable that the proportion shifts towards American works, suggesting again the growing vitality and importance of art in the United States that reached its full stride in the years following World War II.

Even before moving into its new quarters, the NCFA had begun to look upon itself as an institution of inquiry as well as a gallery for exhibitions—and the beginning subject of its inquiry was itself. This was a collection that had grown, rather than one created. It therefore had not been molded by any pre-conceived historical plans and afforded a good many surprises for the innocent modern eye.

Although it retained a fair holding of European art from earlier gifts to the nation, the NCFA, it was determined, would now devote its full attention to American art. As its American works were classified and studied, many names appeared of artists who had long since been forgotten, for example, Lily Martin Spencer, Romaine Brooks, or W. H. Johnson (all of whom would be given exhibitions at the NCFA in the 1970s). The collection invited exploration by scholars and students alike because it became clear that quality was not the exclusive property of works by famous hands. From a quiet repository the collections became the center of expanding activity all across the range of American art.

Where Andrew Carnegie once dwelled—he can almost be seen peering through his New York mansion's windows in the photograph opposite—now dwells the Cooper-Hewitt Museum, the Smithsonian's National Museum of Design. The fantastically rich collection of the Hewitt sisters (granddaughters of philanthropist Peter Cooper) beggars description, especially in the decorative arts. The new museum's opening show examined how designers transform spaces, featuring works of architect/engineers R. Buckminster Fuller (bottom, left) and Hans Hollein (bottom, right), as well as urban images by O. M. Ungers (below); it also showed designers's cloth patterns (bottom, center).

The Archives of American Art, with its several million documents relating to art in America, joined the Smithsonian in 1970, and with this move the Smithsonian declared itself definitely committed to the research and preservation of the American artistic heritage. Toward the same end, a gigantic program was launched in 1971 to get local professionals and amateurs to make an inventory in their areas of the American paintings that had been painted before 1914. Attics and basements and obscure collections were plumbed, as well as the collections of established museums; many communities discovered that they were richer in their American inheritance than they had thought. By July of the Bicentennial year, when NCFA's inventory was opened for the use of scholars, well over 160,000 works were recorded on the computer.

But what happens to all of these unexpected works once they are found? In dealing with works of art, retrieval means more than the acquiring of information; it requires as well the physical recovery of neglected works. Before the National Collection could open in its new quarters in 1968, almost every work from the collection shown had to undergo some degree of cleaning and restoration, and a systematic program of restoration has been going on ever since. In this process the word restore implies two results: not only is the work brought back physically as close to its original condition as possible, but, when layers of dirt and old varnish are

removed, the sensibility of a long forgotten artist is restored to present aesthetic life. The dreary, dark 19th-century paintings we might typically associate with our idea of a Victorian parlor again can speak with a nicety and visual innocence that can only be envied. When it comes to paintings, time tends to be the obscurant, not the revealer of historical truth.

All of this retrieval—through archives, inventories, rehabilitation of works—can have a rather staggering effect on the historian. How does all the new information fit in? This is not so large a problem as might be supposed. Over the last few decades historians have come to doubt the validity of cultural syntheses and have lost a belief in the simple progression of history. In a world of set systems, relative mathematics, and working hypotheses, it is difficult to see the past as a fixed shape of rises and declines or progressive and retrogressive periods. What was once thought of as a closed book has been opened again, and history, instead of being simply a list of facts or the application of known terms to unknown phenomena, is looked upon as a vast and complex field of human experience inviting exploration and continued reformation. The continuous reappraisal of little known works of art in recent years, by collectors as well as historians, is symptomatic of this new freedom from the historical rubric. In addition to the Smithsonian's many temporary exhibitions, several thousand works of art from the permanent

Washington's first major art museum was opened by financier-philanthropist William W. Corcoran after the Civil War in a French Renaissance palace that still stands across from the White House on Pennsylvania Avenue (above). In 1966 the building was renovated by the Smithsonian and named the Renwick Gallery after its architect—who had also contributed the Castle to the capital's skyline (page 30). Below, posters for shows between the years 1972 and 1977 hang on the Gallery's fence.

collections are perennially on exhibit in the institution's museums and galleries, and more than two thousand are on loan for exhibition elsewhere throughout the world. The works shown in the galleries are not there as illustrations to a text book but as bearers of individual experiences to be encountered one by one. The museum staffs have worked to present them to the viewer in this way so that the art that once was rarely seen can now be a part of everyone's personal vision.

One area of study in American art was late in making its appearance in Smithsonian collections, and also in becoming a serious interest of historians and private collectors. That was American folk art, the art of craftsmen—often anonymous—whose traditions lay outside those of the academically trained. Only in the late 1920s were such works sought after, chiefly by artists in the beginning. And it was not until early in the 1930s that comprehensive exhibitions of these delightful works, ranging from highly original weather vanes to candidly painted family portraits, were organized by museums. By earlier historical and aesthetic standards, such works would not have found their way to the Smithsonian. But now they are recognized as a genuine artistic expression and a representative selection of this lively painting and sculpture is handsomely displayed in the National Museum of History and Technology.

To emphasize the force of creativity evident in the crafts and arts of design, the Renwick Gallery was opened in January 1972 as a department of the National Collection of Fine Arts. Its continuous task is to stimulate thinking about the human involvement with design and its impact,

whether through exhibitions of Northwest Coast Indian carvings borrowed from the Museum of Natural History, western saddles borrowed from History and Technology, or through original challenging exhibitions such as *Signs of Life: Symbols in the City* and *The Object as Poet*. The same object exhibited as a work of art in the Renwick Gallery often seems quite different than when it is shown in a social or historical context.

The Smithsonian's commitment to the arts of design was vastly expanded when it took over the Cooper-Hewitt Museum in New York in 1968 and opened it to the public in the renovated Andrew Carnegie mansion in October 1976. Founded as the Cooper Union Museum for the Arts and Decoration in 1895, it has a collection of some 85,000 objects ranging from textiles, metalwork, woodwork, and furniture to paintings, drawings, and prints. Quite aside from the designs relating to the decorative arts, its collection of more than 30,000 drawings includes works by many American artists—most notably Winslow Homer and Thomas Moran—as well as the works of European artists. Like other Smithsonian museums, it is a place for study as well as a place for exhibition, its extensive library and research collections being open to artists, historians, and serious students.

So ideas about what constitutes American art and what is important in its richly textured complexity have changed. And with the changing concepts the Smithsonian's research activity, collections and public programs have expanded to play a leading role. Art is now a major Smithsonian concern as it has become a growing concern among the Smithsonian's public. Certainly art—American art—in its many aspects, will not again be overlooked as an essential part of American life and its cultural inheritance.

An Artful Safari

A very famous and perhaps very lonely teddy bear lives in seclusion at the Smithsonian. And every few decades he comes out to have his picture taken.

The little bear's residence is a wooden storage drawer in the Division of Political History at the National Museum of History and Technology. He is the original teddy bear and

Teddy Roosevelt's own personal teddy bear

belonged to the man for whom all such bears are named, Teddy Roosevelt. For teddies came about partly because Roosevelt saved a bear cub he found during a hunting trip.

The other part of this story concerns a Russian immigrant, Morris Michtom, who ran a candy store in Brooklyn. He and his wife saw a picture of TR and his cub in the newspaper. They designed, cut, and sewed by hand "Teddy's

bear" with his ribbon and his plush fur, and they sent their homemade masterpiece to Roosevelt. Other teddies sold fast, and Michtom went on to found what is today the Ideal Toy Corporation.

Ever since, legions of little plush-furred teddies have gone out to capture the hearts of children. Bully!

Familiarity can blind us to the true nature of things, even of stuffed animals. Teddy bears are an intimate part of America's visual and verbal idiom. And as such they lay as definite a claim to a place in our folk art as they do in the sentiments of our children. Teddy bear number one, to be sure, is an unexpected but authentic artform.

That's no news at Smithsonian where nearly everybody learns to expect the unexpected. So join a safari to discover unexpected art. Some lies concealed behind the scenes. Other art hides, or so it seems, right out in the open.

A famous flea resides in a locked enclave within the Smithsonian, the Dibner Library of the History of Science

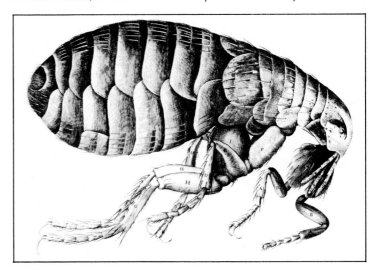

Flea drawn by Robert Hooke, an early English microscopist

and Technology. The flea image was drawn by the English scientist and mechanical genius Robert Hooke, also a pioneer microscopist, and published in 1665 in his book *Micrographia*. Scholars alone can enter the Dibner with its remarkable collection—the cream of early manuscripts and books on technical subjects—but sometimes the flea etching goes on public display in a glass case.

Hooke's flea was one of the early exquisitely drafted works by scientific artists of the western world. And within fields of botany, zoology, and mineralogy, scholars and technicians at the Museum of Natural History carry on the demanding tradition to this day.

Sometimes a specimen or artifact is so valuable (in sci-

Magnificent carved cat god from Key Marco, Florida

graphics painted by James McNeill Whistler. The Freer reveals these hidden masterpieces by appointment only, during a weekly show-and-tell day.

Though not so rare as the Freer's gold, a tiny brooch in sterling silver at the Smithsonian is numbered among the

"Jailed for Freedom" brooch

most treasured mementos of the women's rights movement in the United States. And the proud possessors had to be real insiders to acquire one. It's the "Jailed for Freedom" pin, and was presented by the militant National Woman's Party in 1917 to 97 suffragette demonstrators who landed in the District of Columbia lockup.

Smithsonian visitors need not go to jail to gain access to unexpected art. All it takes is a keen eye to ferret out the thousands of little masterpieces on display. For example, explore the auto section of the Museum of History and

197

Whistler's father

ence's accounting) that pictures of it are about all the public sees. Such is the case with the Key Marco Wooden Cat, an 800-year-old artifact from the Florida Keys.

Who carved the cat? And what for? The answers have been lost with time. The assurance with which the unknown craftsman has executed his design invites comparison with the artists of ancient Egypt, who also excelled at cat sculpture. And on its own merits, the Key Marco Cat expresses the artist's deep feeling for the power and mystery of nature.

A journey into the mysterious Orient, along with sidetrips to other wondrous places, can begin at the Freer Gallery of Art, a museum that's unexpected because of its constantly surprising riches. In the first place, many people would never expect to find a world-renowned collection of classic Chinese, Japanese, and Indian art in the United States capital city, or gold from the ancient Persian Empire.

Also at the Freer, and even more unlikely, hangs Whistler's portrait of his father. And carefully stored in the Freer's vaults are more than 100 other paintings and 1,000

Technology. A stained-glass window, made expressly for the mausoleum of a classic car buff who wanted to take it with him, proudly depicts his super-classy Rolls-Royce Sil-

Mausoleum window depicting a beloved Rolls-Royce auto

ver Ghost of 1907. This classic of the ages was number two of a two-car production run.

But the Silver Ghost's wheels were never destined to roll on heaven's streets of gold. The auto enthusiast and his wife changed their minds and donated the magnificent window to the Smithsonian instead.

The golden age of the great Rolls-Royce Ghost is now accelerating into the past, as is the era of rosy rococo zoo buildings. But reminders of that latter heady epoch live on also, at the National Zoo's Reptile House. Visitors are advised to rise early if they are to see these splendid lizards in all their glory. They appear as decoration on door panels.

By nine each morning, when the doors swing wide, their glittering panels swing back inside a shadowy hall where the shining gold is dimmed. Easier to observe for safari goers to the zoo, and at the Reptile House also, are sleepy-looking monsters. They were carved from stone and perch

Golden lizards adorning a door panel at the National Zoo

atop pillars, perhaps ready to pounce—as might some vengeful creature from prehistory.

At the Smithsonian it's hardly any leap at all from the far past to the far future. Tomorrow lies within the walls of the National Air and Space Museum, ready for visitors to discover. For instance, within an angular capsule of crystal can be found a little green creature. He peers into a tiny model of the very same crystal capsule. It is a hypothetical message pod sent by a big green intelligent creature of a far planet and intercepted by earthmen. The little green creature in the block is a scale model of its "maker." He stands beside a model of his solar system, complete with planet positions. Next to his extraterrestrial message to us lies our space post card sent aboard the *Pioneer 10* space probe from the earth to Jupiter, and from there on out of the Solar System, never to return. It too holds a message revealed through art, yielding clues about us and our location in the galaxy, and perhaps a green creature—or one of another color—will find it, and comprehend.

To find these items, step into the gallery that holds the big studio model of U.S.S. *Enterprise*, Captain James Kirk's Starship from the TV series "Star Trek."

Visitors, employees, and volunteer workers at the Smithsonian soon learn of the great depth of many of the collections—treasures heaped upon treasures. For example, consider political campaign buttons. Fifteen hundred and seventy-two—right down to the button—came out of storage to make a colorful mosaic of the American flag. This sampler in painted, punched steel and plexiglass represents but a sample of holdings in the field of political history. But visitors had better hurry to see the button-bangled banner. It belongs to a special display, Nation of Nations, which began in 1976 and will last only 10 years—by Smithsonian standards, a temporary exhibit.

by Joe Goodwin

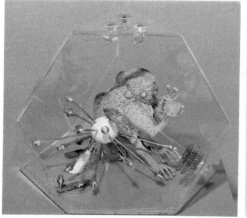

Message pod from a space creature

Earth's greeting card to creatures of distant solar systems

American flag assembled from political campaign buttons

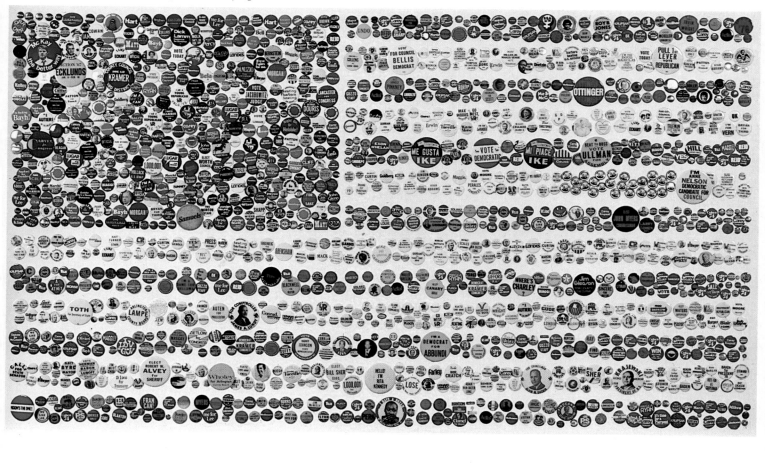

Four Artists In Search of an Author

When Winslow Homer sent the painting "Fog" to his dealer, he added a character-revealing note to explain the asking price of $2,000. "It has taken me a long time and much careful study. Quite different from posing a successful lawyer in one studio light and rattling him off in a week's time to the tune of $3,000. If you want more sentiment put into this picture I can with one or two touches — in five minutes time — give it the stomach ache that will suit any customer."

We are familiar with Homer's seascapes of swelling and bursting waves, boats, fishermen, and billowing clouds. The painter himself—by his own intent—is less known: the complex loner not wholly averse to mercenary consideration, the purist contemptuous of speculators in art and of autograph hunters alike.

In the microfilm treasure trove of the Smithsonian's Archives of American Art, stories about Homer are there for the telling, new dimensions of his character appearing on nearly every page. Go to the Archives (housed in the Old Patent Office Building beyond the Mall in downtown Washington at 8th Street, N.W.) and step into an artist's studio. Have a cup of tea. Chat about the good old days with this artist or that. Glance into his or her personal world of letters, diaries, sketchbooks, records and photographs.

Winslow Homer often wrote with brusque humor. Responding to his dealer's pettifogging request for further information about some paintings, he said: "You may call it a portrait of Paul Smith going out of the woods (after a seven mile tramp) into a 'clearing.' The two fishermen are fishing for trout — call them

The rugged coast of Maine has been a subject dear to the heart of American artists— Winslow Homer pictured it majestically in 1894 (top left); John Marin painted it abstractly in 1921 (top right).

An American in Paris, Mary Cassatt, portrayed society women in repose, as in *The Loge*, 1887 (right). Modern masterpieces in metal (far right) were wrought by the hands of the sculptor David Smith.

Thom, Dick, or Harry. The two log pictures are on the Hudson River anywhere you choose to place them — the trout is a trout."

Homer's first job was as magazine illustrator for *Harper's Weekly,* and during the Civil War he was dispatched to the front as "Special Artist." After the war he settled down to paint the simple pleasures of summer resorts of the 1870s — picnics, hayrides, croquet. Not until his midforties did he begin to express his feeling for the sea. His seas were stormy and treacherous; his fishermen and their wives fought gallantly for their livelihood.

Homer was small, slender, and carried himself very erectly. He lived in a studio cottage on the Maine coast, within sound of pounding waves, as they surged and pounded in his paintings. His days were spent walking along the cliffs with easel and

brushes, searching for a subject. He slept in his attic and cooked over an open fire. In winter he kept warm with a potbelly stove. On his book-

The camera caught a glowering Winslow Homer at 72. At top, a sketch of a painting (rattled off by Homer to his dealer in 1904) exists now on microfilm in the Archives, the largest depository of documents on art in America.

direction of spirit. The society girl from a distinguished Philadelphia family was determined to become a painter. Her father, a broker, complained that he preferred his daughter dead than for her to become an artist. But at 23 she sailed alone to Europe to study the old masters.

Settling in Paris, Cassatt studied on her own and in a few years was invited by the early group of Impressionists to exhibit with them. "I hated conventional art," she exclaimed happily. "I commenced to live."

Women and children in their quiet moments were the creations of her brush and palette. "Women's vocation in life is to bear children," she insisted, yet her own life did not follow this conviction. She had no children, never married, and was an ardent suffragette. Photographs portray her as tall, gaunt, and fond of elaborate hats.

Edgar Degas was a lifelong friend, supporter, and critic. "I do not admit that that woman can draw like that," he said when first seeing her work. Later it was he who drew her into the Impressionists' circle.

In the Archives of American Art letters exchanged with Cassatt's family in Pennsylvania contain chitchat about family and friends, and at least one sample of haute cuisine—a recipe for "Caramels Mous."

George Biddle was another expatriate painter from Philadelphia residing near Mary Cassatt's pink brick country house outside Paris. The two met and reminisced over a bottle of wine. Later he said: ". . . Socially she remained the prim Philadelphia spinster of her generation. When I used to bicycle over from Giverny to lunch with her, she would regale me with

shelves stood Walton's *Compleat Angler, Treasure Island,* Defoe, Washington Irving, Macaulay, Goethe, Shakespeare, Smollett. There were some old guns and swords, a bit of fish net, and a few simple furnishings including a grandfather clock.

Once chided for being antisocial by his friend, the lithographer Louis Prang, he replied: "I deny that I am a recluse as is generally understood by that term. Neither am I an unsociable hog . . . Since you must know it I have never yet had a bed in my house. I do my own work. No other man [or] women within half a mile & four miles from railroad & P.O. This is [the] only life in which I am permitted to mind my own business . . . I am perfectly happy & contented."

Homer could not be bothered with praise or flattery. He shunned exhibitions and other artists. In letters to his dealer, he issued crisp orders regarding the cleaning of pictures, mats, and, frames, and the shipment of pictures. He once warned his dealer off a sale. "I do not like your customer . . . I think this man a speculator . . . thinking he may make a dollar or two . . ."

The artist's papers in the Archives include correspondence, a daybook, and sketches. Letters to his family and friends concern family matters, and those to dealers and collectors contain instructions as to sales, living arrangements, and sketching trips.

Another artist whose treasured memorabilia are guarded by the Archives is the expatriate Impressionist, Mary Cassatt. She was American by birth but French by association and

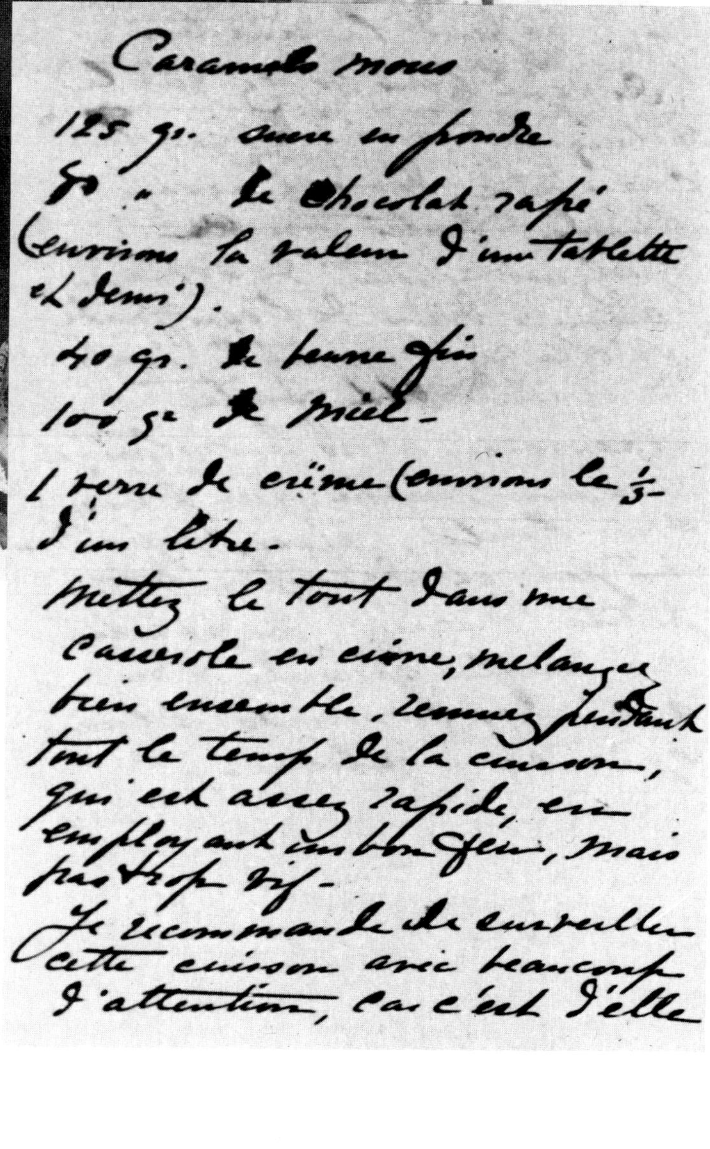

Washington pie and Philadelphia White Mountain cake and sherry. She loved to gossip about Philadelphians and picked with relish on her family, certain of whom she adored. But she would never forgive them for not going to see her exhibition in New York."

At this time, the 1880s-1890s, female painters were not taken seriously, but Impressionists were gaining acceptance in Europe. As one of them, Cassatt was quite well known in France before she won any recognition in the U.S. In her last years Mary Cassatt lost both her sight and her mind; she died in her chateau in 1926.

Because she had ultimately been given the French Legion of Honor, a detail of French soldiers attended her funeral. And because she was chatelaine of the manor, the village band played and townsfolk followed her coffin to the cemetery. But on her tombstone was inscribed this message:
CASSATT, native de Pennsylvanie, États-Unis de l'Amerique.

In the first half of the 20th century John Marin was regarded as one of America's fine avant-garde painters.

He is best known for his seascapes in which a few deft strokes suggest the action of the sea and the pitch of sailboats. A critic has lauded him as the Beethoven of watercolor.

Marin's letters can be as ecstatic as his watercolors. To his friend Charles Duncan he wrote in 1948: ". . . Come with me—just look out of this door—Holy Moses—look out of that door—Holy Holy Moses—now come and look out of this other door— Holy Holy Holy Moses—and—there be other doors—many many more—Hundreds of canvases— many many paint pots—a great stack of brushes and—an extended extended extended—life—."

203

In a letter from Paris, Mary Cassatt (shown above in a self-portrait) enclosed a favorite recipe for candy made of honey, cream, sugar, chocolate and butter.

Caramels mous
125 gr. sucre en poudre
90 g. de Chocolat rapé (environ la valeur d'une tablette et demi').
40 gr. de beurre fin
100 g. de miel.
1 verre de crème (environ le 1/5 d'un litre.
Mettez le tout dans une casserole en cuivre; mélangez bien ensemble, remuez pendant tout le temps de la cuisson, qui est assez rapide, en employant un bon feu, mais pas trop vif —
Je recommande de surveiller cette cuisson avec beaucoup d'attention, car c'est d'elle

Once, pointing to a painting of the end of Manhattan Island, Marin asked him: "Do you know why I didn't use any green in the picture? Because I forgot and left my green at home." Another time, so it was said, Marin set out to paint and had no water to mix his colors. Instead of waiting for another day, he used his own urine. He later sold the painting. The news must have gotten around, for at an exhibition one critic remarked "There goes Marin pissing out art again."

Records in the Archives of American Art relating to John Marin contain letters, catalogs, photographs, and his own scrapbooks of assorted clippings and art reference material.

The sculptor David Smith, born in Indiana, was the first American artist to work with welded metals. Skilled in working bronze, iron, steel, and painted sheet metal, he got his start on the Studebaker automobile production line at a summer job while in college.

"Art isn't made for the wealthy," wrote Smith, who was big, impressive, and self-confident. "It comes from the life of the artist—out of his own life, his own environment." His own environment, his studio as of 1934, was the Terminal Iron Works on the Brooklyn waterfront, which he shared with two affable Irishmen named Blackburn and Buckhorn. Blackburn, he related, was "a big gentle ironmonger" and Buckhorn "white-collar, the job-digger, and checkwriter."

"The Ironworks was inside the gates of the Atlantic Avenue Ferry terminal. George Kieman who ran the 'men only' saloon at 13 Atlantic Avenue had inherited it, Indians in the window and all, from his uncle, Red Mike. We ate lunch, got our mail, and accepted it as a general community house. . . . Those were the De-

A 1912 summer outing in New York includes John Marin at far right. The photo, his caricature, and letter are all contained in the Archives of American Art.

He revealed to a reporter that the New York subway was a favorite place for sketching. But he would quickly turn away if any of his subjects took note of his interest. Around strangers the artist was silent and suspicious; warmed up, he liked to talk. "When I was young, I used to walk in the woods. If I met somebody I was sad. But if I met an animal that wasn't too big, I was glad!"

Marin's shyness permitted him few intimates, but one exception was his friend James E. Davis, who taught art at Princeton and whose papers document at length his relationship with the artist. Said Davis, "I met him once at an exhibition of South Sea Primitives at the Museum of Modern Art. He spoke of the colors used by these primitive people—that they had a good, clean, earthy smell. Then he contrasted this natural smell with the 'sophisticated stink' of the colors in the paintings on 57th Street."

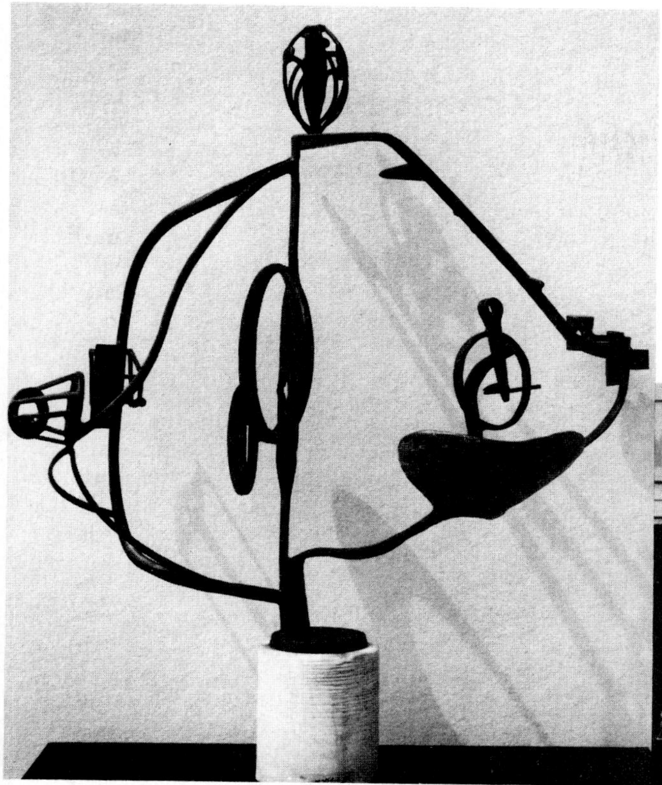

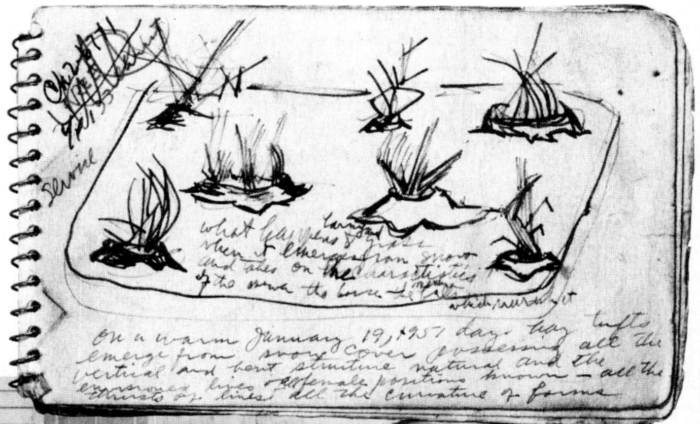

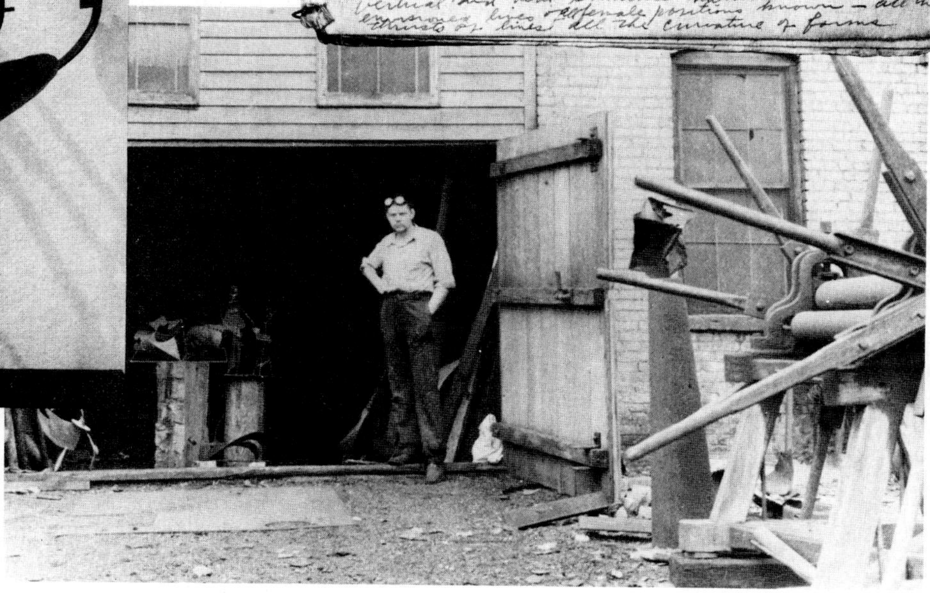

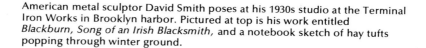

pression days. My sculpture 'Blackburn' was made afterwards in homage. One called 'Buckhorn' I will yet do."

In the 1930s Smith derived a meager income from the New Deal W.P.A. art program. During World War II he worked varying shifts as a welder in a locomotive plant. For a while he carved marble six hours a day at a monument works. He moved permanently to his summer house and studio at Bolton Landing on the shores of Lake George, New York, and earned his living teaching, lecturing, and from the largesse of Guggenheim fellowships.

At Bolton Landing, a typical day went like this: "My work day begins at 10 or 11 a.m. after a leisurely breakfast and an hour of reading. The shop is 800 feet from the house. I carry my 2 p.m. lunch and return to the house at 7 for dinner. The work day ends from 1 to 2 a.m. with time out for coffee at 11:30."

American metal sculptor David Smith poses at his 1930s studio at the Terminal Iron Works in Brooklyn harbor. Pictured at top is his work entitled *Blackburn, Song of an Irish Blacksmith,* and a notebook sketch of hay tufts popping through winter ground.

By the mid-1950s, he had achieved a reputation and his work was beginning to sell. In February, 1965, President Johnson appointed Smith to the National Council of the Arts, and on May 21 the sculptor learned of a forthcoming invitation "to attend the first White House Festival of the Arts." Two days later, his pickup truck ran off a Vermont road and overturned. He died that night from a fractured skull.

David Smith is regarded by some as the outstanding American sculptor of this century and his work will long be examined by critics and scholars. The principal record is in the documentary materials he left which are now preserved at the Archives of American Art—letters written and received, journals and sketchbooks, manuscript drafts of speeches and articles, lists, notes, photographs, scrapbooks, and press clippings. Like the stuff of a good chat, they await only your first question.

by Judy Harkison

PART SEVEN

The Spangled Heavens

**Visit in these pages the Center for Earth and Planetary Studies. Then fall through the eyepieces of a stereoscopic viewer to impact—well, almost—on the lunar surface.
Ages ago, legions of meteorites blasted the moon, shattering rock and plowing the ground. It happened when the Solar System was quite young. Explore that era with curators of meteoritic minerals at the National Museum of Natural History.**

Next,move out of the Solar System with James Cornell of the Smithsonian Astrophysical Observatory. He reports on revolutionary advances in stellar and intergalactic astronomy—"new windows," he calls them, for viewing the endless space of our universe.

207

Then return to earth—almost—to fly low and slow with Edwards Park, Smithsonian's roving correspondent, as he buzzes the National Air and Space Museum in search of the fighter plane he piloted during World War II, a long lost P-39 named Nanette.

Finally, dangle with photographer Ross Chapple from the girders of the National Air and Space Museum and creep into famous cockpits as he reveals details of the paraphernalia of flight. "Truth", they say, "is beauty." So are the heavens—and so, these objects remind us, are the objects that give wings to man's imagination.

I am the Man in the Moon

Remember when Aunt Lucy let you peer into the stereoscope to see Niagara Falls in 3-D? With a newfangled version of Lucy's viewer I sailed to the moon. My guide was Farouk El-Baz, Director of the Smithsonian's Center for Earth and Planetary Studies. Tucked away in the National Air and Space Museum, he and his staff of geologists scrutinize lunar photography.

One duty that Dr. El-Baz finds very pleasant is the assignment of names to lunar surface features on new maps. Craters are assigned the names of distinguished deceased scientists by an international committee of living scientists, of which Dr. El-Baz is a member. Charles Greeley Abbot, Leonard Carmichael, and Samuel P. Langley, former Smithsonian Secretaries, are so honored. Astronaut Michael Collins, Director of the National Air and Space Museum, belongs to the tiny group of living astronauts with lunar landmarks named for them.

At the museum, Dr. El-Baz conducted me to a waiting stereoscope. I leaned forward and put my eyes to the lenses. Geronimo! For a long second I felt as if I were falling right through the eyepieces and diving into the moon, there to make my own crater on its surface.

It was the Apollo 15 landing site at Hadley Rille. The surrounding hills looked round, the craters deep. The rille appeared like a gigantic canyon, with steep slopes meandering through the terrain. The illusion that I was in mid-space was electrifying. Where was the ripcord? Why no parachute?

Just in time I wrenched myself free of the stereoscope and found myself back in Dr. El-Baz's office. Here I settled into a reassuring chair before a mural of the moon that covers one wall of the room. With photos, scientific studies, and experts surrounding me, I'd never have a better chance to get my moon facts straight.

"Tell me, Farouk," I said, "What is the moon really like? I mean, I've even heard it rings like a bell when a meteorite hits."

Man-in-the-moon, once subject of pop songs celebrating the lunar lovescape, turned out to be an astronaut (opposite).

"That's true up to a point," he answered. "Meteors have pounded and fractured the lunar bedrock, creating numerous surfaces that reflect the vibrations."

"I see. Well, then, how did earth get its satellite?"

"We don't know for sure," Farouk replied. "But earth and its moon seem geologically related. Earth received the lion's share of iron and other heavy elements. The moon received a larger proportion of light-weight elements.

Sunlight paints the rim of moon crater Eratosthenes. Such close-ups lay beyond man's reach a few years ago. Through satellite and space-probe imagery, scientists today examine not only earth's moon, but other planets and their moons.

"It all happened about 4.5 billion years ago. This is 100 million years after the best documented estimate for the date of the Solar System's creation.

"And by the way, if you want to be up-to-date," Dr. El-Baz continued, "think of the earth and moon as a dual planet. There is no other moon so big in relation to its planet in the entire Solar System.

"The moon's size and nearness to the earth give its gravitational attraction considerable influence on the earth, particularly on tides. Without its moving waters our planet would be a far less lively place. The moon is a vital part of our life-support scheme."

Dr. El-Baz introduced me to members of his staff, photo-geologists studying the formations of the lunar surface. Priscilla Strain explained that meteoric impacts throughout the eons have repeatedly pulverized and tilled the lunar surface, smashing up old rocks and, through heat of impact, creating new rocks. Rocks so formed are called breccias, each chunk a whole mineral collection fused into one mass. To analyze individual grains, Smithsonian scientists employ an electron microprobe.

I knew I must see this instrument. So, filled with moon images and facts, I departed upon my new quest. But before leaving the Air and Space Museum, I paused to touch the touchable moon rock there, one more time.

Across the Mall at the Museum of Natural History I gained an audience with the remarkable machine. A curator of meteorites, i.e., space minerals, Brian Mason, conducted me into its presence.

Electronics-filled cabinets with oscilloscopes and controls stood near the metal column of the microprobe itself. The room's ambiance resembled that of Dr. Frankenstein's laboratory. But the work is quite innocent, albeit complicated.

Technicians place moon rock or meteorite samples into a chamber and evacuate the air. A microscope focuses on a single grain. The technician fires an electron beam through the microscope. X-rays characteristic of the elements in the grain are produced. Analysis of the spectrographic composition of the X-rays and their concentration reveals what chemical elements are present.

Having already touched a stone from the moon, I yearned to lift a stone that had soloed in the sky—a meteorite. Dr. Mason instantly obliged by offering me an iron meteorite, the size of a fist, blackened by its fiery ride through the atmosphere.

Robert McCall masterpiece, *The Space Mural—A Cosmic View*, inspires visitors to the National Air and Space Museum. McCall's vision captures the awe of man's trailblazing exploration of the moon.

209

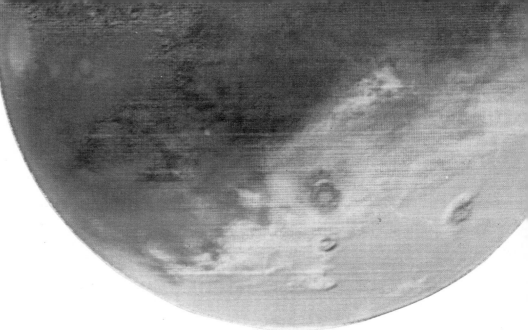

I lifted it. It felt just like ordinary iron and I was sorely disappointed. That is, I was perturbed until I learned the significance of the Solar System's meteoritic connection. Both iron and stony meteorites are probably the oldest things we possess—as old if not older than the earth and the moon. They may have formed at the beginning of the Solar System after a vast cloud of space dust consolidated, heated up, and began to whirl around a young star—our sun.

In a storage area I viewed hundreds of sawn and polished slabs of iron and stone from space. The cutting reveals crystal patterns and other mineralogical features.

Later, in the office of Roy S. Clarke, Jr., one small meteorite caught my eye and imagination. A lattice of gleaming metal held a constellation of transparent crystals, deep olive-

yellow in color. The sun's rays glancing through the window revealed flashes of yellow, green, and deep purple. The remarkable materials seemed to glow with an inner fire.

How were these structures formed? What do they mean? To probe the secrets of creation itself, I attended an intellectual feast served up around the library table in the Division of Mineralogy. Dr. Mason and Dr. Clarke were there with their knowledge of meteorites and moon rocks. Other scholars who deal with craters and earth's geology sat in.

By way of perspective, I learned here that scientists have realized for only 200 years that shooting stars and meteorites are the same things. But the ancient Chinese knew of their celestial origin and revered the iron that fell from the sky. They forged the metal to cast blades for ceremonial daggers.

Left: Early 1900s artwork shows the day's best guess of Mars—a rosy globe laced with canals. Today's multi-sensor imagery depicts details of geology and climate (above).

I had seen two of these artifacts at the Freer Gallery of Art across the Mall. But now, in the clinical presence of these messengers from space, I had that exciting sense of the connectedness of things—art and science—that often occurs at the Smithsonian. It turned out that metallurgical chemists at the Freer had teamed up with Natural History's mineralogists to analyze and verify the use of meteorites in these implements of sacred use.

Some scientists speculate that planetesimals, or mini-planets, were the first heavenly bodies. Such bodies may have impacted, cohered, and melted to form the maxi-planets. The leftovers—asteroids, meteoroids, comets, and assorted junk—retained their original form in the cold vacuum of space. Many meteoroids appear to swing earthward from the Asteroid Belt, a ring of solid bodies that lies between the orbital paths of Mars and Jupiter.

Around the library table, talk turned from meteoroids in orbit to shooting stars in action. The assembled scientists told me that most of the moon's great craters were blasted out during

Smithsonian scientist Brian Mason discovered a meteorite in a scoop of moon dust (above) and dubbed it Mini-moon. Micrometeorite pits on the pea-size metal pellet create an eerie lunar facsimile.

a colossal bombardment four billion years ago. The four inner planets—Mercury, Venus, Earth, and Mars—were also under fire. But since then, Earth's active geology has eroded the old craters.

Battle scars of the shooting-star war remain on the moon, where even the craters have craters. One pea-sized pellet of meteoritic iron came to earth in a sample of moon dust. The iron projectile had melted on impact

Chinese dagger handles in bronze reveal an ancient celestial connection. Under analysis, deposits of iron rust on the handles could have come only from an alloy of iron and nickel found in certain meteorites. Chinese craftsmen apparently melted iron meteorites to cast the dagger blades.

and formed a ball. Micrometeoroids pitted its surface until it became a portrait of the moon itself.

We know more than we used to, but like the tiny metal image of the moon once lost in its dusty grave, many secrets of our Solar System remain as they were, ambiguities engulfed in a mystery.

by Joe Goodwin

211

The New Astronomy: Windows on the Universe

by James Cornell

Sunrise in Arizona is a moment of high drama. The eastern horizon brightens slightly. A grayness wipes away the stars and outlines the distant mountains. Then, almost without warning, the sky bursts into brilliant color. But the sun, so beautiful at dawn, soon becomes an instrument of torture. Within less than an hour, great waves of heat rise from the desert floor, sweeping up the sides of the treeless mountain peaks. Most desert creatures avoid this heat, seeking out shade during the day, emerging only when the parched land rolls away eastward from the sun some 12 hours later.

For a small band of Smithsonian astronomers encamped on Mount Harqua Hala a half a century ago, there was no such escape. The rising sun was a signal to begin the daily task of monitoring and measuring its intensity by noting minute changes and infinitesimal variations in its ovenblast of radiation.

Although only 75 miles west of Phoenix, the solar astronomers might as well have been in the heart of the Sahara. All supplies—food, film, books, clothing, and tools—arrived on the peak in burro packs. Included in these provisions was the 30-gallon-per-week ration of water provided for all drinking, cooking, bathing, dishwashing, and photographic plate developing. The only contact with the outside world was via a telegraph line to Wenden, the nearest town, some 15 miles away.

Today, some 200 miles southeast of Harqua Hala on another Arizona peak called Hopkins, Smithsonian astronomers still monitor the sky, but the routine is quite different. The sky patrol begins at sunset and continues throughout the night, for the distant stars and planets have largely replaced the sun as objects of prime interest. Today, the various buildings for observation are connected by coaxial cable, and one can direct-dial anyone, anywhere in the world, who can be reached via the Federal Telecommunications System. Water is still precious, of course, and food and equipment must still be imported, but now

James Cornell is Publications Manager for the Harvard-Smithsonian Center for Astrophysics in Cambridge, Massachusetts. His publications include *The Great International Disaster Book, The Pulse of the Planet, It Happened Last Year,* and numerous science books for young readers.

they can arrive in less than an hour via an 18-mile-long road smooth enough for any suburban station wagon. The same road links the observatory with U.S. Highway 19 and the booming recreational areas of Southern Arizona's Sunbelt. In fact, Tucson with its restaurants, theaters, and modern university complex is close enough for many astronomers to commute daily.

If the lifestyles of astronomers have changed drastically in the last half century, so has astronomy itself. Whereas the Smithsonian Astrophysical Observatory's research program once was focused on the sun and its effect on the earth's environment, today's program reaches out to literally the entire universe.

In 1890, Samuel Pierpont Langley, the third Secretary of the Smithsonian Institution, who is best known perhaps for his contributions to aeronautics, established the Astrophysical Observatory. For several hundred years before that, astronomers had determined the positions and motions of the celestial bodies, carefully charting the movement of planets and cataloguing the colors, magnitudes, and positions of the stars, thereby intending to define the structure of the cosmos. For Langley, this was not enough; and so he developed what he called "a new branch of astronomy which studies the sun, moon, and stars for what they are in themselves and in relation to ourselves."

Beginning with the external features of the sun, he made discoveries that were "full of novelty and interest." These led to further inquiry as to what the sun was made of, and then to finding "unexpected relations which it bore to the earth and our own daily lives. . . ." Langley came to the conclusion that the sun "in a physical sense made us and recreates us daily . . . the knowledge of the intimate ties which united man with it brings results of the most practical and important kind, which a generation ago were unguessed at . . . this new branch of inquiry is sometimes called Celestial Physics, sometimes Solar Physics, and is sometimes referred to as the New Astronomy."

Langley, of course, was a visionary, and his revolutionary manifesto would lay the foundation for the modern science of astrophysics. Alas, like many other revolutionaries, Langley would not live to see his dream come to fruition. Indeed, for more than 50 years, earth-bound astronomers would be limited to observations of the heavens in the single, extremely narrow spectrum band of visual light. As a result, their concept of the universal grand design would be based on only a fraction of the information available from the stars.

During the past two decades, however, advances in astronomical observing techniques, aided in great measure by space flight, have opened new windows on the uni-

Astronomer and Smithsonian Secretary, Samuel P. Langley peers into a five-inch telescope at Wadesboro, N.C., operations site of a Smithsonian solar eclipse expedition in 1900.

verse. These have revealed a host of exciting, unexpected, exotic, puzzling, and sometimes quite frightening objects in the radio, infrared, ultraviolet, and X-ray regions of the spectrum. And each new discovery has contributed to an understanding of how the universe has expanded, galaxies have formed, and stars have evolved over billions of years. No longer are the heavens considered immutable, or the stars static entities. Instead, the stars are now seen as dynamic bodies that change and evolve—being born, maturing, aging, and dying much like living organisms. The dying stars, in turn, apparently eject new chemical elements into space, where they become available to form new stars and planets—some of them almost certainly supporting life. The mechanisms of this process, this "cosmic evolution," perhaps account for all the structures in the universe—from quasars to planets and from suns to organic molecules.

Could Langley have imagined the extent to which his vision would be realized? Perhaps, but the road to that realization, one to even our present knowledge only just begun, has already been long, difficult, and sometimes circuitous.

In the last years of his life, much of Langley's attention and energies were siphoned off from astrophysics into aeronautics and his pursuit of mechanical flight. The informal shepherding and, following Langley's death in 1906, the full direction of the Astrophysical Observatory fell to his young assistant, Charles Greeley Abbot, a solar physicist.

Abbot's studies of the sun would preoccupy the Astrophysical Observatory for nearly the next half century. Specifically, he attempted to measure the "solar constant," that is, the mean rate of energy received by the earth after corrections are made to allow for variations in the distance between the earth and the sun and the effects of the earth's atmosphere. Observations were made from

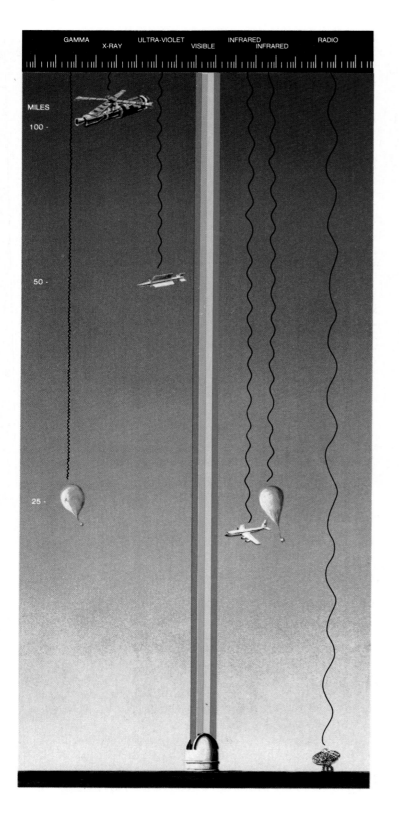

some of the most barren and inhospitable sites ever chosen by science for any investigations: Harqua Hala, Arizona; Montezuma, Chile; Mt. Brukkaros, South West Africa, and Mt. St. Katherine, in the Sinai Peninsula.

Abbot's work came under growing critical attack by the scientific community. His unshakeable belief that fluctuations in the solar constant were linked with sunspot activity caused him to make rather extravagant inferences about the relationship between solar energy and terrestrial climate, particularly regarding short-term weather effects. (For many years, Washington brides-to-be consulted Dr. Abbot for advice on choosing a sunny wedding day.) However, Abbot's sun-weather data are now being re-examined with a number of interesting results. Although he may have misinterpreted the nature of the "solar constant," he apparently discovered other important correlations between the sun's energy and terrestrial phenomena. But more about that later.

By the 1950s, due to lack of funding and problems of logistics, all but one of the solar observing stations had been closed and the Observatory's astronomical research was slight. In 1955, Professor Fred L. Whipple of Harvard was named director of the Astrophysical Observatory and its headquarters were moved to the grounds of the Harvard College Observatory in Cambridge, Massachusetts. Thus began the long and, as Whipple has described it, "symbiotic" relationship between Harvard and the Smithsonian that would culminate in 1973 with the formation of a joint Harvard-Smithsonian Center for Astrophysics.

Whipple's first major act as director was to accept responsibility for establishing and operating a network of optical tracking stations that might observe any artificial satellites launched during the International Geophysical Year of 1957-58. On October 4, 1957, when the Russians rocketed Sputnik I into earth orbit, shocking American politicians and public alike, the Smithsonian stood ready to track it and subsequent spacecraft. Equally important, following a time-honored Smithsonian tradition, the Observatory became America's primary source of information and education about these feats.

Under Whipple's guidance, the Astrophysical Observatory grew in concert with the national space effort. From a staff of five in 1955, the Observatory swelled to nearly 500 scientists, technicians, and administrators both in Cambridge and abroad by the late 1960s. The optical tracking program, originally designed for an 18-month lifetime, has

Optical telescopes gather radiation only from the narrow light spectrum (above). With new devices including space satellites, astronomers today tap the entire electromagnetic spectrum—gamma rays to radio waves—to gain facts on the universe.

continued for two decades. Transcending that first mission merely to track the skies, the Observatory used the precise determination of satellite orbits in relation to the earth below to produce the most detailed representation ever devised of this planet's shape, size, and gravitational field. Today, with its original Baker-Nunn cameras supplemented by laser tracking systems, the network contributes to the international programs of geodesy and geophysics, with the measurement of continental drift a major goal.

While encouraging the continuation of such traditional Smithsonian interests as the earth sciences and meteoritics, Whipple also promoted new ventures in space science: cooperation with Harvard in a joint program of radio astronomy; the development of orbiting space observatories; and the founding of the Mt. Hopkins Observatory near Tucson, where the Smithsonian would eventually embark on a series of pioneering experiments in ground-based high-energy and infrared astronomy. At the Astrophysical Observatory, the new windows on the universe had begun to open.

The first, in the radio band of the spectrum, had actually opened earlier. In the late 1930s, while experimenting with techniques for long-distance communication, a Bell Telephone engineer named Carl Jansky noticed that his crude antenna often registered a strange, inexplicable buzzing noise when scanning the skies. After searching unsuccessfully for possible terrestrial sources of electrical interference, Jansky stumbled on a seemingly impossible explanation. The radio noise coincided with the rise of the Milky Way above the horizon. His discovery was duly noted in a technical journal for radio engineers where it was read by amateur astronomer and radio buff Grote Reber of Wheaton, Illinois. Reber, working in his spare time in his backyard, built the first crude radio telescope, a parabolic receiver looking very much like those used at radio observatories today. And, more extraordinary, he produced the first rough radio guide to the heavens—that is, a contour map showing those areas of radio emission.

The discovery that celestial objects emit radio waves seemed simply too unbelievable for many traditional astronomers. Moreover, the advent of World War II demanded that the talents of America's scientists and technicians be directed into other areas. Following the war, however, and in part aided by the technology developed to wage it, several groups at American universities, including Harvard, began to pursue the potential of radio astronomy.

Early efforts concentrated on observing thermal radiation, that is, radio emissions produced under high-temperature conditions, such as those on the surface of Venus, in the solar flares, in the nuclear processes in the cores of distant stars, and in the hot clouds of gas between the stars. In addition, a group at the Harvard College Observatory discovered that ordinary, neutral hydrogen gas emits radio waves in a single frequency, the so-called 21-centimeter line. By tuning antennas to that radio wavelength, astronomers were able for the first time to measure the Milky Way's extent and structure, looking even to the distant far side which is normally hidden to optical telescopes by thick clouds of interstellar dust.

The 21-cm line discovery prompted searches for other molecules that might transmit at specific frequencies. Soon after the Astrophysical Observatory moved to Cambridge, Smithsonian and Harvard scientists began collaborating on a program to identify and isolate promising

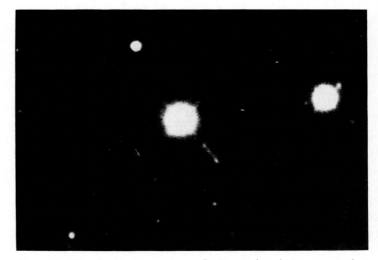

Quasar in Virgo (center) poses a puzzle. Spectral analysis suggests that quasars may be the remotest objects visible from the earth, yet they seem to shine brighter than a host of galaxies.

radio frequencies in the laboratory and then to search the skies at the appropriate wavelengths for such emissions. The results have been astounding: here, and at other observatories, more than 35 interstellar molecules, many of them complex organic structures, have been identified. The Smithsonian-Harvard team has itself discovered some of the most interesting: formic acid, formaldehyde, methyl alcohol, and even ethyl alcohol. (Of the last, one Smithsonian astronomer was moved to estimate that if it could be condensed and distilled, the vast cloud of alcohol molecules near Sagittarius might produce 10 billion billion fifths of 80 proof whiskey!)

The implications of such discoveries are far reaching, for they suggest that the basic building blocks of life on this planet also exist between the stars. The discovery of water vapor in interstellar space of our own Milky Way Galaxy by a group at Berkeley in 1969, and then its detection outside the Milky Way by a German group in 1976, give further support to the possibility that life can form elsewhere than on earth.

The radio window has produced other surprises. For example, observations of powerful radio sources in otherwise unremarkable regions of the sky led to the identification of quasars, extremely distant objects of unusual optical brightness. Although mere pinpoints of light when compared with normal stars, they must be incredibly brilliant to be seen across distances measured in billions of light-years. Although the precise nature of the quasar remains unknown—indeed, the question of their true distances is still the subject of heated debate—they are generally thought to be the oldest objects in the universe, perhaps representing material produced during the primordial explosion—the Big Bang—15 to 20 billion years ago and ever since outwardly receding at nearly the speed of light.

In addition to the optical and radio windows on the universe, there is also another small window available for ground-based observers. At certain high-altitude locations, well above the water vapor levels of the earth's atmosphere, it is possible to observe infrared radiation from celestial sources.

An obvious location for making such observations is on platforms suspended from balloons, and Smithsonian astronomers, again in concert with Harvard colleagues as well as with other researchers from the University of Arizona, have developed a series of balloon-borne experiments for infrared astronomy. Despite these flights, the infrared window so far has barely opened a crack. The field has awaited the development of new and larger ground-based telescopes. Such an instrument now exists at the Smithsonian's Mt. Hopkins Observatory in Arizona. The Multiple Mirror Telescope, a joint project with the University of Arizona, is the world's third largest optical telescope and the largest ever designed for optimum performance in the infrared band of the spectrum.

Although satellites and radio telescopes have revealed objects and conditions never before even imagined, each of these new discoveries has demanded even more extensive use of ground-based optical instruments to elucidate the nature of the underlying phenomena. The need for larger telescopes also results from the need to seek out fainter and fainter objects for study.

Unfortunately, the engineering complexity of large, Palomar-type telescopes has made it extremely difficult—and very expensive—to build single mirrors larger than 200 inches. The Multiple Mirror Telescope is an innovative ap-

Rotating building on Mt. Hopkins, Arizona, houses a "six-gun telescope," or MMT, the Multiple Mirror Telescope. The innovative device consists of six telescope mirrors that beam light to a single focus.

proach to overcoming that problem. Rather than using one huge mirror, the MMT combines six, 72-inch (1.8 meter) Cassegrain telescopes mounted symmetrically around a central axis in "six-gun fashion" with the optical beams of the six telescopes brought to a single focus. The combined apertures of the six mirrors are equivalent to a single 176-inch (4.5-meter) reflector.

In addition to avoiding many of the problems, particularly those of weight and handling usually associated with large, single-mirror telescopes, the MMT costs only a fraction of the production expense for a conventional telescope of similar size. Moreover, since the focal length of the MMT is essentially that of a 72-inch telescope, it is extremely compact and relatively lightweight.

If the MMT is a unique telescope, then its housing is also one of the world's most unusual. Instead of a conventional dome, the MMT housing is a rectangular, four-story, barnlike structure. And, unlike the normal telescope housing where the domed roof turns separately, the entire MMT housing rotates via wheels on a stationary track to follow the motion of the telescope as it scans the heavens. Housing and telescope thus are inseparable, working together as a single instrument. The rotating structure also permits placement of the control and service areas adjacent to the telescope itself. During operation, these offices, control rooms, laboratories, and public areas all turn slowly with the telescope.

Research with the MMT includes daytime observations of infrared objects, as well as traditional optical and infrared astronomical objects. Equally important, the success of the MMT could revolutionize all telescope construction in the future. In fact, the Kitt Peak National Observatory already has begun planning a 1,000-inch instrument of similar design.

Beyond the optical, radio, and infrared bands of the spectrum, other new windows on the universe have been opened by space satellites. The Smithsonian entered this field early, developing detectors for ultraviolet observations that flew on the first series of Orbiting Astronomical Observatory (OAO) satellites in the late 1960s. The Smithsonian-designed Celescope Project produced the first ultraviolet map of the heavens and has provided the basis for continuing studies of young, hot stars emitting most of their energy in the form of ultraviolet light. In the late 1960s, Harvard used ultraviolet detectors aboard rockets and also the Orbiting Solar Observatory (OSO) satellites to gain new insights on the physical processes determining energy production in the sun. Then, in 1973-74, a Harvard-designed ultraviolet spectroheliograph was flown as an experiment on Skylab. This project produced more than 100,000 detailed ultraviolet photos of the solar disk.

If this advanced space-study of the sun sounds reminiscent of the early research by Langley and Abbot, the coincidence has not been lost on Smithsonian and Harvard astronomers. In 1975, the two observatories established a joint Langley-Abbot Program of Solar Research, named in honor of those two solar pioneers. Funded by the institution and using Harvard satellite data, the program attempts to integrate current theories and observations of solar phenomena with historical data of solar variability produced by Abbot and his dedicated band of sun watchers. The goal is a critical assessment of the interrelationship between solar and terrestrial phenomena, particularly long-term climatic change.

So far the Langley-Abbot Program has included an analysis of possible "solar constant" variations using both 50 years of Abbot data and more modern data from the Mariner and Nimbus spacecraft. Other related studies have included measuring the rotation of solar magnetic fields and the effects on the sun's photosphere, theoretical studies of the interaction of the solar plasma and magnetic fields in the sun's active regions of prominences and flares, and an intensive analytical comparison of long-term climatic variations with solar activity. This program has produced some significant (and possibly chilling) results.

The historical analysis of sunspot activity is based on direct observations of the sun's surface that have been made almost continuously since the telescope was introduced in 1610. Reports of unusual auroral displays, which are related to solar activity, can be traced back at least to the time of Christ. There is also a history of the sun locked into the ring of patterns of bristlecone pines, some of which are nearly 7,000 years old. The record is not in the width of the rings but rather in their content of carbon-14, or radiocarbon. Because the production of radiocarbon in our atmosphere is regulated by solar activity, and since trees absorb this chemical as carbon dioxide in photosynthesis, the trees record in each annual growth ring a measure of the solar activity of that time. Comparison of the tree rings with the observational record clearly suggests that periods of low solar activity, or sunspot minimums, correspond closely with times of cold climate on earth. One period when sunspots disappeared completely, the so-called "Maunder Minimum" of the 16th to 18th century, exactly matches the severe dip in temperature known as "the Little Ice Age." This was a time of severe Northern Hemisphere winters, when the Norsemen abandoned their Greenland colonies and the Pilgrims shivered at Plymouth. Solar physicist Jack Eddy has said, "Our present era—a period beginning in the mid-1700s—stands out as abnormal, in the sense that solar activity has been unusually high. We have lived our lives and built our explanations of the sun during solar conditions that really have applied for only ten percent of the time, or less, in the long run of history. Moreover, although it is still difficult to evaluate our present period, the general level of solar activity appears to be falling again after an unusual peak that was reached in the late 1950s."

If the new window opened onto the sun has revealed a somewhat uncomfortable vision of an inclement earth, the window opened by high-energy astronomy, particularly in the X-ray band, has revealed a most inhospitable and hostile universe. This new view could even have profound effects on our philosophical conceptions of existence. Ancient man lived in an anthropocentric universe, in which the earth was surrounded by crystalline rings carrying stars, planets, sun, and moon. The Copernician version of the solar system shattered those rings by shifting the sun to the center. Although this realignment simplified the explanations for how the system worked, it complicated man's explanation of his situation in creation. Our place in the great cosmic scheme was shown to be still more peripheral early in this century by Harlow Shapley and Edwin Hubble, who demonstrated that our Milky Way Galaxy was neither alone nor at the center of the universe. In fact, our galaxy was but one of uncounted (and probably uncountable) billions of other galaxies, all rushing headlong away from each other. For the insecure and tremulous, only one feature of the universe remained certain: the stars, galaxies, and constellations of this vast universe were at least relatively permanent, constant symbols of stability promising a sense of eternity. Alas, observations in the X-ray band of the spectrum reveal the universe to be dynamic and explosive, turbulent and chaotic. Most disturbing, the violent changes occur on time scales measured not in millions or billions of years, but often in millionths of seconds.

A rocket flight in 1962, carrying experiments designed by a group now associated with the Smithsonian, detected Scorpius X-1, the first strong X-ray source in our galaxy to be identified optically also. Other rocket experiments detected some 30 discrete points of X-ray emission scattered about the sky. About a half-dozen of these could be identified with known optical or radio objects.

In 1970, the *Uhuru* satellite (bearing the Swahili name for "freedom" in honor of its unusual floating launch site off the coast of Kenya) produced the first true X-ray map of the heavens, showing over 340 sources of X-rays. A series of other space flights including the Astronomical Netherlands Satellite (ANS) and the Small Astronomy Satellite (SAS) series found still other X-ray objects. And, in almost all these programs, Smithsonian astronomers played major roles, either preparing the experiments or analyzing the results.

The X-ray sources so far discovered fall into four major classes: (1) the remnants of supernova explosions, (2) clusters of galaxies, (3) single galaxies apparently related to the mysterious quasars, and, perhaps best known to the public, (4) objects such as Scorpius X-1 and Cygnus X-1 that have been classified as "neutron stars" or "black holes."

The neutron star is the next-to-final stage of a dying star. The star's normally gaseous material has condensed, or collapsed, into a tiny sphere of extreme density, with a correspondingly strong gravitational field. Imagine our sun shrinking to the size of Manhattan, yet maintaining all its mass, or all the automoblies in the world being squeezed into a thimble.

The black hole is a dying star that has gone even further into decline. Indeed, its collapse is so complete that all material has been squashed into a virtual pinpoint and the gravity field has become so intense that not even light rays can escape; thus its name.

Both the black hole and the neutron stars are thought to be parts of binary systems (twin stars) in which the material from a nearby normal—and visible—star is sucked into the cosmic sink hole. The violent, tumultuous gush of stellar material between the two objects produces the X-ray emissions seen by the space satellites.

In addition to the major X-ray sources, some oddball objects have been seen. For example, Smithsonian astronomers were the first to identify the "cosmic bursters," X-ray sources that suddenly and inexplicably send out massive doses of X-ray emission, comparable to the 30-fold brightening of a visual star, and, then, just as suddenly and as inexplicably, fade back to normal levels. Other even more transient sources have been seen to flare dramatically and then disappear, apparently forever, almost as if a black hole had turned itself inside out and completely left this universe to pop up in another dimension of time and space. (This is a possibility at least semi-seriously considered by some otherwise very serious theoreticians.)

By the mid 1970s, the Astrophysical Observatory had emerged as the leader in this exciting field, with the scientists and technicians working here under the leadership of Riccardo Giacconi literally responsible for first opening the windows on this violent universe. During the next decade, this same team will construct experiments for a series of High Energy Astrophysics Observatories (HEAO) to be flown by NASA, each promising an impact on space astronomy similar to that of the MMT concept on ground-based research.

The first of this series, the HEAO-A, was launched in 1977 and carried four experiments prepared by various scientific groups in the United States. The Smithsonian package was a detector designed to obtain highly precise positions for X-ray sources which can provide ground-based astronomers with the pinpoint accuracy necessary for optical and radio identifications of the same objects. Within less than two decades, the instrumentation developed by X-ray astronomers should achieve a view of the sky comparable to all the improvements in optical telescopes from the time of Galileo to the present.

Modern astrophysical research obviously has become much more complex since Langley's day. Each new window on the universe has spawned a host of new and specialized fields that often appear unrelated and unconnected to the layman.

Only those organizations with a broad research program encompassing many fields are capable of pursuing the many-faceted approach demanded by today's astrophysical problems. Recognizing the need for such an organization, the Smithsonian Astrophysical Observatory joined in 1973 with Harvard College Observatory (HCO) to form, under a single director, George B. Field, the Center for Astrophysics for the pursuit of "excellence in astrophysical research." Today, this joint venture is represented by more than 125 scientists and 350 supporting staff members, both in Cambridge and at field stations around the world. Combining the resources of HCO with those of SAO, the Center for Astrophysics may be considered the largest single enterprise dedicated to astronomical research in the nation if not the world.

Arizona sun sets. Astronomer's workday begins. The structure (here under construction) now houses the joint University of Arizona-Smithsonian Multiple Mirror Telescope.

The "new astrophysics" may also seem far removed from Langley's "new astronomy," yet the goals of the Smithsonian Astrophysical Observatory are essentially unchanged from those established by him nearly a century ago: to understand the basic physical processes determining the nature of the universe. In other ways, too, astronomy is unchanged. Despite a modern tendency to speak of research "groups" or "teams," most men and women still find astronomy a highly personal endeavor. Certainly its rewards are mostly intellectual, with its insights often sounding esoteric and arcane to the outsider, and its advances somewhat unrelated to the normal concerns of society. To be sure, some applications of the research, such as the relationship between the sun and weather, could have a direct effect on the quality of life, but more often goals are pursued solely for the sake of the knowledge. The exploration of the heavens is, in a sense, a philosophical endeavor. Ancient observers attempted to explain their roles in the cosmic mystery by giving the stars familiar names and recognizable shapes. Langley sought those "intimate ties which united man" with the sun. Few modern scientists can forget these cultural and spiritual bonds with the past, because to look deep into space is also to look back into time.

At the Smithsonian the bonds are especially strong—and personal. Astronomers at telescopes on Mt. Hopkins are directly linked with those astronomers who once manned instruments 200 miles away and 50 years before at Mt. Harqua Hala.

The same mountain ranges are outlined by a crimson glow as the sun drops behind the horizon. The same stars appear in the east as the air grows crisp and cool. Another observing night begins. The roof of the instrument house opens and the telescope swings into position. Alone under the great dappled dome of sky the astronomer of today—just as his counterpart of yesterday—looks out across the boundless distances of space and wonders about those forces "that made and recreate us daily."

My Aircraft Is Missing

Years ago, at a moment of great national peril, I was taught to fly. The process was known as "scraping the bottom of the barrel." And when to everyone's surprise—especially my own—I survived it, I not unnaturally sought reasons for having been spared.

In retrospect, it became clear that I had returned safely to the ground because of my association with a certain aircraft which had a soul like mine. She was as hesitant at her job of flying as I was at my task of flying her. I was the sort of pilot who bobbled uncertainly around the sky, allowing a wing to sag, the nose to drop, the compass to wander. She, similarly, left the ground in a rush of blind terror, sniffed and choked at the prospect of getting too high and overreacted hysterically to any attempts at guidance.

The great thing we shared was a powerful sense of survival. We were equally reluctant to get involved in nasty situations. We quailed together and so lived on.

This marvelous aircraft was a Bell P-39, sometimes called "Airacobra." Understandably, I have kept an eye peeled for one ever since those reck-

less days, so that we could nod surreptitiously to one another. The trouble is, the Bell P-39 seems to be rarer than the whooping crane. Other ancient warplanes are cherished. But P-39s seem to have disappeared, petulantly kicked to pieces, one presumes, by their former pilots.

On my first visit to the Smithsonian's National Air and Space Museum, I still hoped that I might meet my old and disreputable companion. I was one of a group of staff people being shown through the building before

its opening, and while doing the rounds and listening to the guide I kept staring into shadowy corners. Nothing.

In the great entrance hall—the Milestones of Flight—I stared up at the Wright Brothers' original *Flyer,* hanging just a little higher than it flew on its epochal flight at Kittyhawk in 1903. I saw above it, and off its left wing, Lindbergh's *Spirit of St. Louis* appar-

ently about to land at Le Bourget after its flight from Long Island in May of 1927. Under it, directly behind the Wright plane, stood the Apollo 11 spacecraft, a fat, blunt-ended cone, tilted upward on the museum floor. Its broad end is discolored from the blazing heat of re-entry after that 1969 mission that put astronauts Armstrong and Aldrin on the moon. About 15 feet separates its rim from the tail of the Wright *Flyer.* Two giant strides for mankind. My P-39 was never in this league. She was no milestone of flight. More likely a roadblock. The parade of famous craft stirred endless memories. I looked up at the bullet-shaped X-1 in which Chuck Yeager blasted past the speed of sound, and recalled dark stories of the strange "sound barrier" that seemed to limit the speed of World War II fighters. The sound waves, it was said, would be jammed together by the hurtling air-

craft, building up a wall which it could not penetrate—which, in fact, would lock its controls in a weird grip that we called "compressibility."

A little of this was a little true. But the solution was a relatively simple marriage of power and design. The X-1, *Glamorous Glennis* (named for test pilot Yeager's wife), slipped away from the B-29 mother ship that had carried her high over the Mojave Desert, shot forward under rocket thrust, and reached Mach 1.06—700 miles per hour. The black X-15, hanging near the X-1 among those milestones of flight, went six times as fast.

To consider Mach figures is difficult to one trained in the 1940s. My P-39 used to chug around, belly tank and all, at about 170 miles per hour. When the enemy struck, she would retreat precipitously, belly tank gone and nose straight down, at a blistering 360 miles an hour. This speed could be increased some as the amount of panic grew. But Mach 6 —4,534 miles per hour! One gulps.

Of course the X-15 was a research aircraft. Yet hanging near it I saw a Lockheed F-104 Starfighter, a standard operational plane. This one bears NASA markings and was used by the agency for research, some of which involved flying chase missions with the X-15, howling along beside it to check up on it. It couldn't go so fast, but it could go more than 1,400 miles an hour. Its little wings were so sharp along their leading edges that a shield had to be fitted over them on the ground so that the ground crew wouldn't slice themselves up by leaning against the wrong part. On the leading edge of my wing I used to slap chewing gum for luck.

Experiments with the X-15 helped lead us into space just as displays of experimental supersonic planes led me toward the space section of the museum. I stood amid vast gleaming cylinders and burnished tailpipes— the Apollo-Soyuz spacecraft, the Skylab Orbital Workshop, a cluster of giant rockets and, in nearby galleries, a veritable skyful of satellites plus the

entire story of the Apollo moon flights. My favorite piece of hardware turned out to be a thing called the M2-F3 Lifting Body. It's a test device that NASA dreamed up for the space shuttle program, where a combination air and spacecraft is to go hurtling into orbit under its own rocket power; then, without power, hurtle back down again into the atmosphere and glide in for a landing. It can't afford much in the way of wings, since they would hold down its speed. But it has to have enough lifting surface for that re-entry and landing so it won't glide like a lump of wet cement. Answer: a fuselage designed to provide part of the lift.

This Lifting Body, then, gave the scientists a chance to see how one fuselage shape would work. And the reason I feel warmth and kinship for this particular curious, delta-shaped chunk of metal hanging in Space Hall is that it *didn't* work, at least once. On its 16th flight, it spread itself all over the landscape when it tried to land. The crash, in fact, was so spectacular that a film of it became the opening shot of a television series: *The Six Million Dollar Man*. The pilot recovered, fortunately, though in the TV story he is rebuilt into a ''Bionic Man''. The plane *was* rebuilt and flew again. Here it is—a nice reminder to us fliers of an earlier and more harebrained generation that today's young tigers can goof things up, too, despite all their computers and simulators and graduate degrees.

221

There are plenty of reminders of the hairy old days toward the other end of the three-block-long building. In the Hall of Air Transportation, I looked up at the Ford Trimotor hanging from the tubular trusswork ceiling and thought of the airline ads of the early '30s: smart ladies in fox furs accompanied by sleek gentlemen in wide-brimmed fedoras, all smiling tensely as a stewardess with movie-queen teeth welcomed them aboard for the hop to Chicago. It was some hop: frantic chewing of gum to allow lots of pressure-relieving swallows, cotton for the ears because

being enclosed in that metal fuselage was like putting your head inside a kettle drum, and the slow, lurching flight, with often a good deal of need for those little waxed paper bags.

No wonder the DC-3 suspended nearby (the heaviest craft to hang in the museum) was greeted as the ultimate in air transport and set an unparalleled record of achievement.

During World War II, these Douglas airliners were converted to carry troops or drop supplies ("biscuit bombing"), and their pilots took them daily over some of the world's most wretched country. Our squad-

ron of P-39s (sigh!) escorted them in New Guinea, and I remember returning to base late one afternoon as the tropical clouds were mounting high in the sky and everyone was tired after a long day. The C-47s (military version of the DC-3) had been ferrying troops; the big, awkward looking planes were headed for the barn, empty. And suddenly the lead transport dove slightly to get ahead of its formation, pulled its nose above the horizon and executed a perfect slow roll while we in our little fighters cheered on our radios.

I suppose every nation in the world has flown or is still flying the DC-3. Again, during that same war, I watched from the ground a squadron of them return from a mission. They fell into line astern as they entered traffic for their airstrip—13 big lumbering planes, all in olive drab. Thirteen? There were only 12 in a squadron. And sure enough, the last plane turned away and headed back north where only the Empire of Japan held the air bases. As I said, every country flew the DC-3.

In the Exhibition Flight Gallery, among the films of barnstorming and acrobatics, there is a Waco 9, a graceful old biplane with a two-place front cockpit. It was designed in 1926 and took passengers for rides around country airfields during the barnstorming days. I knew an old pilot who once owned a Waco 10, a somewhat more comfortable model. He used to tell how he got caught in a fog bank one morning and began following the course of a river because the water was the only thing he could see. He dipped low between the banks and swung from side to side as the stream twisted beneath him. And suddenly, one twist was so sharp that the Waco couldn't make it. What's more, a steep cliff rimmed the riverbank at this bend.

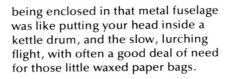

Seeing that he would splatter himself against that cliff, my friend climbed straight up to skim over the top. The clouds swallowed him, but not before he'd realized that he'd cleared the top and that right ahead of him was a smoothly harrowed field, just sprouting with corn. So he chopped the throttle and simply put his wheels on the ground, blindly, the fog shrouding what lay ahead of him. He shut off his engine and rolled quickly to a stop. And then he just sat in his cockpit for a moment in the white silence, at the end of a short trail of ruined corn, and he patted the side of his Waco.

He's getting on, now. If he visits the National Air and Space Museum and talks to the right people, maybe they'll make an exception and let him pat the Waco 9, very gently.

Among the balloon and airship exhibits is a small Curtiss Sparrowhawk, a light-weight biplane adapted to be carried aboard one of the huge naval airships of the '30s. It's equipped with an overhead hook allowing it to clamp on to a trapeze on the under-side of the airship. The idea was that while the USS *Akron* or USS *Macon* were on patrol, rumbling along over the ocean, seeming to fill about half the sky, they could lower their Sparrowhawks, which would then start engines and release themselves. When they'd finished scouting around, they'd fly back under the mother airship, match speed with her, and deftly hook on to be drawn back into her innards.

As a boy I wanted to be a Sparrowhawk pilot—to have that dainty little ship to fly, to test skill with that demanding hook-up and then to be drawn back to the comforts and cuisine of airship life (I was convinced that the Navy airships were just as luxurious as the *Graf Zeppelin* and *Hindenburg*). Instead I got a P-39.

In a corner gallery on the second floor I found at last my own era— World War II. Memories swamped me. Here stood a German ME-109, there an Italian Macchi, here a Spitfire, there a P-51. And overhead hung a beautiful Japanese Zero; I had the feeling that I had fled from it many times in the distant past. By the door was part of a famous old B-26, and on the wall was a mural of B-17s. There wasn't a P-39 anywhere. Not even a mention of one.

But by then I had forgotten my longed-for reunion. Like everyone else I was mind-blown by the film, "To Fly," stirred by the Spacearium, moved by the Life in the Universe Gallery. I renewed acquaintance with Amelia Earhart, Wiley Post, Jimmy Doolittle, Roscoe Turner, Howard Hughes, Eddie Rickenbacker, Otto Lilienthal, our own Professor Samuel Langley, and Dr. Robert Goddard. This place has collected them all, and many others. It contains just about every aircraft and spacecraft that ever made a "breakthrough."

It does not contain a P-39, which, after all, never did anything very notable except scare a lot of pilots and save the worthless neck of at least one of them.

by Edwards Park

223

To Fly, To Fly

Photographs by Ross Chapple

During the most recent tick of the universal clock humanity has learned how to rise above the earth, to travel through the air, and to carry its curiosity to the moon and beyond. In less than one hundred years human flight has progressed from a crazy idea to an everyday fact. We have applied our newfound gift both creatively and destructively. In our time, flight has been used to obliterate entire cities, to revolutionize the world's commerce and communication, to give mankind entirely new dimensions in recreation, and to begin the exploration of the planets, perhaps of the stars.

The Smithsonian chose to recognize the significance of flight by establishing the National Air and Space Museum in a new building on the Mall in Washington. As Deputy Director, one of my main responsibilities has been the development of the exhibits for this museum.

Since its opening on July 1, 1976, our museum has conveyed to millions of visitors the theory, the history, and the splendor of flight. Our exhibits are designed around thousands of specimens including such unique flying machines as the Wright Flyer, the Apollo 11 Command Module, Lindbergh's *Spirit of St. Louis;* the Bell X-1, the first supersonic flyer; *Friendship 7,* the first American manned orbiter, and many more. It's a source of great pride to us that all of our airplanes are genuine. Our spacecraft are genuine—when it's been possible to bring the originals back to earth. The rare exceptions are carefully labeled.

Our artifacts have been brought together in 23 exhibit galleries, each of which tells a part of the story of flight. We have worked to be a museum of history and of ideas, as much as a museum of things, and we've developed many special exhibit and presentation techniques such as automated dioramas and shows, giant motion pictures, and entertaining mechanized demonstrators. Our goal has been to make the museum visit a pleasurable and inspiring educational experience.

How should such a giant of a museum be represented on these few pages? The photographer of this essay has wisely decided not to try to show our exhibits, which take days to observe firsthand. Instead he has developed an extraordinary photographic portfolio, featuring a few of our objects, arranged to commemorate certain themes of flight.

Text by Melvin B. Zisfein

225

The Wright Brothers to Gemini 4: 61 years of flight.

The Dreamers

Out of man's mind have come the dreams from which flying machines have sprung.

The Montgolfier brothers, two paper manufacturers from Annonay, France, noticed that smoke rose into the sky; as a consequence, they designed and built the first balloon, with hot air providing the lift. The Wright brothers, two bicycle manufacturers from Dayton, Ohio, developed and applied concepts that outdid the leading scientists of their day; they made and flew the first successful airplane. Robert Hutchings Goddard and Konstantin Eduardovich Tsiolkovsky, an American physics professor and a Russian mathematics professor, recognized that space travel absolutely required reaction propulsion.

From progressive successes larger dreams have grown.

Grim 13th-century Chinese rocketeer with black-powder rocket lance (left) was created in paper by artist Leo Monahan. Probable inventors of the rocket, the Chinese early recognized the military potential of today's tyrant of the battlefield. When Russian space flight theoretician Konstantin Eduardovitch Tsiolkovsky (above, with spaceship model) published his concept of a liquid propellant spaceship in 1903, people sneered. Yet on April 12, 1961, Soviet cosmonaut Yuri Gagarin became the first man to leave the earth, boosted into space atop a liquid propellant rocket. Right: Gasoline and liquid oxygen tanks of the oldest surviving liquid propellant rocket. The rocket was built by American rocket pioneer Robert H. Goddard, from parts of the world's first liquid propellant rocket, launched by Goddard on March 16, 1926. Two attempts to fly the rocket at right failed.

Opposite: As ballooning became a sport in the late 1700s, balloonamania burgeoned (top) with snuff boxes and picture puzzles part of the rage. Gondola of scientific balloon, Explorer II (bottom) rose to 72,395 feet in 1935.

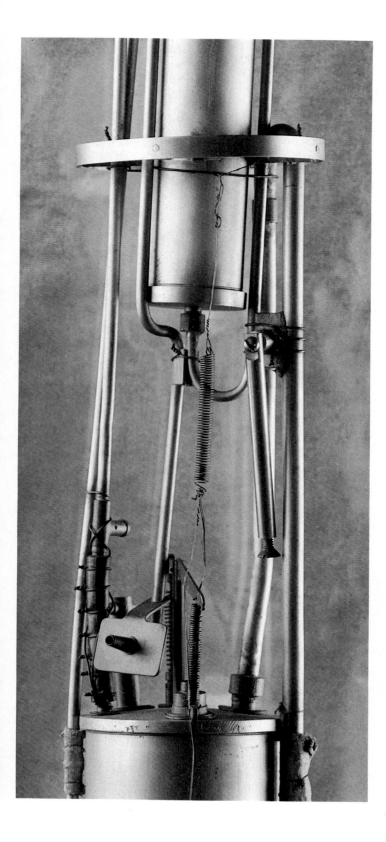

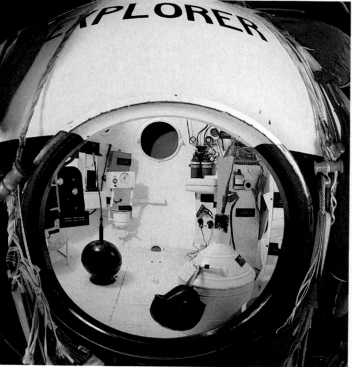

War

Initially the gods of war were reluctant to accept flight. Napoleon disbanded his balloon observation corps despite its utility at the battle of Fleurus. In the American Civil War, General Winfield Scott wouldn't even discuss a balloon corps with Thaddeus S.C. Lowe until Lincoln instructed him to do so. "We do not consider that aeroplanes will be of any possible use for war purposes," said the British War Secretary in 1910. However, once the airplane joined the Four Horsemen of the Apocalypse, it set new records for devastation.

To this day, the machines of flight continue to play a critical role in war. Consider the irony of Orville Wright's statement during World War I: "When my brother and I built and flew the first man-carrying flying machine, we thought that we were introducing into the world an invention that would make further wars practically impossible."

Considered by many to be the best German fighter of World War I, the Fokker D-VII (below) was sturdy and easy to fly and maintain. This D-VII was captured on November 9, 1918, when Lt. Heinz von Beaulieu-Marconnay mistakenly landed on an American airstrip.

An American airfield, somewhere near Verdun in late 1918: in the maintenance hangar (above) an 80-horsepower French Le Rhone rotary engine (foreground) is ready for reinstallment while a Nieuport Type 83 E2 scout awaits new fabric covering.

Vestments of war in the air, reminders of World War II: against a leather jacket background lie a pair of goggles, flying helmet, Distinguished Flying Cross, gauntlet, and cockpit clock.

American volunteers in the Royal Air Force's Eagle Squadron hoped to evade capture if shot down over the Continent with such aids as this silk map-scarf and compass button.

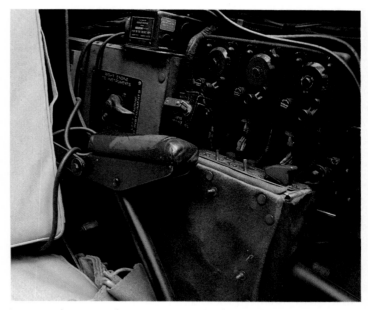

Weary and worn, a pilot's armrest speaks eloquently of hundreds of hours of combat during World War II. "Flak Bait," a Martin B-26 Marauder medium bomber, carried 8th and 9th Air Force crews on 202 missions over Northern Europe between June 1943 and May 1945.

Brain of a missile, the Mark 3 inertial guidance system could direct its Poseidon C-3 nuclear missile to Armageddon with pinpoint accuracy. The 65,000 pound Poseidon is a two-stage, nuclear submarine-launched rocket with a range of 2,875 miles.

In the Pilot's Seat

After the scientists, engineers, designers, and craftsmen have fulfilled their roles, a flying machine emerges from the factory to be servant, companion and, on occasion, master to its pilot. The pilot operates in and out of the cockpit, which is sometimes referred to as "the office."

The photograph of the *Spirit of St. Louis* cockpit below tells an intimate story; the feeling is one of cramped confinement, no place for a claustrophobic. Amazingly, our entrapped eyes find no windshield, no direct way to see forward. Lindbergh planned it that way. He eliminated the windshield during design and replaced it with a necessary additional fuel tank. For forward vision he planned to use a small periscope or simply to thrust his head out through the opened side window. Compare his primitive approach with any of the more modern cockpits shown here; he rightly earned his nickname, "Lucky Lindy."

Below: Charles A. Lindbergh's view of the Atlantic Ocean during his 3,610 mile flight from New York to Paris, May 20-21, 1927. Lindbergh piloted his Ryan NYP *Spirit of St. Louis* for 33 hours, 30 minutes— the first nonstop, solo flight across the Atlantic. A plumber's nightmare of fuel lines and valves can be seen beneath the simple instrument panel.

In quarters as cramped as Lindbergh's, Alan B. Shepard, Jr., made the first U.S. space flight in his Mercury spacecraft, *Freedom 7*, (above) on May 5, 1961. Only 15 minutes, 22 seconds long, Shepard's flight was the first step toward Neil A. Armstrong's "giant leap for mankind." The lunar module cockpit simulator (below) evokes memories of Apollo 11 and the exultant cry, "The *Eagle* has landed!" In all, six crews landed on the moon at the controls of lunar modules. Skylab's Airlock Module (back-up at right) served as laboratory for three teams of three crewmen each during 1973 and 74.

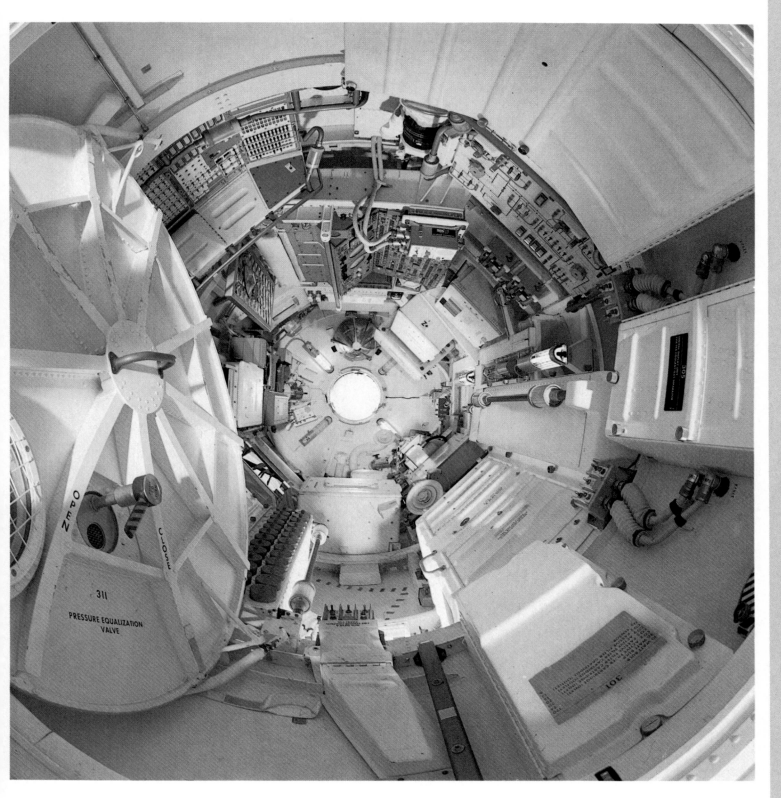

Power

There is a sculptural beauty within the machines of flight—propellers, propellant pumps, rocket engines, jet engines, and control systems—waiting for the eye of the artist. It's one thing to have an engineer's familiarity with such items as the fan end of a fanjet or the cooling tubes inside a rocket engine; it's another to look at these objects as art subjects after the photographer has added composition and lighting.

In the National Air and Space Museum we too have had some successes in imparting reality to the powerful objects displayed. Though neither earplugs nor goggles are required yet, few visitors leave the museum without feeling that, in some way, they've been carried farther into the true dimensions of flight. Hang on, it's taking off!

Thirsty F-1, main engine for the Apollo Saturn 5 rocket, carried a 60,000-horsepower propellant pump (below, sectioned) to force 6,000 pounds of propellants into the combustion chamber each second.

The Hamilton-Standard constant-speed propeller (above, sectioned) permitted maximum use of engine power, increased propeller efficiency, and reduced engine wear.

Surveyor spacecraft carried three of these 15-inch rocket engines for control during moon landings. Five Surveyors landed and sent to earth 87,632 TV images.

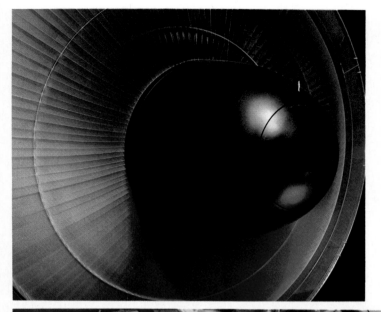

Power for the jumbo-jet age—the six-foot fan section (left) of a Pratt & Whitney JT9D turbofan jet engine, original equipment for some Boeing 747s and DC-10s. Above: Sectioned cooling tubes and combustion chamber of an RL-10 rocket engine. First liquid hydrogen-liquid oxygen-burning engine to fly, it powered the upper stage of the Atlas-Centaur rocket. Bewildering complexity of spacecraft is revealed under the skin of back-up Skylab's Airlock Module (below).

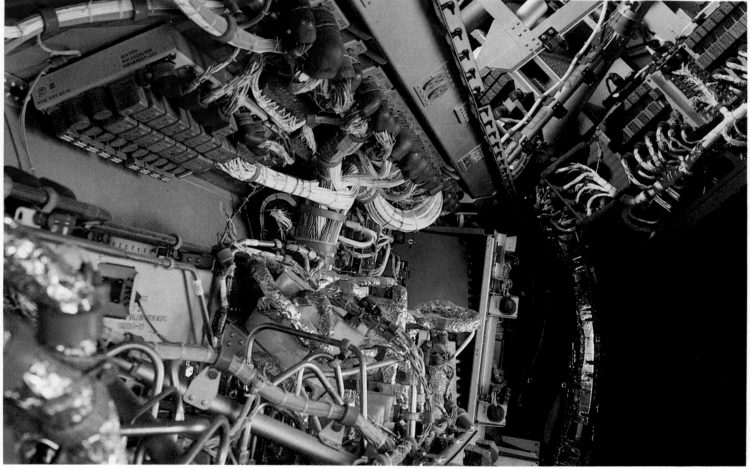

Quo Vadis?

The best machines of flight usually display such balance and grace that they look, for want of a better word, "right."

The early Wright gliders and airplanes were intensely fundamental. Flight itself was the only objective. The Hughes H-1 Racer, made during the 1930s, reflects an ever increasing emphasis on performance.

The third flight machine shown here, the back-up Pioneer 10 spacecraft, designed to fly by Jupiter, represents some of today's objectives of flight.

So there we are: now our machines carry messages to the peoples of the stars. We of the National Air and Space Museum look at the patterns of history in our exhibits and await the revelations of the future.

The Wright brothers conducted thousands of wind tunnel experiments and flew a number of gliders (model, far right) before their powered flights on December 17, 1903. January 19, 1937: in the beautiful Hughes H-1 Racer (below), Howard Hughes flashed across America in seven hours, 28 minutes, averaging 332 miles per hour. His record stood for 10 years. Pioneer 10 (back-up spacecraft, right) was the first spacecraft to probe Jupiter. Launched on March 3, 1972, it passed the giant planet on December 4, 1974, only 82,000 miles from the surface. In 1990, Pioneer 10 will cross the oribit of Pluto and leave the Solar System to fly forever among the stars.

PART EIGHT

To The World's Farthest Corners

Under donkey power, an expedition truck lurches through South-West Africa's flooded Great Fish River in 1972. Smithsonian geologists trekked on to Mt. Brukkaros, site of a strange crater. Oddly enough, back in 1929-30, Smithsonian's Charles Greeley Abbot built an observatory on the wild, remote peak.

These Smithsonian people . . . a curious lot. They continue to span the globe in search of . . . well, almost everything.

And as a result of such explorations, the Smithsonian has become something of a lodestar for foreign visitors, including royalty. To the delight of our impressionable correspondent, Edwards Park, kings and queens come to visit the Smithsonian. Indeed they come every day—though most have no crowns and most are not from foreign lands. They are you.

And what of the future? Secretary S. Dillon Ripley looks back at another impressionable correspondent, a boy who learned to love museums. He suggests that the destiny of the institution is to be sought both within and without: not only in clearer perceptions of ourselves and more intimate connections with the Smithsonian's Washington neighborhoods, but also in a better understanding of the neighborhood we all share, the planet Earth.

237

Kings and Queens I Almost Met

In the early days of the institution, no Visiting Dignitaries from Far Off Lands paid much attention to it. Washington was the half-baked capital of a second-rank nation. The city was a sprawling village punctuated by unfinished edifices and marred by quagmire streets and a noxious canal that bred malarial mosquitoes. The citizens lacked couth. Even plain Henry Adams from Boston took a

type and he felt himself duty bound to see all he could of the United States and then write exhaustively detailed letters home to Mama (Queen Victoria). But the Prince apparently never ventured into the Smithsonian. His letters fail to mention it, and any record the institution may have had of such a visit would have gone up in smoke when the Castle suffered a devastating fire five years later.

Being by nature a gawker at the great, I have kept a sort of log of the visiting dignitaries that have been browsing through our halls lately. I venture out of my office to stare at First Ladies giving gowns to our collection, to admire the shoulders of Muhammad Ali donating his robe

dim view of the place where he later came to live. But *visit* Washington? The mere thought caused a raising of perfumed handkerchiefs to aristocratic European nostrils.

In 1860 the Prince of Wales (later King Edward VII) *did* visit Washington. He was no lace handkerchief

It really took the flowering of the museums in the 20th century to lure the crowned heads of Europe and Asia to our spread along the Mall. (By then, incidentally, that canal had been covered over and the streets paved.) So the solid stream of royalty that we have lately enjoyed here began only quite recently—linked, especially, to our national Bicentennial celebrations.

Muhammad Ali presents his gloves to Carl H. Scheele and Ellen R. Hughes.

and boxing gloves, to gaze at everyone from astronauts and actors to xylophone players and zoologists. But the best gawk of all is royalty.

There is something about kings and queens and emperors and empresses that stirs me deeply. Maybe it's the realization that they still exist at all. I find myself scrutinizing them with the intensity that an ornithologist would save for an ivory-billed woodpecker. So when, in 1975, Emperor Hirohito of Japan dropped in at the

Emperor Hirohito studies a marine specimen at the Museum of Natural History.

Museum of Natural History, I was on hand in classic rubberneck pose, eyes aglaze, mouth agape, and posture aslouch. The Emperor had come to check out his identification of some of his hydroid collection. He is a better than average marine zoologist and like any scientist wants to check his taxonomy of these tiny animals against the collection of a well equipped lab. Sure, he has his own lab back in Japan, but it may not be quite so complete in every way as our Smithsonian facilities. (I say this in trepidation, not wanting to see Japanese heads roll.)

So, while the Washington cops mounted appropriately on Hondas kept crowds of us rubbernecks at bay, Hirohito, the Mikado himself,

swept up to the Museum of Natural History in an 80-foot-long limousine, waved a little nervously at us all, and disappeared inside surrounded by Smithsonian dignitaries, all in dark suits and regimental ties. There, according to my inside sources, he sat himself down at a microscope and checked his drawings of hydroids as he had identified them against the Smithsonian's specimens, all positively and indisputably identified.

He got through seven of his 10 drawings and found he had made a mistake on one of them. He had mixed

up an *Aglaophenia elegans* with an *Aglaophenia floweri*. These days even an Emperor can make a mistake and no one need commit hara-kiri.

When his allotted time was up—the time, that is, for fun—Hirohito emerged from the Museum of Natural History, bade farewell to all the dark-suited dignitaries and thanked them, waved again nervously to us rubbernecks, and went swishing off in the limousine with the Hondas muttering along in escort. All in all, it was a great day.

During the Bicentennial year, a couple of Scandinavian monarchs dropped by our museums. King Gustaf of Sweden wanted to see the National Air and Space Museum, even though it wasn't yet finished. What King Gustaf wants apparently King Gustaf gets. He was shown through those fabulous halls while the workmen were still putting it all together. Then Queen Margrethe of Denmark brought her royal yacht up the Potomac River to Washington, brav-

Hirohito—Emperor of Japan and noted marine biologist—meets Secretary S. Dillon Ripley at the Museum of Natural History. He came to check his identification of sea creatures.

ing the stench of pollution, to pay a visit to the capital with her tow-headed little children. On her agenda was an exhibit of Danish design at the National Portrait Gallery. She spent a fair amount of time there, even making the museum director a Knight of Dannebrog—a distinction that will doubtless prove useful to him in some unusual way. She charmed everyone and seemed to leave with real reluctance. I expect anyone would be reluctant to return to a yacht moored in the Potomac.

King Juan Carlos of Spain whispered up to the Museum of History and Technology in the same limousine that Hirohito had used. He got a special tour of the exhibit of maps and documents and armor and gold that dated from the time of Columbus—a Bicentennial exhibit made possible by the King himself. Carlos is pretty much what you'd expect your everyday king to look like—tall and upright and handsome and curly haired and broad-shouldered. His queen is

lovely and blonde and smiling. But it wasn't until another rubberneck asked me whom we were looking at that I realized that his real glamor lies not in his looks but in his title. "The King of Spain!" I said, "That's who."

The name came out like a fanfare on a score of heraldic trumpets, "Oh, wow!" responded my fellow rubberneck. "King of Spain." Whoo boy. It really is a honey of a title.

Queen Elizabeth's title doesn't have the same ring to it now that they've dropped "Empress of Injah" from the phrase. What is she now, anyway? Queen of Great Britain and Northern Ireland or something awkward like that. But aside from that failing, she's got a very special place with us Americans who have always had a national love-hate thing about British royalty. As an old Elizabeth-watcher (I recall seeing her and her sister

Danish Queen Margrethe II, (above) visits the National Portrait Gallery. Director Marvin Sadik welcomes her (below).

Juan Carlos, King of Spain (top), came to the Smithsonian during his visit to the United States in 1976—the first visit of a Spanish King to the New World. At Museum of History and Technology, Secretary S. Dillon Ripley greets the king.

when they were two little kids in the back seat of a 25-foot-high Daimler), I can report that there isn't a king or queen around who makes a visit with such precision of timing and such polish of execution. She purred up to the front door of the Smithsonian Castle exactly when she was supposed to, raised her hand to the waiting crowd in that splendid royal gesture of greeting—the gesture one would make to steady the broad brim of a royal hat in a wind storm—and alighted to receive the deferential greetings of the tall, dark-suited Smithsonian dignitaries in their regimental ties.

Elizabeth had some rather dull stuff to look at, including James Smithson's tomb, which hardly wins any Oscars. But she attacked the whole project with that same determined interest she shows when she opens a handicraft exhibit in North Wales. Then Mr. Ripley, who towers above her, cracked some private joke, and she looked up at him with a wide grin and a look in her eye that can only be described as mischievous. I had the feeling that behind the regal manner and the precise little voice that can be so devastatingly imitated, there stood a nice, warm-blooded lady who would probably be a lot of fun to have a drink with at a Georgetown bar I know of.

Elizabeth did her stuff with her usual cool competence, zinging through the allotted exhibits on the tick of her schedule (pronounced "shedule") without the tiniest bead of—um—perspiration daring to gleam upon the royal brow. She left the Castle at the correct second, whispered off to the National Gallery, and there put in another meticulously prescribed tour of a Jefferson exhibit.

In reading over this catalogue of regal visitors, I realize that each one I mentioned went to a different museum and concentrated on a different subject. Royalty is obviously limited in what it can see at the Smithsonian, and that's a disillusioning thought for anyone who remembers the omnipotence of the Red Queen in *Alice's Adventures in Wonderland* shouting "Off with her head!"

It occurs to me that the real power wielders around here are the everyday tourists who arrive from Des Moines or Cleveland or Albuquerque. These kings and queens from not-so-distant lands may struggle to find a place to park, but then they wander happily *and at will* around the Mall, visiting every museum they want, staying as long as they want in front of an exhibit that tickles them, moving on as soon as they like from one that doesn't. Royalty is great stuff for a rubberneck but, perhaps, not so great for royalty. The Red Queen is long gone. She left her freedom of choice to the rest of us.

by Edwards Park

241

Queen Elizabeth II, accompanied by Prince Philip (above). The Queen chats with Vice President Nelson Rockefeller and Secretary S. Dillon Ripley (below).

The View of Tomorrow

by S. Dillon Ripley

In the Smithsonian Institution's heartbeat there is an emotional reverberation of how all of us, citizens, feel about ourselves. The Smithsonian is history. Its pulse, like the ticking of a clock, records our past hopes, aspirations, successes, and failures. It harbors the material results of our gradual ascent from primeval lands and forests to open spaces surmounted with the evidences of our presence, our inventive genius, and our increase. The Smithsonian's tangible objects represent in a hundred thousand ways the long passage of time, the strivings of our ancestors, the terror and the glory of our past. But the institution is more than history. Beyond the past is the present.

What is the present? To most of us it is a kind of vacuum chamber in which we live, day to day, as insubstantial as a dream. We wake, shower, and work. The accoutrements of conscious life surround us with forced busyness; there are too few moments in any day for reflection, or peace, or calm. I am reminded of a phrase from Cardinal Newman's evensong prayer: "the busy world is hushed."

All of us need quiet, for in reflection comes thinking, and thinking is in itself refreshing. Only pauses in continuous motion tend to promote thoughts. A museum then, like a planetarium, is a place where one sits alone for a moment as the lights dim and the hush descends. The past lies before one in this theatrical museum, and the stage is set for vital events. Stimulated, the viewer responds and reflection flows.

There are myriad images: paintings in which one can immerse oneself; objects which speak of the past or present. There are stunning experiences of sound and sight. In our new Air and Space Museum, almost unbelieving, one can stand at a mock-up of a spacecraft descending onto the surface of the moon, the console buttons at hand and the windows mirroring the image of the lunar landscape as the machine settles miraculously and safely onto a hitherto unknown celestial body. For me, such experiences do far more than remind me of history or light up the past. Rather

Eighth Secretary of the Smithsonian S. Dillon Ripley regularly contributes comments to the Smithsonian's associate membership on the institution's development in his Smithsonian *magazine column, "The View from the Castle." His publications include* Handbook of the Birds of India and Pakistan, Rails of the World, *and* The Sacred Grove. *Since 1964, when his stewardship of the Smithsonian began, the institution—by new buildings, extensive research, lively exhibits, and magazine, TV, and book programs—has dramatically augmented its contributions to the ultimate goal, which Mr. Ripley calls "public enlightenment."*

they project me as if from a springboard, from a vantage point in time, towards the future.

It is my belief that a museum is a social planetarium. Why social? Because it is not subjective. It is a shared experience, even though each sharer has the privilege of having an inward individual reaction to every fraction of its meaning. There is no regimentation in that.

A museum is not didactic, like a classroom. The message is there for all, but it does not subjugate or compel.

To enter a museum is to enjoy an open experience. No one tells you exactly where to go or stop. School classes often exasperate the teacher; the children are not all safely in their seats, alphabetically, two by two. The children wander out of the lines giggling or tickling, but even within the limits imposed they are on their own, able to absorb something without being told. Being open is a view into the future. It is already an option, a chance to integrate a few impressions of the past vested in one's present being (pinch yourself if necessary to remember you're alive) and, from that springboard, to float out and off into the future. The view of the past coupled with the experience of the present, points the way towards tomorrow.

Thus museums in themselves do far more than preserve in isolated splendor the artifacts of the past, whether artifacts made by the miraculous processes of natural creation, or creations of mankind made by the unimaginable achievements of the greatest computer of all, the human brain. By preserving such things, museums lead us inevitably into synthetic reasoning about where we are going.

As the previous chapters have shown, the vast, almost overwhelming museum functions of the Smithsonian, so appropriately supported as a public trust, are tangible. They are the contact points for people, visitors from everywhere, schoolchildren and others of all ages, led by curiosity or bent on reflective learning. What enables the Smithsonian to provide these experiences is the tradition of research and teaching which not only affords the authority for our collections and their appropriate care, but also the seeds of innovation and forward-reaching thought which maintain the impetus to the future. As history shows, interactions among people cannot be static any more than a plant can survive without watering or a marriage without freshness and vitality.

Our exhibits are a testament to the need to reinterpret the past, to correct errors, to act in awareness of the constant need for measured truth and relevance. Like collections, exhibits lose their value if they are not nurtured. And so there is nothing essentially static about museum-keeping. Museums evolve as much as life itself. That is a sure presentiment for the future.

She rides her zebra into skies of imagination, over the towers of the Smithsonian's Arts and Industries Building. For many, the Castle's carousel offers a first glimpse of the institution's varied realms.

Open education seems to me the most powerful tool for the reinforcement of learning. It provides a continual resource, never ending, to be tapped like a drinking fountain, on demand. When I was a child I felt that the museum was as much fun as the carousel in the nearby park. One sensation transposed itself into the other: to ride on the carousel, jousting for the gold ring (which if caught gave an additional ride free), then to leave and go inside to look at paintings, sculpture, ship models, or panelled rooms . . . what could be more fun? Why do we dissociate learning from fun? Why is it not fun to learn? Should it be serious? Pompous? No museum-keeper can believe it. We learn things when we are excited. Nowadays, it is called being turned on. A museum must be fun. To learn is to increase the possibilities of enjoying our individual, single trip.

I have always wondered why more people are not aware of museums as a resource and as fun. When I was growing up in New York before World War II, museums were popular, the Metropolitan Museum of Art especially, but also the American Museum of Natural History where I worked for a time. And to many, the exuberant and then new galleries and collections and museums of modern art were another resource for delight. Yet my impression is that most curators did not care as much about the visitors then as they do now. They felt perhaps less involved in teaching, less socially obligated than they do today. The exhibits were just put up and left. That was that. Take it or leave it. Many curators seemed not to look at what had been wrought; perhaps like a writer upon finishing a book, they felt a kind of emotional catharsis. Certainly people didn't worry then so much about changing or improving exhibits.

In addition, schools paid far less attention to museums then than now. There was less coordination with the school systems, especially with inner-city schools. Visits had almost a segregated quality. Busses rolled in from the wealthier school systems of the suburbs or from the private day schools. This always worried me. How could children, and adults too, from poorer neighborhoods be persuaded that museums belonged to them just as much as to anyone else? Why did the museum conjure up visions of marble palaces? How could the delights within be shared openly and the horizons of the world revealed?

Coming to Washington in the mid-1960s, I felt that the Smithsonian, in addition to being looked to as the National Museum, had an obligation to lead in museum techniques. Not for nothing was the nation's museum part of an institution held as a public trust for the "increase & diffusion of Knowledge among men." We should have a message for everyone.

I remember so well going to a discussion in 1966 with two of my colleagues, Charles Blitzer and Frank Taylor. It was one of those dreary think-tank affairs, this time on the future of museums. Everyone strained to utter weighty or symbolic things, vying in a kind of intellectual badminton to outdo each other with cleverness. It came over me suddenly that the way to solve the problem of having the alienated come in and share with us the fun of going to a museum would be to start a branch in a neighborhood that was in the midst of the urban crisis. When I broached the subject of a neighborhood museum I realized that a nerve had been touched.

"What would happen to our masterpieces?" one man said. What indeed? If one confines one's thought to the acquisition and care of masterpieces, it is obvious that such a vision of a museum is a limited street indeed. If, on the other hand, museums are to be fun for everyone of all ages and conditions, then it follows that we should all be enticed into belonging to this universal club.

Over the succeeding months, with the help of a number of volunteers from those conversant with the city and its districts, notably Caryl Marsh and some District Government officials, we finally found our setting—a section of the city called Anacostia, along the river, full of history and life and tradition, threatened by urban blight but proud of its roots. The neighborhood, of course, is what counts—the neighborhood and the strengths that lie in its personalities. After some discussion, an Anacostia neighbor-

"I respect the ideas put across to our black children . . . to establish an identity and pride in blackness." said an observer of the 1973 African heritage exhibition staged by the Anacostia Neighborhood Museum.

hood group voted to ask the Smithsonian to help them set up their own museum. That was the beginning.

Now our neighborhood Anacostia Museum has an identity of its own, a training and exhibits center, identification with its own history (The Anacostia Historical Society started in 1974), and a keen sense of belonging to a larger extended town, the United States. A moment of pleasure came later when one of the Anacostia Museum visitors said to me: "You know, I used to drive a truck by those big buildings on the Mall and I thought that's where other folks go on the weekend, but now I know we are a part of the whole thing, and so I take my kids over there." Statements like this are an answer to prayer.

Just as the Smithsonian has helped connect the people of Anacostia with the entire nation, so the institution has long been a link between the nation and the rest of the world. Having collected papers and books and correspondence from nations all over the world for more than 130 years, the Smithsonian has always been a force for international scholarship and exchange, though few people

are aware of this role. Nowadays, foreign activities seem to be a purely government responsibility, or a question of business or tourism.

And yet the Smithsonian has played an important part at all levels. In 1878 the Smithsonian advised the Department of State on how to set up a protocol for dissemination of research papers and the like under the authority of what would be called today a "Freedom of Information Act." At that time it was a novelty. All during the last decades of the 19th century, the institution played a crucial part in mapping the resources of the West and neighboring areas in disciplines ranging from anthropology to zoology, A to Z. It was our scientists—William H. Dall, Henry M. Bannister, Robert Kennicott, to name a few—who visited Alaska and created such interest in its resources that the government of the time finally agreed to purchase it from Russia.

Nor were we confined to the continental limits in the thirst for knowledge. Smithsonian scientists combed the Pacific from Kamchatka to the South China Sea and the Austral latitudes searching for facts of the world of nature as well as artifacts of man's presence. What better way could the advancement of knowledge be prosecuted than by studying the dimensions of our planet and at the same time working on the rudiments of flight? What could be more reasonable than for a Secretary of the Smithsonian Institution, that *omnium gatherum* of curiosity seekers, like Samuel Pierpont Langley to be an astronomer and an experimenter in heavier-than-air flight, to start a zoo for public instruction and conservation, to be the curator of a children's museum, and to be the administrator of a forward-looking institution with publications flowing to the four corners of the earth? What better than to have an institution in Washington, belonging to the people everywhere, capable of doing so many things on so many levels at the same time? Nothing could be more appropriate; a far-ranging institution is yet another reminder that a vital resource of mankind is to be interested. That is certainly what we are all about and a lesson never to be forgotten. For in forgetfulness, in the loss of interest, lies an abnegation of our birthright.

Sometimes I have been impatient at the thought of accepting too little, of assuming that our horizons are not boundless. In the same way the Smithsonian has always promoted an active interest in knowledge about the rest of the planet, as well as the universe. In foreign affairs our role has always been the exchange of letters and documents, constructing in that way a network of interest and friends and communication *outside* the realm of foreign affairs. This is as it should be, for individual or scholarly discourse is often a more effective means to understanding than formal, politically organized agreements, so often subject to gaps and electoral lapses, to say nothing of wars. There are far fewer wars in international intellectual affairs, where jealousies are subordinated to honest curiosity and a measure of objective assessment.

Thus it seemed to a number of us that there was a great need in the America of the '50s and '60s of this century for a revival of one of the Smithsonian's earliest functions under its first Secretary, Joseph Henry—an international, scholarly traveler's aid. By post-World War II Washington City had attained a critical mass in scholarship and scholarly resources; could it not serve as an intellectual hospice?

We spent a summer in the middle '60s assessing the scholarly resources in Washington: we found more Ph.D.'s in science spread throughout the government laboratories and kindred institutions in this city and its surrounding communities than any university cluster in the nation. There were great library and collection resources in Washington, and yet Washington's intellectual community as a whole was spread out, unintegrated, and largely submerged by the numbing presence of vast bureaus of the government. With this in mind, a group of men and women in and out of government thought together over the years, usually at dinner in the Cosmos Club, that traditional originator of academic organizations, and finally gave birth to an idea. We would appeal to the then-existing Presidential Commission on a Memorial for the late scholar, President Woodrow Wilson, for whom a memorial was to be designated in the District of Columbia. Our group visualized no traditional equestri-

Woodrow Wilson Center scholars confer on a bibliography for the 1972 Stockholm Conference on the Environment.

an statue for this forceful creator of the graduate school at Princeton and the League of Nations, but rather an international center for scholars. The hearings went very well and in October 1968 the Congress approved the creation of the Woodrow Wilson International Center for Scholars as a "living memorial expressing the ideals and concerns of Woodrow Wilson . . . symbolizing and strengthening the fruitful relation between the world of learning and the world of public affairs."

The center was placed in the Smithsonian Institution under the administration of its own 15-person, mixed, public and private Board of Trustees appointed by the President of the United States. The first chairman was then Vice President Hubert H. Humphrey, and funds were to be provided directly to the center by Congress, as well as by grants from foundations and the public. And thus the center, created in this manner, has seemed to me to evoke the aspirations of Joseph Henry, first Secretary of the Smithsonian, who in the 1850s dreamed of the institution as becoming his "College of Discoverers."

Now after some nine years of existence, we are finding that the Woodrow Wilson Center, in the words of its able Director, James H. Billington, is "a place which makes a difference" . . . a center which "is a creative mix . . . people who can think, ideas that matter, and communication that gets through." With the addition of a Kennan Center for Advanced Russian Studies, and a projected plan for other regional groups, we hope to synthesize the unmatched documentary resources of Washington City to better understand our neighbors on this beleaguered planet.

Now in the closing years of this turbulent 20th century of ours how fares the Smithsonian? It is alive and well, its heartbeat mirroring the times. New buildings have risen for public service, new research programs suit the tides of events of our nation—solar radiation studies, studies in ecology and environmental monitoring, studies in the history of American art, in history itself, the history of science, technology, and medicine. We are vigorously pursuing studies in American Indian history and culture, reviewing as we do so the encyclopedic publications of the Smithsonian on all the tribes of North America, classic research going back more than 100 years.

We are preserving and documenting objects and studying their conservation, a task of incredible complexity and increasing priority with every tick of the clock. For we are beginning to know something of the inscrutable processes of aging in objects, a subject as mysterious these days as the aging of individual humans or animals.

We are deeply concerned with the fate of the living creatures of this earth. Our museum collections form a kind of National Bureau of Standards on the health of the planet itself. We can document that state of health as surely as a patient might have a physical check-up, through presence or absence or the rates of decline or disappearance of the living ecosystems of this earth.

The opportunities that lie ahead for the Smithsonian exist not so much in novelties as in maintaining our traditional excellence in doing what we do: preserving and studying collections, making them known to all the people both in and out of Washington, and drawing where necessary the appropriate conclusions from those things we have and know about.

That is part of my dream of the future, to be able to show the past and present so accurately that the prediction for the future will be plain. Through its activities abroad in the land, traveling exhibitions, our Associates publications, perhaps TV eventually, we can help to keep more people interested and alert to the future than ever before, fulfilling in this way Mr. Smithson's dream for the institution of "increase & diffusion." Of course all this takes money, and so far the United States Congress, mindful of its obligation to the Smithsonian trust, and appreciative of the respect which our citizens have for the institution, has been generous in its support for buildings and collections. None of this would have been possible without the original Smithson gift and all the subsequent private gifts of great magnitude and incomparable value over the years. That the gifts have been given is symbolic of the faith of individuals in the trust responsibility of the institution.

I am reminded of the fact that since my predecessor Dr.

Langley in 1896 started experimenting with heavier-than-air flight, the Smithsonian has been accepting gifts in kind and in money for what would be, one day, a great temple dedicated to the fulfillment of his dream: that one day man would be girdling the earth in a twinkling and reaching out to land on nearby planets, even as we plumb the secrets of the universe. As the Viking spacecraft circled Mars on July 1, 1976, 80 years after Langley's experiments on the Potomac River, a signal from the craft cut the ribbon across the door of the new National Air and Space Museum,

From morning until evening of every day except Christmas, the Smithsonian—and particularly the Castle, its information center and administrative heart (above)—remains open for all.

opening it to resounding public approval. At that moment I thought to myself that everything in the building was free. These were all gifts from 100 sources—objects, books, manuscripts, artifacts of every kind as well as endowments of money from the public for research. All of this had poured in like a stream, to be encompassed in a single building costing about 40 million dollars, created and endowed with funds appropriated for the Smithsonian from the United States. And what was the value of those gifts which the Smithsonian had husbanded all the years? No one can set a value, except perhaps in a hazarded conjecture, like billions of dollars, a figure as mysterious as time in outer space.

This then had come to fruition in a way as inadvertent and unexpected as Mr. Smithson's will itself. The Smithsonian exists, and in its mysterious ability to distill an essence of thought and interest for every human who enters its doors, it gives a dividend to all those who over the years have nurtured its progress and provided its support. Surely in that success lies our view of the future.

AMERICA'S PAST IN PERSPECTIVE

Because the Smithsonian Institution probes and expounds the American experience in terms of science, society, and the arts, the editors have chosen to end this book with a review of American history which presents events in those three parallel channels. And because people are the dynamic factor in all of these activities, portraits of significant Americans from the 18th, 19th, and 20th centuries, highlight the time chart. The portraits are drawn from the National Portrait Gallery collections—but one section of the Smithsonian, which helps put the nation and its life story into perspective.

THE ARTS

Advocate of the discovery and advancement of American artists, the Smithsonian also celebrates writers and musicians, sculptors and painters, dancers and actors, playwrights and craftsmen.

SCIENCE

Just as Joseph Henry and Samuel P. Langley epitomize Smithsonian scientific contributions, so is American science marked by Eli Whitneys, Cyrus McCormicks, and Thomas A. Edisons.

SOCIETY

The diverse backgrounds of the American people—a Smithsonian theme—are reflected on the chart in lives as varied and significant as Alexander Hamilton and Lucretia Mott.

THE ARTS

1653 Boston Public Library opens			1784 Charles Willson Peale opens "Peale's Museum" in Philadelphia		1816 John Trumbull paints murals of the Revolution in U.S. Capitol rotunda
1716 First theater in English America built in Williamsburg	Matthew Pratt 1734-1805, Self-portrait; Colonial Artist	1760-80 Gilbert Stuart, John Copley portrait painters		1806 Noah Webster's first dictionary	
1730 Ben Franklin publishes *Pennsylvania Gazette*		1781 Philip Freneau, poet of the Revolution	Phillis Wheatley c., 1753-1784, Engraving; Colonial poet		1817 W. C. Bryant's "Thanatopsis" published in *North American Review*

SCIENCE

		1750 Conestoga wagon in use		1787 John Fitch launches first steamboat	1800 Oliver Evans constructs first high-pressure steam engine in America
1643 Saugus Iron Works, Massachusetts	1728 John Bartram establishes botanical garden in Philadelphia		1754 Benjamin Banneker makes the first American clock		
1721 Zabdiel Boylston inoculates patients against smallpox		1752 Ben Franklin conducts kite experiment	1767 David Rittenhouse builds first orrery in America	1793 Eli Whitney invents the cotton gin	1807 Robert Fulton launches steamboat "Clermont"

SOCIETY

1636 Harvard College established		1765 Stamp Act tax on British imports		1803 Louisiana Purchase; and Lewis and Clark expedition to Northwest	1811 Henry Clay, John C. Calhoun promote war with England
1735 Zenger Trial for "press freedom"		1773 Boston Tea Party	James Monroe 1758-1831, by John Vanderlyn; Fifth President of the U.S.		1817-18 Seminole War
	Alexander Hamilton 1755-1804, by James Sharples; First Secretary of the Treasury	1776 Declaration of Independence	1781 Cornwallis surrenders to Washington at Yorktown, Virginia	1806 Zebulon Pike reaches Pike's Peak, Colorado	1821 First public high school

1819
Thomas
Jefferson
designs
University of
Virginia

1848
Stephen Foster
composes "Oh!
Susannah"

1852
Harriet Beecher
Stowe publishes
*Uncle Tom's
Cabin*

1861
Winslow Homer
sketches the
Civil War

1820
Washington
Irving writes
The Sketchbook

1836
Essay *Nature*
published
by Ralph Waldo
Emerson

Harriet B. Stowe
1811-1896, by
Alanson Fisher;
Novelist and
humanitarian

1845
Edgar Allen Poe
publishes
The Raven

1855
Leaves of Grass
by Walt
Whitman

1843
Hiram Powers'
"Greek Slave"
most popular
statue of the
period in U.S.
and Europe

1846
James Renwick
designs the
Smithsonian
Institution
Castle

1851
Moby Dick by
Herman
Melville

Henry David
Thoreau
1817-1862,
daguerreotype;
Author of
Walden

1871
Little Women
published by
Louisa May
Alcott

1825
Erie Canal com-
pleted; and
John Stevens
builds his first
locomotive

1825
Robert Stevens
develops T-Rail
for rail track
construction

1830 s
John Hall uses
interchangeable
parts in gun
manufacture

1863
National
Academy of
Sciences
founded

1866
Cyrus Field's
Atlantic cable
completed

1827-38
Audubon paints
Birds of America

1846
Elias Howe
patents sewing
machine

Benjamin
Silliman
1779-1864, by
John Trumbull;
Chemist,
geologist

1856
Gail Borden
patents first
evaporated milk

1868
Westinghouse
invents air
brakes

John C. Warren
1778-1856, by
Francis
Alexander;
First anesthesia
demonstration

1831
Joseph Henry
publishes a
paper on the
induction coil

1859
Drake drills first
oil well,
Pennsylvania

Elisha Kent Kane
1820-1857, by
Giuseppe
Fagnani;
Physician and
Arctic explorer

1869
Golden Spike
driven at Prom-
ontory Point,
Utah

1823
Monroe
Doctrine

1833
American
Antislavery
Society

1830-60
Underground
Railroad

1858
Lincoln-Douglas
debates

1862
Emancipation
Proclamation

1846
Smithsonian
formally
dedicated

1852-54
Commodore
Perry trip to
Japan

Daniel Webster
1782-1852, by
G.P.A. Healy;
Statesman,
lawyer, and
orator

1830
U.S. Capitol
completed

Lucretia C. Mott
1793-1880, by
Joseph Kyle;
American
feminist
and reformer

1848
California
Gold Rush

1857
Dred Scott
Decision

1860
Pony Express

Abraham Lincoln
1809-1865, by
John Henry
Brown; Repub-
lican party
nominee

1870
Hiram Revels
first black
Senator; J.H.
Rainey first
black
Congressman

THE ARTS

- **1825-75** Hudson River School of New York landscape painters
- **1884** John Singer Sargent paints "Madame X"; shocks public
- **1890** Emily Dickinson's first poetry published 4 years after her death
- **1913** New York Armory Show of Impressionist painting
- **1918** George M. Cohan ushers in an era of spectacular musicals
- **1923** George Gershwin's *Rhapsody in Blue*
- **1872** James McNeill Whistler finishes a painting popularly known as "Whistler's Mother"
- **1903** Henry James writes *The Ambassadors*
- **1925** F. Scott Fitzgerald's *The Great Gatsby*
- **1885** Scott Joplin plays ragtime in St. Louis honky-tonks
- Charlotte S. Cushman 1816-1876, by William Page; Great actress of 19th century
- **1893** Premiere of Anton Dvorak's *New World Symphony*
- **1908** "Ashcan" school of art
- **1915** *The Birth of a Nation*, film, premieres at Clune's Auditorium in Los Angeles
- Ruth St. Denis 1877-1968, Drawing; Exotic Dancer
- **1927** Al Jolson performs in *Jazz Singer*

SCIENCE

- **1878** Albert Michelson, first U.S. Nobel laureate measures speed of light
- **1885** John Montgomery early glider flight
- **1904** New York subway opens
- **1920** Radio station KDKA begins operation
- Isaac M. Singer 1811-1875, by E. H. May; Patented practical sewing machine
- **1889** George Eastman invents flexible photographic film
- **1892** Duryea brothers operate first American auto
- **1909** Robert Edwin Peary reaches North Pole
- John Wesley Powell 1834-1902, by Edmund C. Messer; Geologist and ethnologist
- **1876** Alexander Graham Bell demonstrates telephone
- Cyrus McCormick 1809-1884, by Charles L. Elliott; Inventor of the reaper
- **1883** Brooklyn Bridge opens
- **1903** Wright Brothers fly at Kitty Hawk
- **1914** Henry Ford operates an assembly line at Highland Park
- **1927** Charles Lindbergh flies Atlantic

SOCIETY

- **1877** Rail strikes paralyze nation
- **1888** Washington Monument opens
- **1870-1900** Almost 12 million immigrants enter United States
- **1904-14** Panama Canal
- **1881** Clara Barton founds Red Cross
- **1894** Coxey's "Army" marches on Washington, D.C.
- **1912** Sinking of the *Titanic*
- John J. Pershing 1860-1948, by Sir William Orpen; World War I commander in Europe
- "Stonewall" Jackson 1824-1863, daguerreotype; Confederate general
- **1886** American Federation of Labor (AFL)
- **1892** Homestead Strike at Carnegie Steel Mills, Pittsburgh
- Chief Joseph c. 1840-1904, by Cyrenius Hall; "I will fight no more forever."
- **1898** Spanish-American War
- **1906** San Francisco earthquake
- **1914-18** World War I
- **1918** Air Mail

1929 Museum of Modern Art established in New York				1949 Arthur Miller wins Pulitzer Prize for *Death of a Salesman*	1959 Guggenheim Museum opens; designed by Frank Lloyd Wright;		1971 Bernstein's *Mass* performed at opening of Kennedy Center
1930 Grant Wood exhibits "American Gothic"	Huddie Ledbetter 1888-1949, by Berenice Abbott; Singer and guitarist, jazz artist	1944 Aaron Copland's *Appalachian Spring* performed by Martha Graham troupe	Countee Cullen 1903-1946, by Winold Reiss; Lyric poet of Harlem Renaissance				
1936 Margaret Mitchell's *Gone With The Wind*		1947 Tennessee Williams wins Pulitzer Prize for *Streetcar Named Desire*	1948 Andrew Wyeth paints *Christina's World*	1954 Ernest Hemingway wins the Nobel Prize for Literature	1962 John Steinbeck wins Nobel in Literature	Richard Wright 1908-1960, by Miriam Troop; the author of *Native Son* and *Black Boy*	1976 Saul Bellow wins Nobel for Literature
1927 H. Campton, Nobel Laureate, successfully demonstrates television	1934 Harold Urey, Nobel laureate in chemistry	1937 Golden Gate Bridge dedicated	1945 Atomic bomb	1954 Jonas Salk introduces a vaccine for poliomyelitis		1960 First weather, communications, and navigation satellites launched	1969 Neil Armstrong walks on Moon
1930 Ernest Lawrence develops cyclotron		1938 Dupont introduces nylon		1956 Transistor developers win Nobel prize	Albert Einstein 1879-1955, by Julius C. Turner; Theory of Relativity	1961 Alan Shepard becomes first American in space	1976 Viking lands on Mars
1931 Empire State Building completed	Thomas Alva Edison 1847-1931, by Abraham Anderson; Genius of invention	1944 First information-processing digital computer	George Washington Carver c. 1864-1943, by Becky G. Reyneau; Agricultural chemist	1958 Explorer I, first U.S. Satellite, orbited		1962 Rachel Carson publishes *Silent Spring*	1977 Alaska Pipeline opens
1920 League of Nations	1930 s Franklin D. Roosevelt and "New Deal"	1950 Korean War	1960 s Lyndon B. Johnson's "War on Poverty"		1964 Civil Rights Act	1968 USS *Pueblo* captured by North Korea	
1925 Scopes "Monkey Trial" Tennessee	1949 North Atlantic Treaty Organization	1954 Supreme Court rules segregated schools to be unconstitutional	1961 U.S. troops sent to Vietnam	W.E.B. DuBois 1868-1963, by Winold Reiss; Civil rights leader	1965 Ralph Nader publishes *Unsafe at Any Speed*	1969 SALT talks begin in Helsinki	1973 Vietnam ceasefire
1929 Stock market crash		1960 U-2 plane shot down over Russia	1963 John F. Kennedy assassinated		1967 Detroit scene of worst race riot in history	1970 Kent State student riots	1974 Watergate Cover-up Trial

INDEX

illustrations and caption references appear in *italics*

253

255

Text Credits

Page 164: C. Wilkes, *Narrative of the United States Exploring Expedition*, 1845, Vol. III. 165: *The Japan Expedition, 1852-54, The Personal Journal of Commodore Matthew C. Perry*, edited by Roger Pineau, Smithsonian Institution Press, 1968. Journal excerpt courtesy of Mrs. August Belmont. 166: E. Nelson, *The Eskimo About Bering Strait*, 18th Annual Report of the Bureau of American Ethnology. 167: W. W. Rockhill, *Diary of a Journey Through Mongolia and Tibet in 1891 and 1892*, Smithsonian Institution, 1894. 169: R. Hitchcock, *The Ainos of Yezo*, Report of National Museum, 1890. 169: D. C. Graham, *Folk Religion in Southwest China*, Smithsonian Miscellaneous Collections, Vol. 142, No. 2. 170: William Louis Abbott Papers, 1892-1917, National Anthropological Archives. 171: A. Hrdlicka, *The Aleutian and Commander Islands and Their Inhabitants*, Wistar Institute of Anatomy and Biology, Philadelphia, 1945. 172: M. Stirling, *Historical and Ethnological Material on Jivaro Indians*, Bureau of American Ethnology Bulletin 117.

Photo Credits